E for Environment™

E for Environment™

An Annotated Bibliography of Children's Books with Environmental Themes

Patti K. Sinclair

R. R. Bowker

New Providence, New Jersey

Published by R. R. Bowker, a division of Reed Publishing (USA) Inc.
Copyright © 1992 by Reed Publishing (USA) Inc.
All rights reserved
Printed and bound in the United States of America

Library of Congress Cataloging in Publication Data

Sinclair, Patti K., 1949–
    E for environment : an annotated bibliography of children's books
with environmental themes / by Patti K. Sinclair.
        p. cm.
    Includes bibliographical references and index.
    ISBN 0-8352-3028-7
    1. Children's literature–Bibliography. 2. Environmental
protection–Juvenile literature–Bibliography. 3. Environmental
literature–Bibliography. 4. Ecology in literature–Bibliography.
5. Nature in literature–Bibliography. I. Title.
Z1037.9.S57 1992
[PN1009.A1]
011.62–dc20   91-39577
                                                        CIP

This book is printed on 55-pound, cream white Miami Book paper
containing 50% de-inked, recycled fibre, which includes 10%
post-consumer waste and is acid free.

ISBN 0 - 8352 - 3028 - 7

9 780835 230285

To my parents

Contents

Preface

Locating books on the many topics that fall under the subject of environment can be a challenge. The interdisciplinary nature of this subject means that books not only in science but also in art, literature, philosophy, technology, economics, sociology, and politics may have something to say about our understanding of and respect for the environment and the problems we face today.

While current interest in the quality of the environment is high, concern for the earth and its creatures is nothing new, and children's books are becoming a rich source of information and inspiration. From ecology to eco-activism, from pollution to people, from endangered animals to energy, from respecting the earth to recycling, the issues and themes are endless. This bibliography brings together some of the best books published for children on these and other selected environmental themes and issues. Librarians, teachers, parents and other environmental educators will find it a valuable tool in locating books to help children appreciate, know, respect, and care for the earth.

The 517 titles selected for this bibliography of trade books are drawn from a variety of subject areas. They include fiction, nonfiction, and a handful of titles for adults who work with children. The bibliography is targeted at children from preschool through age 14. One of the purposes of the bibliography is to offer a balance of books in subject and age level.

Primary focus is on books published within the last ten years, from 1982 through mid-1991. However, several pre-1982 titles found a place in the bibliography. For example, Jorg Müller's *The Changing Countryside* and its companion *The Changing City* (both Macmillan, 1977), were landmark works, are still in print, and say much about our influence on the land. Robert McCloskey's *Time of Wonder* (Viking, 1957) conveys the wonder of the natural world as memorably as any book published since. The conservation message in Dr. Suess's *The Lorax* (Random, 1971) continues to entertain and educate children today. And in some subject areas, such as energy alternatives, relatively little was published during the 1980s; for that reason a few 1970s titles were included.

Although the majority of books in the bibliography are in print, readers will discover about two dozen out-of-print titles. This may be inconvenient for those who wish to use *E for Environment* as a guide to collection development, but many will find the bibliography helpful in making better use of titles already in their collections. And with the current demand for children's books on environmental issues, publishers are already bringing some older titles back into print. They should!

With such a broad topic, narrowing the scope of this bibliography was a challenge. Five general areas were chosen, although many other themes and topics could have comfortably fit into this selection.

Books that help foster positive attitudes about nature and the environment are the focus of Chapter One. I am indebted to Rachel Carson whose oft-quoted words from *The Sense of Wonder* convinced me that the path to responsible adult stewardship of the earth lies in the affective realm. Said Carson,

> It is not half so important to *know* as to *feel*. If facts are the seeds that later produce knowledge and wisdom, then the emotions and the impressions of the senses are the fertile soil in which the seeds must grow. The years of early childhood are the time to prepare the soil. Once the emotions have been aroused . . . then we wish for knowledge about the object of our emotional response. . . . It is more important to pave the way for the child to want to know than to put him on a diet of facts he is not ready to assimilate.

Love, respect for, and appreciation of nature and the environment may not be the dominant theme of every book in Chapter One, but at least one of these themes underlies each story.

Many fields of science could be incorporated into an environmental curriculum—natural history, geography, geology, meteorology, botany—but the branch of biology called ecology, the study of the relationships between all living things and how they interact with their environment, is the heart of environmental education. Chapter Two focuses on books about ecological communities, books that emphasize the interrelationships between plants, animals, and the environment or highlight how one plant or animal fits into its biotic community.

Environmental issues rise and fall in popularity, in the amount of media attention devoted to them, and in the government's commitment to them. Chapter Three, the largest chapter, comprises selected books on issues of current concern. Fiction, nonfiction, and picture books are included.

We are part of the environment, too. How do we see ourselves in relation to the natural world? How have we shaped and changed it? Who are the people most influential in nature and environment? Books in Chapter Four attempt to answer these questions.

Ideally children will have frequent opportunities as they grow to experience and learn from nature directly. But books are powerful tools, and a large field of "how-to" books helps readers make the most of these experiences whether children are at home, in the classroom, or outdoors. The books in Chapter Five will help both children and adults become involved in nature and the environment through crafts and other activities; titles in the final section show how to become active in helping protect the environment.

Outside the scope of this bibliography are most field guides; career books; general natural history, botany, biology, and geology books; and books on natural wonders.

The search for titles included a systematic look at review journals including *School Library Journal, Booklist, Horn Book, Appraisal,* and *Science Books and Films;* recently published bibliographies on the environment; and winners of awards such as ALA Notable Children's Book, Outstanding Science Trade Book for Children (OSTB), Notable Children's Trade Book in the Field of Social Studies (NSSB), and Newbery and Caldecott awards. I also turned to librarians for suggestions, searched public library collections and, for newer titles, visited bookstores and publisher's booths at the American Library Association conferences. I also utilized the Cooperative Children's Book Center, a children's and young adult literature research library and examination center at the University of Wisconsin – Madison. My own professional experience as a librarian and my personal interest in environmental issues and education were a great help and motivating factors.

Books included in this bibliography are recommended—some more enthusiastically than others. Because there was less to choose from in some subject areas, some titles appear here that will probably be replaced by better efforts when the next edition of *E for Environment* is published. Read the annotations carefully.

Because the topics covered are so broad and interrelated, readers will find a great deal of interconnectedness in *E for Environment.* Refer to the index or scan other chapters when looking for books on a particular topic. Many of the books in Chapter Five's "Taking Action" section, for example, include information on current issues such as pollution, recycling, and animal rights. The threads of Chapter One are also seen throughout the bibliography.

For adults who wish to educate themselves about the environment or for students who wish to read further, the short list of books in the Appendix, "Environmental Classics," suggests some of the definitive titles in adult environmental literature along with a few newer titles.

To assist users, author, title, and subject indexes are included.

Because the primary intent of *E for Environment* is to pull together more recently published books on the environment, many fine older titles, particularly fiction titles with environmental themes, were omitted. I welcome suggestions for titles or topics you wish to see included in future editions of *E for Environment*.

Entries

Book entries are arranged alphabetically by author within each section of a chapter. A typical entry includes: (1) author's name; (2) title; (3) other contributors such as editor, illustrator, or translator; (4) publisher; (5) date of publication; (6) number of pages (Unp. = unpaged); (7) ISBN (LB = library binding; o.p. = out of print); (8) series title, if any; (9) fiction or nonfiction indicator; (10) interest level (e.g., Ages 8 – 10); and (11) annotation.

Publisher's imprints are listed under the parent company. For example, Scribners' will appear as Macmillan. Addresses are provided after lesser-known publishers.

For award-winning books, the awards and years are listed following the annotation (NSSB = Notable Children's Trade Book in the Field of Social Studies; OSTB = Outstanding Science Trade Book for Children).

Acknowledgments

Many people helped in the preparation of this bibliography.

Jane Roughen, a librarian at Madison (Wisconsin) Public Library, researched titles and wrote the annotations for Chapter Five. Her care and excellent judgment were great assets and her support and good humor were greatly appreciated.

Kären Richgruber, a librarian at Duluth (Minnesota) Public Library, contributed annotations to sections in Chapters Three ("Pollution" and "Garbage and Recycling") and Four ("The Changing Landscape"). Her creativity, fine writing, and sense of humor were also invaluable to this project.

Another librarian without whom I could not have completed this project is Jeannie Gartman, whose diligence in tracking down hundreds of reviews and books throughout the duration of the project was essential and is greatly appreciated.

Through Madison Public Library, a member of Wisconsin's South Central Library System, I was able to obtain the majority of books requested. Special thanks to the Interlibrary Loan staff, who handled several hundred requests, the Children's Services staff for their help, and to Dorothy Batt and the staff at the Monroe Street Branch Library for their professional and cheerful attitude over the past year.

I was fortunate to have access to the Cooperative Children's Book Center on the University of Wisconsin—Madison campus. The collection of basic titles and newly published books made my research much easier. Special thanks to Ginny Moore Kruse, Kathleen Horning, and Merri Lindgren.

Several publishers graciously and promptly sent me review copies of books. Marion Sader, Roy Crego, and the staff at R. R. Bowker also have my gratitude for their help.

My husband Tom, whose environmentalism shines both at work and at home (and who still reminds me to turn off the lights), was an inspiration for this bibliography. He contributed the appended list of environmental classics and spent many additional hours caring for our son Colin during the research and writing of this book.

1

Planting the Seeds of Environmental Awareness
Introducing Young Children to Nature

> *If a child is to keep alive his inborn sense of wonder . . . he needs the companionship of at least one adult who can share it, rediscovering with him the joy, excitement and mystery of the world we live in.*
>
> Rachel Carson *The Sense of Wonder*

This chapter was inspired by the ideas so eloquently expressed in Rachel Carson's *The Sense of Wonder*. Here are books that reinforce familiar experiences in nature like Catherine Stock's *Sophie's Knapsack* or Anna Grossnickle Hines's *Come to the Meadow*. Here also are books that will inspire children and their parents to develop a sense of wonder at the natural world, like Robert Welber's *The Winter Picnic* or Byrd Baylor's *I'm in Charge of Celebrations*. Other books help sharpen the senses like Millicent Selsam's *Keep Looking!* or Bruce McMillan's *Growing Colors*. And, perhaps most important, there are books that will help develop empathy and respect for all life, as exemplified in Julie Brinkloe's *Fireflies* and Denis Cazet's *A Fish in His Pocket*.

Most of the titles in this chapter elicit an emotional response from their readers. They do not *tell* children to save the earth or to be kind to animals, but as they foster a positive attitude toward the natural world, they work their own magic. For more ideas on sharing nature with children, see Chapter Five—It's Your Turn.

A Sense of Wonder

■ Aragon, Jane Chelsea. SALT HANDS. Illus. by Ted Rand. Dutton, 1989. Unp. (0-525-44489-0) Fiction. Interest Level: Ages 3–7
Aragon creates magic in this story narrated by a young girl who wakes up one summer night to see a deer nibbling fallen pears under a tree in her backyard. Sprinkling salt on her hands, the girl quietly heads outside. There she softly sings a song and offers the salt to the deer. Aragon's text is spare but filled with the excitement and anticipation that comes from such a

1

unique encounter. Rand's watercolors capture the magic of the moonlit night, the joy of the young girl, and both the wariness and gentleness of the deer. This book is summer magic. For winter magic, see Aragon's *Winter Harvest* (Little, 1988) in which a family in the country regularly feeds a family of deer.

■ Baylor, Byrd. I'M IN CHARGE OF CELEBRATIONS. Illus. by Peter Parnall. Macmillan, 1986. Unp. (0-684-18579-2) Fiction. Interest Level: Ages 6–9

Teachers looking for alternatives to traditional holiday celebrations or ways to incorporate environmental awareness into their curriculum will find inspiration in this Baylor and Parnall collaboration. The narrator, a young girl or woman, has an enthusiasm for the beauty and wonder of her desert environment that readers will find contagious. She describes several of the 108 celebrations she gave herself last year. Among them are Dust Devil Day, when she saw seven dust devils, or whirlwinds, and Rainbow Celebration Day, when she saw a jackrabbit looking at a triple rainbow. What qualifies as a celebration? "You can tell what's worth a celebration because your heart will POUND and you'll feel like you're standing on top of a mountain and you'll catch your breath like you were breathing some new kind of air," she says.

Parnall's characteristic line drawings are washed with intense desert yellows, blues, and greens. This book is an inspiration for everyone, no matter where they live, to observe, explore, discover, and celebrate.

■ Carlstrom, Nancy White. WILD WILD SUNFLOWER CHILD ANNA. Illus. by Jerry Pinkney. Macmillan, 1991 (repr. of 1987 ed.). 32pp. (paper 0-689-71445-9) Fiction. Interest Level: Ages 3–7

Energy flows through Carlstrom's fast-paced, free-form verse about the joy a young girl named Anna takes in the flower-filled meadow where she spends an early summer day. Pinkney's exuberant, summery illustrations burst off pages where greens and yellows predominate. Anna, a young black girl in a bright yellow dress, is the focus of each vibrant illustration set in this flowery meadow. In Anna's world, the meadow is a place to frolic, daydream, and observe the life around her. She picks berries, digs in the garden, goes barefoot across a creek, climbs a tree, rolls down a hill, watches insects, and eventually falls asleep. Readers will feel the sun, smell the flowers, and want to head outside to enjoy a warm, sunny meadow after reading *Wild Wild Sunflower Child Anna*.

■ Carrick, Carol. IN THE MOONLIGHT, WAITING. Illus. by Donald Carrick. Clarion/Houghton, 1990. Unp. (LB 0-89919-867-8) Fiction. Interest Level: Ages 3–7

Anticipation and wonder characterize this lovely, small-size picture book about lambing time on a family farm. The story is told from the point of view of a young girl who wakes her brother up in the middle of the night to go out and welcome the first lamb of the season. Once the lamb is born, Mom and the two children carry the lamb to the barn, show him off to the horse, and then see that the lamb and ewe are comfortable in their pen. Back inside the house, the girl describes how Mom makes a cup of tea and takes a nap, and brother goes back to sleep, "while I watch in the moonlight, waiting for more lambs." Donald Carrick's watercolor sketches capture the atmosphere of a late winter night and the closeness this family shares as lambing season begins.

■ Clifton, Lucille. THE BOY WHO DIDN'T BELIEVE IN SPRING. Illus. by Brinton Turkle. Dutton, 1973. Unp. (LB 0-525-27145-7) Fiction. Interest Level: Ages 4–8
In this picture book, wonder is evident on the face of a boy called King Shabazz and his friend Tony Polito when they find spring. After hearing about spring both at school and home, King Shabazz decides he's going to find some. Having grown up in a big city, he's not sure what to look for or where to look. So he and his friend Tony venture further from home than they ever have before. Eventually they come upon a vacant lot with an abandoned car in the middle. "Oh man, oh man," whispers King. And as they walk toward the car, they discover not one but two signs of spring. Clifton writes with freshness and humor of two friends from a multiethnic city neighborhood. Turkle's charcoal and watercolor drawings capture the city environment and the magic to be found in such everyday signs of spring as a clump of flowers or a nest of eggs. Clifton knows that children everywhere are drawn to the natural world and that spring can be found even in a big city.

■ Frank, Josette, comp. SNOW TOWARD EVENING: A YEAR IN A RIVER VALLEY. Illus. by Thomas Locker. Dial, 1990. Unp. (LB 0-8037-0811-4) Nonfiction. Interest Level: Ages 8 up
Frank's selection of 13 short poems "reflecting the feeling" of each month and of the New Year includes poems by N.M. Bodecker, Elizabeth Coatsworth, William Wordsworth, Rachel Field, and Christina Rosetti. Each poem is set on the left-hand page; on the right a full-page print of an oil painting by landscape artist Thomas Locker invites study and reflection. Set in the Hudson River valley, the large, often panoramic views dominate the small figures that appear in some scenes as if to show that, in the end, nature prevails against any human trespassers. Magnificent skies, subtle changes in light, and little evidence of human encroachment characterize the paintings. Most successfully used with one child at a time, these nature poems

combine with Locker's view of nature to offer the observant child an opportunity to see the natural world in a new light.

■ **Hasler, Eveline. WINTER MAGIC. Illus. by Michele Lemieux. Morrow,
1984. Unp. (LB 0-688-05258-4) Fiction. Interest Level: Ages 5–8**
When you're not shivering in the cold, there is something magical about
northern winters, especially as portrayed in Eveline Hasler's *Winter Magic.*
Young Peter, sitting in a window seat with his white cat Sebastian, com-
plains, "The grass is gone. The animals are gone. There's nothing but snow.
I hate winter." But after dinner, his mother tells Peter and his brothers and
sisters a story about the winter king. That night Peter dreams of the icicle
kingdom where he and Sebastian dance in the snow with other forest
animals. Waking up to check on Sebastian, Peter is transported by a now
much larger cat into winterland, where they discover some of winter's
secrets: tree roots that store food, mice and badgers in burrows under the
snow, the sound of birds rustling their feathers, glistening ice on the
branches of trees. Lemieux's soft watercolors express the sparkling, magical
quality of the winter night and young Peter's newfound delight in the
season. A simple, charming fantasy that will stimulate readers to find their
own magic in winter (or in any other season).

■ **Hoban, Julia. AMY LOVES THE SUN. Illus. by Lillian Hoban. Harper,
1988. Unp. (LB 0-06-022397-9) Fiction. Interest Level: Ages 2–5**
This small, cheerful book conveys the joy a young child experiences on a
warm and sunny summer day as she romps through the grass picking
dandelions and daisies for her mother. Her simple observations and activities are those of a young child—the dandelions are yellow, the daisies white,
with yellow centers. Lillian Hoban's sunny illustrations capture Amy and
her world at her close-to-earth level. The Hobans also collaborated on *Amy
Loves the Wind* (Harper, 1988), *Amy Loves the Snow* (Harper, 1989), and
Amy Loves the Rain (Harper, 1989).

■ **Hughes, Shirley. OUT AND ABOUT. Illus. by author. Lothrop, 1988. Unp.
(LB 0-688-07691-2) Fiction. Interest Level: Ages 2–6**
Eighteen short poems describe the delights of the outdoors for a rosy-
cheeked little girl and her brother. Their pleasure in mud, rain, rainbows,
sand, wind, cold, and such spans the seasons in and around their busy
neighborhood. Hughes captures the world of the preschool child with her
characteristic robust, colorful, and playful kids. Perfect for one-on-one sharing and reading aloud.

Award: ALA Notable Children's Book, 1988

■ Keats, Ezra Jack. THE SNOWY DAY. Illus. by author. Viking, 1962. 32pp. (LB 0-670-65400-0) Fiction. Interest Level: Ages 3 – 7
Published 30 years ago, *The Snowy Day* remains fresh and inviting, like the snow outside Peter's house. Keats captures Peter's delight during a winter day spent in his city neighborhood making tracks, angels, and snowballs. The experience is extended as he tells his mother about his adventures and thinks about them in the bathtub. When he discovers the snowball he put in his pocket has melted, he's sad and that night he dreams that the sun has melted all the snow. But he wakes up to discover that new snow is falling, an invitation to share another snowy day with a friend. Keats won the Caldecott Medal for this, his first picture book, which portrays with simple lines and bright colors an African-American child experiencing the essential pleasures of any northern child's winter.

Award: Caldecott Medal, 1963

■ Livingston, Myra Cohn. A CIRCLE OF SEASONS. Illus. by Leonard Everett Fisher. Holiday, 1982. Unp. (LB 0-8234-0452-8) Nonfiction. Interest Level: Ages 8 – 11
Each season comes alive and is seen as busy and purposeful in Livingston's energetic celebration of the seasons. Her images are strong, vivid, and refreshing, conjuring up baseball players, anglers, and artists involved in the things that make each season special: "Spring brings out her baseball bat, swings it through the air, / Pitches bulbs and apple blossoms, throws them where it's bare, / Catches dogtooth violets, slides to meadowsweet, / Bunts a breeze and tags the trees with green buds everywhere."
    Fisher's impressionistic paintings do not attempt to compete with or realistically portray Livingston's word images, but they suggest the spirit of each stanza with strong, abstract shapes and colors, allowing readers to create their own visual images. This is a fine collaboration.

Award: ALA Notable Children's Book, 1982

■ Locker, Thomas. WHERE THE RIVER BEGINS. Illus. by author. Dial, 1984. Unp. (LB 0-8037-0090-3) Fiction. Interest Level: Ages 6 – 8
Two young brothers, who live on the banks of a river, ask their grandfather to take them to the river's source. The three set out on a trip that takes them through field and forest up to a high meadow where the ever-narrowing river begins in a small pond. There they wait out a pounding thunderstorm in their tent before heading back down the next day. Locker's prose is formal and detached, but his magnificent full-page landscapes, unusual in children's picture books, will draw some readers in. Children will be drawn to the idea of following a river to its source and the somewhat rugged trip

with this adventurous grandfather. The story also suggests the grandfather's close relationship to both the land and his grandchildren.

Award: OSTB, 1984

■ McCloskey, Robert. TIME OF WONDER. Illus. by author. Viking, 1957. 64pp. (0-670-71512-3) Fiction. Interest Level: Ages 5–8
McCloskey's award-winning story is as fresh today as it was when published over 30 years ago. *Time of Wonder* is about spending a summer on an island off the coast of Maine. It describes the excitement of watching storm clouds gather, feeling rain on your skin, hearing porpoises splash, fiddlehead ferns unfurl, hummingbirds hum, and the many other explorations and discoveries a child experiences throughout the summer. The islanders prepare for a big storm. "We're going to have some weather," they say. As a hurricane develops and pounds the island, the family takes shelter and keeps safe inside their summer home. The aftermath provides more opportunities for exploration and, as the family packs up to leave the island, it is a "time of quiet wonder—for wondering, for instance: Where do hummingbirds go in a hurricane?" McCloskey's outstanding watercolors are matched by his lyrical prose; these lasting images will expand a young child's awareness and appreciation of nature. This is a classic.

Award: Caldecott Medal, 1958

■ Martin, Bill, Jr., and John Archambault. LISTEN TO THE RAIN. Illus. by James Endicott. Holt, 1988. Unp. (LB 0-8050-0682-6) Fiction. Interest Level: Ages 3–8
With the freshness of a summer shower, *Listen to the Rain* reminds readers that the sounds of nature are as exciting as the sights. Martin and Archambault's rhythmic ode to the sounds of rain is fun to read and, like a tune you can't get out of your head, it will stay with you awhile. Each refrain begins, "Listen to the rain," as it whispers, sings, roars, pours, pounds and eventually stops. Endicott's original, somewhat abstract illustrations will be enjoyed, but the poem stands on its own, begging to be read aloud. This book can be used with poetry and nature study classes.

■ Radin, Ruth Yaffe. HIGH IN THE MOUNTAINS. Illus. by Ed Young. Macmillan, 1989. Unp. (0-02-775650-5) Fiction. Interest Level: Ages 6–9
A young girl spends a day in the mountains near her grandfather's house and describes her observations and activities. Late in the afternoon, the girl's grandfather says, "Let's go," and they take off to camp overnight: "Up to the clouds, then down again / to a place just right to pitch a tent / facing

toward the morning sun." Young's impressionistic paintings are vibrant. His mountain landscapes are softly defined. Misty vistas, alpine meadows, luminous streams, even soft-edged boulders match the dreamy quality of the brief text, in which the young girl appears only occasionally, a small out-of-focus figure surrounded by the color and splendor of the mountain scenes.

Awards: NSSB, 1989; OSTB, 1989

■ Ryder, Joanne. INSIDE TURTLE'S SHELL: AND OTHER POEMS OF THE FIELD. Illus. by Susan Bonners. Macmillan, 1985. Unp. (0-02-778010-4) Nonfiction. Interest Level: Ages 6–10
These free-verse poems by nature writer Joanne Ryder describe, from the point of view of meadow animals, their activities during night and day. Wit and drama characterize the poems that chronicle life cycles and behavior with a dose of meadow ecology along the way. The poems start in spring and continue through summer and fall. Bonners's delicate black-and-white pencil drawings often add the perfect comment to the poems. In a poem about a frog, Ryder says, "Frog sings so pretty, / fox comes to listen. / Where's that frog now?" Bonner shows two frog legs disappearing in a splash of water. *Inside Turtle's Shell* will enrich both poetry and ecology classes.

Award: OSTB, 1985

■ Ryder, Joanne. STEP INTO THE NIGHT. Illus. by Dennis Nolan. Macmillan, 1988. Unp. (0-02-777951-3) Fiction. Interest Level: Ages 4–8
At dusk a young girl "steps into the night" and stands quietly beneath a tree outside her home watching and listening as animals of the day find places to rest and night creatures begin to stir. As she waits, she enjoys the sights, sounds, and smells of the evening and her observations lead her to imagine being the creatures she sees. On one page the girl smells the flowers along a fence. A scent of skunk wafts by and on the next page a skunk emerges from the leaves hunting for food, then sprays a dog that startles it. Other animals include a young mouse, a firefly, a spider, a bat, a mole, and a green frog.

Ryder's narration in the second person gives continuity to the observations of the girl and the animals she "becomes." Finally she is called home and she "leaves the night behind." The deep blacks and blues of Nolan's nighttime scenes illuminated by the moon create a still, shining quality. The combination of prose and illustrations evoke a sense of wonder about the natural world at night that will make young children want to step out into their own backyards some summer night to experience the sights, smells, and sounds of nature. Companion books include *Under Your Feet* (Macmillan, 1990) and *Mockingbird Morning* (Macmillan, 1989).

Award: OSTB, 1988

■ **Rylant, Cynthia. NIGHT IN THE COUNTRY. Illus. by Mary Szilagyi. Bradbury, 1986. Unp. (0-02-777210-1) Fiction.** Interest Level: Ages 3–6
Young children will enjoy discovering an alternate world of life and activity that carries on during a night in the country. They'll find that although the night is dark, many animals are awake and active. Frogs sing songs, owls swoop among the trees, rabbits patter, a raccoon mother licks her babies. There are sounds too—an apple falls, old houses squeak, a dog's chain rattles, and just before dawn a small bird chirps, signaling the end of night. Szilagyi's rough, colored pencil illustrations are deep and dark with night color, but the close-up views of owl, rabbit, and frog are not scary, and the overall effect is comforting. By intermingling people and nature noises and sights, Rylant creates a sense of harmony between people and the natural world.

Award: OSTB, 1986

■ **San Souci, Daniel. NORTH COUNTRY NIGHT. Illus. by author. Doubleday, 1990. Unp. (LB 0-385-41320-3) Nonfiction.** Interest Level: Ages 3–6
San Souci recreates the hushed, snowy world of a north country winter as he follows several nocturnal animals searching for food—a great horned owl, a coyote, a red fox, a mountain lion, a porcupine, a cottontail, and others. The animals are realistically drawn on double-page spreads. Snow, represented by white flecks of paint, falls throughout the night on woodland scenes washed in blue. Oddly, these snowy scenes are also washed in moonlight. The illustrations are framed in pale blue and the book is visually very appealing.

Award: OSTB, 1990

■ **Shulevitz, Uri. DAWN. Illus. by author. Farrar, 1974. Unp. (0-374-31707-0) Fiction.** Interest Level: Ages 4–8
A mood of expectation infuses *Dawn*, a simple story based on an ancient Chinese poem. In it Shulevitz lyrically tells of an experience a young boy and his grandfather share. Camping along a small lake, they rise while it is still dark and quietly push their boat into the water. They reach the middle of the lake just as the sun comes up. Through prose and soft watercolor illustrations, Shulevitz captures the quiet, subtle changes that take place before dawn—a bird calls, a bat circles above the lake, the mist rises, and ever

so slowly it gets lighter until the lake and mountain are washed with bright morning colors. *Dawn* is a companion piece to *Rain Rain Rivers* (Farrar, 1969).

■ **Skofield, James. ALL WET! ALL WET! Illus. by Diane Stanley. Harper, 1984. 32pp. (LB 0-06-025752-0) Fiction.** Interest Level: Ages 4–8
A little boy in a yellow slicker and rain boots walks through meadow and woods on a rainy summer day observing animals in their natural habitats. The story is quiet and lyrical. It describes, from the animals' point of view, their search for food and shelter and some of their interactions. Late in the afternoon the rain stops, the sun breaks through the clouds and the boy heads home. Stanley's subdued illustrations reflect the understated text. In each scene the boy is shown unobtrusively watching the animals. Children who have taken a rainy day hike in the woods will appreciate his luck in observing so much activity. Others may be inspired to don slicker and boots for a wet walk on the next rainy day. Skofield's *Crow Moon, Worm Moon* (Macmillan, 1990), illustrated by Joyce Powzyk, is a poem welcoming spring, which is quite different in tone.

Award: OSTB, 1984

■ **Tejima, Keizaburo. FOX'S DREAM. Trans. by Susan Matsui. Illus. by author. Putnam, 1987. Unp. (LB 0-399-21455-0) Fiction.** Interest Level: Ages 4–10
Do animals have emotions? Do they experience the wonder and beauty of their environments? For author-illustrator Tejima the answer is yes as he takes readers into a magical world filled with breathtaking images of a lone fox's journey through a snow-covered woods at night. In a strange part of the woods where "the frozen trees glitter in the moonlight," the fox sees icy images of birds, deer, and a family of foxes. These images remind him of spring and the family he came from. The fox continues on until dawn when he sees a vixen in the distance and the promise of spring and companionship. Tejima's striking woodcuts washed with blues and lavenders and his quietly told story combine to elicit understanding and empathy for these animals and the beauty of their natural habitats. Other works by Tejima with similar spirit and style include *Owl Lake* (Putnam, 1987), *Swan Sky* (Putnam, 1989) and *Woodpecker Forest* (Putnam, 1989).

Award: ALA Notable Children's Book, 1987

■ **Yolen, Jane. RING OF EARTH: A CHILD'S BOOK OF SEASONS. Illus. by John Wallner. Harcourt, 1986. Unp. (LB 0-15-267140-4) Nonfiction.** Interest Level: Ages 7–12

Four animals poetically celebrate their place in the natural world in Jane Yolen's exuberant, *Ring of Earth: A Child's Book of Seasons.* Each animal chosen represents one season—the weasel in winter, the spring peeper in spring, the dragonfly in summer, and the goose in autumn, and for each a short poem spreads over six colorful pages. Yolen's verse is lively and moving, with rhyming couplets broken by the "Pe-ep, Pe-ep, Pe-ep, Pe-ep," of the frog or the "Kerhonk, Kerhonk. Kerhonk." of the goose. She also incorporates much information about the life cycles, behavior, and environment of each.

Wallner's detailed watercolors reflect the circular nature of the seasons with circled insets and vine wreaths throughout. The animals celebrate themselves with joy and drama. An author's note provides more information about each animal. This book is a creative addition to natural history and ecology studies. It may be used with Marilyn Singer's *Turtle in July* (Macmillan, 1989).

■ Zolotow, Charlotte. SOMETHING IS GOING TO HAPPEN. Illus. by Catherine Stock. Harper, 1988. Unp. (LB 0-06-027029-2) Fiction. Interest Level: Ages 3–8
Most of the action in Zolotow's picture book takes place indoors, yet her story convincingly communicates an appreciation of the natural world. As each member of a family (including the dog) wakes up and begins to get ready for the day, they sense that "something is going to happen." Anticipation mounts until the whole family converges at the front door to discover that it is snowing. The last illustration shows the dog frolicking in a neighborhood covered with snow.

Children will like this story; it is told from the point of view of each family member, and anticipation builds at just the right pace to keep them interested. Stock's watercolors depict a traditional middle-class family. See also Zolotow's *The Storm Book* (Harper, 1952) to experience from a little boy's perspective a summer thunderstorm as it passes over countryside, city, and seashore.

Enjoying Nature with Family and Friends

■ Adoff, Arnold. IN FOR WINTER, OUT FOR SPRING. Illus. by Jerry Pinkney. Harcourt, 1991. Unp. (LB 0-15-238637-8) Nonfiction. Interest Level: Ages 6–9
Narrated by Rebecca, the youngest in her family, this series of poems celebrates life in a rural African-American family throughout the seasons. The family's respect for nature and their close connection to the land is

evident as they work in the garden, harvest fruits and nuts, take in a stray dog, and observe changes in weather and the activities of birds, insects, and mammals around them. Rebecca remembers special moments—feeling the wind in her hair on a sled ride with her brother in the snow, digging in the earth to transplant saplings with her dad, and watching a chipmunk digging tunnels in the yard. She also remembers smelling the foul breeze from a nearby paper mill that keeps the family indoors one summer day. Pinkney's watercolor, pencil, and pastel drawings are vivid, and they enhance Adoff's free-flowing poems.

■ Caudill, Rebecca. A POCKET FULL OF CRICKET. Illus. by Evaline Ness. Holt, 1989 (repr. of 1964 ed.). Unp. (0-8050-1200-1) Fiction. Interest Level: Ages 5–8

In this endearing school story, children will respond to the love Jay, a young farm boy, has for his rural world. Caudill takes readers along on a sensory filled afternoon walk with Jay. He visits the pasture where he hears, smells, sees, feels, and collects bits and pieces of his world—a hickory nut, a goose feather, an arrowhead, some speckled beans, and a cricket. He puts the cricket in his pocket, takes it home, and keeps it as a pet. When the first day of school arrives, Jay takes his cricket with him to school, a comforting reminder of home and farm. When the cricket's chirping disrupts the class, his perceptive and understanding teacher suggests he share his cricket and his world with his classmates.

Award: Caldecott Honor Book, 1965

■ Coutant, Helen. THE GIFT. Illus. by Vo-Dinh Mai. Knopf, 1983. Unp. (LB 0-394-95499-8) Fiction. Interest Level: Ages 7–10

Fifth grader Anna is friends with Nana Marie, an elderly neighbor who teaches her to observe and enjoy nature. Anna is upset when she learns that Nana Marie is now blind. Invited to attend a party for her friend, she spends a long day trying to think of an appropriate gift. At the end of the day spent in the woods near their neighborhood, Anna thinks of the perfect gift. She will tell her old friend about the sights and sounds of the day she day spent in the woods, returning the gift Nana Marie had given her, the ability to appreciate the natural world.

This short fiction work, illustrated with black and white drawings, sensitively depicts an intergenerational friendship strengthened by Anna and Nana Marie's love of nature. Another story that captures the closeness a girl feels for her recently deceased grandmother and their shared closeness to nature is *Nana* by Lyn Littlefield Hoopes (Harper, 1981).

Award: NSSB, 1983

■ Day, Alexandra. RIVER PARADE. Illus. by author. Viking, 1990. Unp. (0-670-82946-3) Fiction. Interest Level: Ages 4–8
A young boy and his father go for an outing in a rowboat. The boy takes three wooden toy animals along. One by one they land in the river where they float, connected by a rope. When the boy reaches out to move a branch he falls in, but like the animals, he floats too because he's wearing a life jacket. Says the boy: "We were like a parade. It's wonderful to swim in the river, as long as you're on a string." The story is told from the boy's point of view and Day turns what might be a frightening experience into a small adventure. Day's watercolors capture the light reflecting off the blues and greens of this inviting river. Boats and water can be scary and this book may help some young children get over their fears and realize that even a dunk in the river can be fun.

■ Denslow, Sharon Phillips. AT TAYLOR'S PLACE. Illus. by Nancy Carpenter. Bradbury, 1990. Unp. (0-02-728685-1) Fiction. Interest Level: Ages 5–8
A warm story for a cool day that portrays a friendship between a young girl, Tory, and her elderly neighbor, Taylor, and their shared enjoyment of woodcrafts. Taylor's hobby is woodworking, and Tory helps him as he makes wooden weather vanes for neighbors and friends. Tory makes little baskets out of peach stones for each of the weather-vane animals to wear. While the emphasis of the story is on an intergenerational friendship, the setting is a rural landscape in which Taylor, who is portrayed as a gentle man in tune with his rural surroundings, passes on his love of animals and woodcrafts to his young friend. Carpenter's soft pastels complement this gentle story.

■ Denslow, Sharon Phillips. NIGHT OWLS. Illus. by Jill Kastner. Bradbury, 1990. Unp. (0-02-728681-9) Fiction. Interest Level: Ages 4–7
For some people nighttime *is* the right time. In *Night Owls,* night is the best time for Charlene and her nephew William who visits her each summer. Charlene bakes, walks her dog, and pots her plants all after the sun goes down. William is another night owl, and when he visits, they enjoy a night picnic, build a bonfire, count lightning bugs, and listen to cricket and frog voices nearby. They also climb a tree and blow bubbles from the branches. Charlene writes to William (at night) after he's gone, describing the night deer, the snow, and in early spring, the spring peepers she sees and hears from her house. While not as strong or magical a story as Yolen's *Owl Moon,* *Night Owls* entices readers to the delights of nature experienced at night, right out the back door. Kastner's rough pastels are striking and rich with color.

■ Griffith, Helen V. GEORGIA MUSIC. Illus. by James Stevenson. Greenwillow, 1986. Unp. (LB 0-688-06072-2) Fiction. Interest Level: Ages 5–8
A little girl spends the summer with her grandfather in a small house in Georgia. Grandfather gets much pleasure from tending his garden, and he and his granddaughter spend the summer working there. During the day the sounds of birds, bees, crickets, and grasshoppers serenade them. In the evening grandfather gets out his mouth organ and plays tunes "for the crickets and the grasshoppers because they [had] made music for him in the daytime." When he is too ill to live alone the following summer, he goes to Baltimore to live with his daughter and granddaughter. Away from the things he loves best, he seems to lose interest in life until his granddaughter gets out the mouth organ and recreates the sounds of birds and insects they had enjoyed so much in their Georgia garden. The "Georgia music," like a photograph or painting, brings back to both the special summer they had shared. Stevenson's pen and watercolor drawings, with a touch of whimsy, lighten the tone.
Award: ALA Notable Children's Book, 1986

■ Hamerstrom, Frances. WALK WHEN THE MOON IS FULL. Illus. by Robert Katoma. Crossing Press, 1975. 64pp. (0-912278-69-2) Nonfiction. Interest Level: Ages 7–11
"Do we have to go to bed early every single night until we are old?" asked Frances Hamerstrom's son as he looked out the farmhouse window one winter night. The question led naturalist Hamerstrom to begin the first of 13 moonlit walks with her two young children, one for each full moon of the year. They explored the land around their 240-acre Wisconsin farm: listening for the mating call of woodcocks in April, swimming in the pond with frogs in August, watching weasels play on the marsh on a frigid December night, always listening, watching, smelling the activity of the natural world. Written in short chapters, one for each full moon walk, this makes a wonderful read-aloud book and inspires one to take similar walks with one's children. The book is illustrated with pencil drawings.

■ Haseley, Dennis. MY FATHER DOESN'T KNOW ABOUT THE WOODS AND ME. Illus. by Michael Hays. Macmillan, 1988. Unp. (0-689-31365-9) Fiction. Interest Level: Ages 6–8
Experiences with nature are sometimes transforming. In this story a young boy and his father go on walks in the woods near their home. The boy wishes his father knew how he feels about the woods, because on their walks, the boy is transformed (in his imagination?) into various animals—a wolf, a hawk and a fish. He feels the changes in his body and sees the world

through each animal's eyes as he becomes each creature in turn. When he comes upon a stag in a clearing, a magical moment transpires. Emerging from the woods, he meets up with his father and realizes that his father, too, is transformed on these woodland walks. Hays's muted oils in autumn colors create a misty forest environment for this imaginative story. The book may lead to discussions of how experiences with nature make one feel. Another nice feature of this story is the illustration on the title page in which the boy is shown painting the stag from the woods, suggesting another response to nature.

■ Henkes, Kevin. GRANDPA AND BO. Illus. by author. Greenwillow, 1986. Unp. (LB 0-688-04957-5) Fiction. Interest Level: Ages 4–7
Bo spends his summers with his grandpa in the country, where they share many outdoor experiences. The book describes how they take walks in the cornfields, work in the garden, fish, wait for a shooting star, and sit under a fir tree telling each other stories and watching the branches "swish in the wind." Grandpa teaches Bo the names of things such as birds, flowers, and grasses. The two also give more personal names to things. They call the Douglas fir next to the house Doug and name the three bluegills they catch before letting them go. When Bo realizes that he won't be spending Christmas with Grandpa, they have a summer Christmas celebration. The night before Bo leaves for home, he and his grandpa sit out under the fir tree where Bo finally sees a shooting star. Henkes's gentle story portrays the warm relationship between this grandparent and grandchild, one in which they share their love of the natural world.

■ Hines, Anna Grossnickle. COME TO THE MEADOW. Illus. by author. Clarion, 1984. Unp. (LB 0-89919-227-0) Fiction. Interest Level: Ages 3–6
Mattie's special place is a nearby meadow. Now that it is spring, she has discovered things that she wants to share with her family: buttercups and shooting stars, a hop toad and a turtle, field mice, birds' eggs, and other wonders. Too busy with their own spring chores or interests, each family member turns her down as she asks, "Come to the meadow, come to the meadow with me." Finally her grandmother is intrigued and gathers together the makings of a picnic lunch to take to the meadow. As Mattie and her grandmother head out the door, the other family members become curious and follow. Then they all enjoy a springtime picnic in the meadow. Illustrated with simple, cheerful line drawings washed in yellow and green, this small book will remind parents how enthusiastic children are about the natural world and how important it is to take time to share nature activities with them.

■ Lattig-Ehlers, Laurie. CANOEING. Illus. by Ivan Gantschev. Picture Book Studio, 1986. Unp. (LB 0-88708-029-4) Fiction. Interest Level: Ages 6–8
Canoeing offers a sensory journey down a moonlit river on a summer evening. At dusk two people head down to the river for an canoe ride. The narrator describes the sights and sounds as they paddle along, floating by people on distant shores, listening to grouse, a heron, bullfrogs, a great owl, and the roar of rapids. How they get back home without a portage back around the rapids isn't explained! Lattig-Ehlers's text is poetic and evokes the quiet thrill of being on the river at dusk. Gantschev's impressionistic watercolors capture the subtle changes in color and shadow as the sun sets and the moon rises.

■ Lionni, Leo. FREDERICK. Illus. by author. Pantheon, 1967. Unp. (LB 0-394-91040-0) Fiction. Interest Level: Ages 3–7
In this now classic animal fable, Frederick the mouse sits out while the rest of the family of field mice are gathering food for the winter. When they ask him why he isn't helping, he replies that he *is* helping. "I gather sun rays for the cold dark winter days." When, at the end of the long winter, the mouse family runs out of food, they turn to Frederick, whose poetry provides them with memories of the warm summer days. His words sustain them through the hard times. His message, that poetry is as important for our nourishment as food, reminds us that our joy in nature can inspire us to write or paint or create. It is something to share and enrich others with. Lionni's simple paper collages and paints enhance the text.

Award: Caldecott Honor Book, 1968

■ Long, Earlene. GONE FISHING. Illus. by Richard Brown. Houghton, 1984. 32pp. (0-395-35570-2) Fiction. Interest Level: Ages 2–5
While fishing may not be everyone's cup of tea, this popular sport attracts many people who grow to cherish unpolluted lakes and rivers and the beauty of unspoiled natural settings. The shared pleasures of an early morning father-and-son fishing trip are told with a touch of humor from a preschool boy's perspective. His pleasure and pride in catching fish is obvious. The concepts of big and little are reinforced throughout: "A big fishing rod for my daddy. A little fishing rod for me, A big lunch for my daddy. A little lunch for me," and finally, "A little fish for my daddy. A big fish for me." Together they watch the sun come up, share lunch, catch fish, and take them home for his mom to see. The brief text and warm, simple pictures make this book good both for story hours and one-on-one sharing.

■ Michl, Reinhard. A DAY ON THE RIVER. Illus. by author. Barron's, 1986. Unp. (0-8120-5715-5) Fiction. Interest Level: Ages 5–8

A German author's recollections of childhood summers spent with friends playing on and along a river form the basis of this picture book story. An inflated inner tube serves as the children's boat as they paddle down the river, fish, swim, and explore, imagining sea monsters, wild men, and treasures. Michl's text is not as engaging as his illustrations, which are attractive oversize spreads that evoke a child's sense of adventure and fun in an unspoiled environment. The back endpaper illustrates and identifies the wildlife the friends encounter along the river. The book is not just a nostalgic look back as Michl notes in an afterword the changes to the stretch of the river he once played in and took completely for granted. He makes a plea for preservation of natural habitats like the one he so vividly remembers. A detachable poster is included.

■ Otto, Carolyn. THAT SKY, THAT RAIN. Illus. by Megan Lloyd. Harper, 1990. Unp. (LB 0-690-04765-7) Fiction. Interest Level: Ages 3–6

A grandfather takes his young granddaughter on a tour of the farm one summer day as a storm builds and finally bursts forth in a torrent. Lloyd's realistic, well-composed watercolors capture the changing light as sun gives way to storm clouds. One can feel the storm coming. The red roofs of the farmhouse and buildings accent the darkening clouds and almost-black tree trunks. Grandfather's simple observations of the farm animals and the rainstorm tell of his close connection to the land and the elements. Lloyd's illustrations reinforce the relationship between grandfather and grandchild suggested in the brief text.

■ Peters, Lisa Westberg. GOOD MORNING, RIVER! Illus. by Deborah Kogan Ray. Little, 1990. Unp. (1-55970-011-4) Fiction. Interest Level: Ages 5–8

Katherine and her elderly neighbor Carl share a friendship and a love of the river that flows near their homes. Each morning Carl's voice booms out over the river, "Good morning!" and a softer voice echoes back. Carl has always told Katherine, whose voice isn't strong enough to get the same response, that the river is talking back to him. Through the seasons Carl shares his knowledge of the river with Katherine, and they enjoy swimming, canoeing, and, in winter, walking on the ice. One autumn, Carl becomes ill and leaves home to live with his daughter for a while. When he returns, he has lost some of his vigor and can no longer muster the energy to greet the river each morning. "Maybe I can," Katherine says. "She turns to face the broad valley, stands tall, and holding her hands around her mouth shouts as loudly as she can: "Good morning!" And the river answers in a softer voice:

"Good morning . . . good morning. . . ." This is a gentle but moving story about friendship between young and old and also about the passing on of knowledge and appreciation of the natural world from one generation to the next. Ray's watercolors are soft and gentle like the story and illustrate the changing of seasons and the close friendship between Katherine and Carl.

Award: NSSB, 1990

■ Rockwell, Anne. APPLES AND PUMPKINS. Illus. by Lizzy Rockwell. Macmillan, 1989. Unp. (0-02-777270-5) Fiction. Interest Level: Ages 2 – 6
A little girl with bright orange hair tells of the outing she and her parents take each fall to a country orchard where they pick apples and pumpkins. They return home with the car loaded down, carve the pumpkin for Halloween, and give out "red and shiny apples for trick or treat." Rockwell's text is simple enough for very young children and, with its large print, it is easy enough for beginning readers. It combines with cheerful illustrations in bright autumn colors to portray from a child's view an annual outing many families enjoy and a tradition every urban and suburban child should experience. Companion books include *At the Beach* (Macmillan, 1987), *The First Snowfall* (Macmillan, 1987), and *My Spring Robin* (Macmillan, 1989).

Award: OSTB, 1989

■ Say, Allen. THE LOST LAKE. Illus. by author. Houghton, 1989. 32pp. (0-395-50933-5) Fiction. Interest Level: Ages 6 – 9
A father takes his son, Luke, who is living with him for the summer, on a camping trip to Lost Lake, a special, remote place he remembers from his own childhood. After a long day's hike they arrive only to find that the lake is not "lost" anymore, but it is crowded with campers swimming, fishing, and sunbathing. Disappointed and disgusted, the father leads his son away and they camp in the rain somewhere further up the mountain. They decide to look for another lake and, after another day of trekking cross-country, they again make camp. The following morning they awake to discover that they've camped on the shores of a new "lost lake." Say shows the importance of children and parents sharing time together and the closeness that comes with spending time in the wilderness together. Luke's father is so absorbed in his career that, until the camping trip, it seems he doesn't really know his son at all. The story is narrated by Luke, who cherishes the time spent with his father, which was made possible by this trip. "It really seemed as if Dad and I were all alone in the world. I like it just fine." The clean, often spare, watercolor illustrations glow with light from the sun or from the campfire at night.

■ Stock, Catherine. SOPHIE'S KNAPSACK. Illus. by author. Lothrop, 1988.
Unp. (LB 0-688-06458-2) Fiction. Interest Level: Ages 3–7
A city girl's first camping trip in the mountains with her family is the simple,
happy story of *Sophie's Knapsack*. Sophie's dad decides it is time to show
her some real sky, and the family prepares for a weekend trip to Purple
Cloud Rock. Stock describes Sophie's preparations, the family's car ride,
and their arrival at the trail head. "I feel like a tortoise carrying his house
on his back," says Sophie. "Sing Ho for the life of a Bear!" her dad sings
out. They camp, see the Big Dipper, and the next day make it to Purple
Cloud Rock. One more night of camping (this time in the rain) and they
head back down the mountain and back to the city with the "green scent
of pinecones" to keep them company. This is a gentle story showing a family
enjoying an outdoor adventure together. Stock's colorful, cheery watercolors are very appealing. See also *Sophie's Bucket* (Lothrop, 1985), a story
about Sophie's trip to the seashore with her family.

■ Tafuri, Nancy. DO NOT DISTURB. Illus. by author. Greenwillow, 1987.
Unp. (LB 0-688-06542-2) Fiction. Interest Level: Ages 2–7
People often forget that while they are enjoying the outdoors, their presence can be disturbing to the local wildlife. Tafuri reminds young readers
of this in a clever, humorous picture book. She pokes fun at the members
of a family who spend the first day of summer at a campground, oblivious of
the effect they are having on the animals who dodge stray balls, splashes in
the water, fishing hooks, or the family's dog. Told almost entirely in pictures, the story progresses with bold watercolors that convey both the
enjoyment of the family and the discomfort of the animals. In one spread,
the father is cooking fish over the campfire, while an owl in a nearby tree
closes an eye to avoid the smoke coming its way. The animals get their
revenge that night, however, when their chorus of hoots and howls keeps
the family awake in their small tent. The final spread showing raccoons,
frogs, loons, grasshoppers, owls, and a coyote making their calls, offers an
opportunity to discuss animal calls as well as the playfully given message.
Award: OSTB, 1987

■ Welber, Robert. THE WINTER PICNIC. Illus. by Deborah Ray. Pantheon,
1970. Unp. (LB 0-394-90444-3) Fiction. Interest Level: Ages 3–6
If it were not for their children, some parents would *never* get out to enjoy
snowy winter days. *The Winter Picnic* reminds young children and their
parents that winter can be fun. A young boy wants to have a picnic in the
snow. After repeated assertions from his mother, who is busy cleaning
house, that you can't have a picnic in the winter, he takes matters into his

own hands. After making snow plates and pretending that he is having a picnic, he comes inside and prepares a picnic lunch, takes it outside, and at last convinces his mother. "I was wrong," his mother says. "You *can* have a picnic in winter." And they share peanut butter sandwiches, lemonade, and potato chips on snow plates in their snowy backyard. Colorful illustrations with lots of white space create a festive air. As in Grossnickle's *Come to the Meadow* (Clarion, 1984), the child takes the initiative in bringing family members out to enjoy the season.

■ Williams, Vera B. THREE DAYS ON A RIVER IN A RED CANOE. Illus. by author. Greenwillow, 1981. Unp. (LB 0-688-84307-7) Fiction. Interest Level: Ages 6–9
This story of a canoe trip taken by a girl, her cousin Sam, and their mothers is a charming journal-style account describing their adventure. Their experiences include a treacherous rainstorm in the night, a portage over a waterfall, and a dunk in the river for Sam. Included too are recipes for fruit stew and dumplings and directions for making knots and putting up a tent. Although they are never too far from civilization, they do see moose, herons, Canada geese and other birds, and lots of fish, which they catch and cook for supper. Williams's crayon drawings document each part of the trip and are a perfect complement to the text, as is the cover, which is designed to look like a school notebook. This book will inspire children to recount their experiences in nature through writing and art.

■ Wolff, Ashley. COME WITH ME. Illus. by author. Dutton, 1990. Unp. (0-525-44555-2) Fiction. Interest Level: Ages 4–8
A young boy tells his new puppy all of the things they will do together when the puppy is old enough to come and live with him, such as walking through the meadow down to the sea, visiting the ducks in the pond, feeling the wind blowing from "across the Pacific," watching sea lions, and hunting for shells on the beach. The close and classic relationship between a boy and his dog is warmly conveyed here as is the boy's happiness in sharing the things he most loves in the natural world with his pet. Children will respond to this fetching black-and-white pup and her new owner. Wolff's soft watercolors on two-page spreads are very appealing. The story line is direct and simple and can be used to initiate discussions of caring for pets and enjoying activities in nature with them.

■ Yolen, Jane. OWL MOON. Illus. by John Schoenherr. Putnam, 1987. Unp. (0-399-21457-7) Fiction. Interest Level: Ages 3–8
Owl Moon captures a special experience in this beautifully illustrated picture book. A young girl tells of her walk in the woods with her father one

moonlit winter night to call down a great horned owl. Perhaps the youngest in her family, she has been waiting "to go owling with Pa for a long, long time." It is cold, a time when they must be very quiet, and it's a bit scary, too. But what a wondrous experience. Her father calls out several times, "Whoo-whoo-who-who-who-whooooo" from different places in the woods. At last they are rewarded when an owl returns their call, flys near, and perches on a branch where "for one minute, three minutes, maybe even a hundred minutes," they stared at one another. At last the owl flies off, and father and daughter head home. Yolen's prose captures the wonder and magic of the moonlit walk and encounter. Schoenherr's pen-and-ink washes depict the snow-covered, moonlit fields and the deep-dark woods from varying perspectives with a bundled up father and daughter walking quietly through.

Awards: ALA Notable Children's Book, 1987; Caldecott Medal, 1988

A Closer Look

■ **Allen, Marjorie N., and Shelley Rotner. CHANGES. Photos by Shelley Rotner. Macmillan, 1991. Unp. (0-02-700252-7) Nonfiction. Interest Level: Ages 3–5**
Razor sharp photographs illustrate the concept of changes in nature in this handsome picture book. From pinecone to tree, egg to bird, caterpillar to butterfly, baby to toddler, and fall to winter, Rotner's richly-colored images record and illuminate growth and seasonal changes. Allen's minimal text supports the photographs in a well-designed format. Preschool and primary teachers will find this book useful in developing units on seasons and growth; beginning nature watchers will find *Changes* helps them to focus their observations.

■ **Arnosky, Jim. COME OUT, MUSKRATS. Illus. by author. Lothrop, 1989. Unp. (LB 0-688-05458-6) Nonfiction. Interest Level: Ages 2–5**
Although they are nocturnal, it is not unusual to see muskrats early or late in the day along rivers and marshes, especially if you are out in a canoe or rowboat. Young children who have seen muskrats will enjoy Arnosky's close-up observations of the activities of a family of muskrats in their marshy habitat. It is a pleasing introduction to wildlife watching. Softly colored but detailed drawings of muskrats show them coming out at dusk to swim, eat, and play through the night. The brief, rhythmical text in large print adds to the charm of the illustrations. This is similar to Arnosky's *Watching Foxes* (Lothrop, 1985).

Award: OSTB, 1989

■ Coxe, Molly. WHOSE FOOTPRINTS? Illus. by author. Harper, 1991. Unp.
(LB 0-694-04837-8) Fiction. Interest Level: Ages 2–5
It is a winter day on a snow-covered farmstead, and there are lots of animal
tracks for a mother and her preschool daughter to follow. The tracks lead
them through the barnyard and into the barn. The question, "Whose footprints?" is posed on one page and answered on the next. Mother and
daughter discover tracks belonging to a cat, a rooster, a mouse, a pony, a
sheep, a dog, and even their own and the father's footprints. At the end of
the day, the family enjoys popcorn together by the wood stove. A simple
family story for very young children, *Whose Footprints?* suggests a way for
families to enjoy and observe nature in winter through animal tracking. The
illustrations are bright and appealing, although they do not provide enough
detail to be used as an identification guide.

■ Ehlert, Lois. FEATHERS FOR LUNCH. Illus. by author. Harcourt, 1990.
Unp. (0-15-230-550-5) Fiction. Interest Level: Ages 3–8
A clever "cat tale" about a cat looking for an easy lunch, this picture book
will introduce young children to bird watching and sharpen their observation skills at the same time. In rhyming verse and large type, Ehlert describes the antics of her cat, who sneaks out of the house and stalks the
neighborhood birds. On each two-page spread, readers see a different bird
portrayed life-size in a natural setting. Each bird is identified, its own
particular call is given (for example, "what cheer, cheer, cheer" for the
cardinal), and plants or trees it frequents are named. A mini-field guide is
appended. Titled "The Lunch That Got Away," it provides field notes and a
small picture of each of the birds stalked by the cat: northern cardinal,
northern oriole, red-winged blackbird, blue jay, American robin, mourning
dove, ruby-throated hummingbird, American goldfinch, house sparrow,
house wren, northern flicker, and red-headed woodpecker. Bright, bold
colors create flat shapes on a white background with enough detail to
identify. The book is a creative blend of fiction and field guide information.
Award: OSTB, 1990

■ Florian, Douglas. NATURE WALK. Illus. by author. Greenwillow, 1989.
Unp. (LB 0-688-08269-6) Fiction. Interest Level: Ages 2–6
An excellent beginning nature book for the youngest, *Nature Walk* helps
young children with observation and identification skills while presenting
animals typical of a forest habitat. A mother and two children take a walk
through a forest on a summer day observing the wildlife. Young children
will enjoy the brief, rhyming text in large print, which calls attention to some
of the things in the forest. On the final page Florian shows 20 plants and

animals and ask readers to find them elsewhere in the book. Florian's roughly sketched crayon drawings outlined in black are appealing. Share this with children before and after a walk in the woods. Companion volumes include *A Summer Day* (Greenwillow, 1988), *A Winter Day* (Greenwillow, 1987), and *A Year in the Country* (Greenwillow, 1989).

Award: OSTB, 1989

■ Hoban, Tana. LOOK AGAIN! Photos by author. Macmillan, 1971. Unp. (0-02-744050-8) Nonfiction. Interest Level: Ages 2–6
For more than 20 years photographer Tana Hoban has been creating books that encourage observation and discovery. *Look Again* invites participation through its unusual format. Cutouts expose only a small square of a photograph and reveal an interesting pattern that is part of something or somebody larger. When the page is turned, the whole object appears (a dandelion, a zebra, a shell, a peacock, and so forth). On the following page the same object is seen from even farther away, providing three perspectives. Subjects are all taken from the natural world and have patterns and textures that could be part of something else, helping to create a sense of mystery. Black and white photographs effectively highlight the patterns and textures in nature.

■ McMillan, Bruce. COUNTING WILDFLOWERS. Illus. by author. Lothrop, 1986. Unp. (LB 0-688-02860-8) Nonfiction. Interest Level: Ages 2–5
Counting Wildflowers is a counting book that also helps children sharpen their observation skills. Wildflowers common to roadsides, thickets, vacant lots, and gardens grow at a young child's eye level and will attract their attention while on nature hikes or on neighborhood walks. McMillan encourages name and color identification and an awareness of the variety of sizes and shapes in nature through his exquisitely photographed wildflowers. The flowers are labeled with common names, one species per page (one fragrant water lily, two spiderworts, three true forget-me-nots, and so on). The photographs of up to twenty flowers are followed by a list for adults of the flowers' common and scientific names, blooming season, and habitat. Clean design and excellent color reproduction make this book a good choice for nurturing young nature lovers.

Award: ALA Notable Children's Book, 1986

■ McMillan, Bruce. GROWING COLORS. Photos by author. Lothrop, 1988. Unp. (LB 0-688-07845-1) Nonfiction. Interest Level: Ages 2–6
Not just a color identification book, *Growing Colors* teaches young children about the variety of color in nature and also about the places where fruits and vegetables grow—in the ground, on the ground, and even up in trees. Carefully designed with sharp, clear photographs, the book includes 14

fruits and vegetables in 10 different colors. Because some colors repeat, children can look for differences in the yellow of a squash and of an ear of corn or the purple in a plum and the purple of an unusual purple bean. Each spread includes a full-page close-up photograph of the fruit or vegetable on the right. On the facing page a smaller photograph shows the whole plant. Each color is written out and printed in the color of the fruit or vegetable, reinforcing the color concept. All the plants are pictured and identified by name and color on the last two-page spread.

■ **Peters, Lisa Westburg. THE SUN, THE WIND AND THE RAIN. Illus. by Ted Rand. Holt, 1988. Unp. (0-8050-0699-0) Nonfiction. Interest Level: Ages 3–7**
Children will look at mountains in a new light after reading *The Sun, the Wind and the Rain*, a story that describes how mountains are formed and shaped by the elements over time. A young girl named Elizabeth spends a day on the beach building a sand mountain. By comparing the growth of a real mountain with that of Elizabeth's sand mountain, and discussing how both are shaped by the sun, the wind and the rain, Peters makes a geologic concept accessible to children. Rand's pictures of Elizabeth and her sand mountain are set within the illustrations of the big mountain, a technique that is effective in showing the changes that have occurred to both. This book is perfect to share before a trip to a hilly or mountainous terrain.
Award: OSTB, 1988

■ **Robbins, Ken. A FLOWER GROWS. Photos by author. Dial, 1990. Unp. (LB 0-8037-0765-7) Nonfiction. Interest Level: Ages 4–8**
For those children who do not have easy access to backyards or city parks, growing plants indoors is one way to see and observe nature. Photographer Ken Robbins chose an amaryllis, an elegant, beautiful, and easy-to-grow flower, to show the life cycle of a plant. Grown from what he calls an ugly bulb that thrives in tropical forests, the amaryllis emerges dramatically on a tall stem with large, showy flowers that last about two weeks. Although more expensive than a packet of marigold seeds, an amaryllis bulb provides a radiant example of the stages of development in a plant and its growth is exciting for both parent and child to observe. Robbins's hand-tinted photographs and elegant design capture the amaryllis' growth and make an attractive presentation. His simple well-written text describes the plant's life cycle, and an afterword explains how to plant and care for the bulb.
Award: OSTB, 1990

■ **Ryder, Joanne. WHERE BUTTERFLIES GROW. Illus. by Lynne Cherry. Dutton, 1989. Unp. (0-525-67284-2) Nonfiction. Interest Level: Ages 5–7**

Ryder's technique of encouraging readers to imagine what it is like to become a particular animal will help them improve their powers of observation. In *Growing Butterflies* the reader learns where caterpillars live, what they eat, and how they grow, change, make a cocoon, and eventually become butterflies. Cherry's lush illustrations detail the swallowtail butterfly's habitat and show its life cycle from egg to caterpillar to butterfly, making it easy for readers to find and identify them in their own backyards, if conditions are right. In an afterword, Ryder describes which plants to grow that will attract swallowtail butterflies and how to watch a caterpillar grow and change.

■ **Selsam, Millicent, and Ronald Goor. BACKYARD INSECTS. Photos by Ronald Goor. Scholastic, 1988. 40pp. (paper 0-590-42256-1) Nonfiction. Interest Level: Ages 3–8**
Backyards are a natural choice for beginning nature watchers. They are accessible to many children and, as Selsam and Goor suggest, their insect populations are quite high. Over 1,000 insects can be found in a single backyard. This book, about the ways in which insects defend themselves, will give young readers a close-up look at several common insects like caterpillars, spittlebugs, bees, beetles, and butterflies. The clear, colorful photographs show different types of insect defenses such as camouflage, warning colors, and copycat coloration, and illustrate how well-protected some insects are. The simple text invites close observation and identification and makes the book a good companion for backyard nature explorations. Older children will enjoy Norsgaard's *Nature's Great Balancing Act: In Our Own Backyard* (Cobblehill, 1990).

■ **Selsam, Millicent, and Joyce Hunt. KEEP LOOKING! Illus. by Normand Chartier. Macmillan, 1989. 32pp. (0-02-781840-3) Nonfiction. Interest Level: Ages 3–7**
The snow-covered yard outside a house in the country is the setting for this inviting picture book, which introduces children to a variety of winter creatures and their habitats. Subdued watercolors create a naturalistic landscape where animals blend in with their surroundings but are never too difficult for young children to find. Selsam and Hunt invite readers to keep looking on each page as they describe active and hibernating animals both above and below ground. In a final spread, the authors ask readers to find the animals pictured (a squirrel, a rabbit, and a junco). An index lists all the animals pictured and their locations. The book provides an appealing way to encourage observation of animals in winter.
Award: OSTB, 1989

■ Showers, Paul. THE LISTENING WALK. Illus. by Aliki. Harper, 1991. Unp. (LB 0-06-021638-7) Fiction. Interest Level: Ages 3–6
In this update of a classic first published in 1961, author Paul Showers reminds readers that they can use their ears as well as their eyes to experience their environment. This new edition benefits from Aliki's cheerful, fresh, full-color illustrations done in pen and ink, watercolor, and crayon. In this version, the boy who took a "listening walk" with his pipe-smoking father through their city neighborhood to a nearby park is replaced by a young girl walking with a nonsmoking dad. "On a Listening Walk I do not talk," she explains and she listens to many different sounds including lawn mowers, sprinklers, and cars. In the park she listens to birds, bees, and crickets. *A Listening Walk* is a good choice to use in conjunction with neighborhood walks for preschool and early primary grades. This new edition is worth the upgrade.

■ Wexler, Jerome. FLOWERS, FRUITS, SEEDS. Photos by author. Prentice, 1987. Unp. (LB 0-13-322397-3) Nonfiction. Interest Level: Ages 2–6
Colorful photographs show the shape, color, and size of flowers, fruits, and seeds in this attractive introduction to variations in plants. The brief text, geared to young children, describes additional physical characteristics such as taste, smell, and texture with just a bit of information on function, i.e. "mostly flowers are for producing fruits that contain seeds", and "mostly, fruits are to protect the seeds inside them," and "mostly, seeds are for growing new plants." A final page pictures a pear tree's flower, fruit, and seeds to illustrate the cycle. Photos are captioned with common names and include many flowers, fruits and seeds young children will be familiar with—dandelions, watermelons, acorns.

■ Wilson, April, and A.J. Wood. LOOK! THE ULTIMATE SPOT-THE-DIF-FERENCE BOOK. Illus. by April Wilson. Dial, 1990. Unp. (0-8037-0925-0) Nonfiction. Interest Level: Age 6 up
Spot-the-difference pictures have long been popular. April Wilson and A.J. Wood take the concept to new heights and to new places in a lushly illustrated picture book that invites readers to compare bordered pictures on facing pages in 12 diverse habitats around the world. Readers must look carefully to note a frog catching a fly in the mountain scrub of Australasia, crocodiles hatching in the Australian rain forest, pepper-vine fruits ripening from green to red along a river's edge in South Asia, or a spotted crab camouflaged in the ocean. The key to the color plates that follow is a bit confusing. Differences are highlighted in red (but not explained) on small black-and-white reproductions. The reproductions also include a numbered guide with brief notes on the flora and fauna of each habitat. Both illustra-

tions and notes emphasize the richness and diversity of life on earth and acquaint readers with symbiosis, camouflage, predator-prey relationships, and seasonal changes. A little more emphasis on the fragility of the habitats would have been welcome, but as it is, the book will keep young people and their parents busy for hours.

■ **Yabuuchi, Masayuki. WHOSE FOOTPRINTS? Illus. by author. Putnam, 1985. 30pp. (0-399-21209-4) Nonfiction. Interest Level: Ages 2−7**
The simple, clean format of this brief book will appeal to young children beginning to notice animal tracks. Six large-size footprints are illustrated (duck, cat, goat, horse, bear, and hippopotamus), each on a double-page spread. To find out what animal has made the tracks, readers turn the page and see the animal pictured against a white background. Although no information on the animals' habitat is included, and children are not likely to come across the tracks of some of these animals, *Whose Footprints?* introduces young children to the different tracks animals make in an appealing way. Children will enjoy the format and the realistic illustrations. Yabuuchi's companion volume, *Whose Baby?* (Putnam, 1985) has a similar format and identifies the parents of several baby animals.

■ **Ziefert, Harriet. SARAH'S QUESTIONS. Illus. by Susan Bonners. Lothrop, 1986. Unp. (LB 0-688-05615-6) Fiction. Interest Level: Ages 4−6**
Tired of gardening, young Sarah asks her mom to play I spy. Soon they are taking a walk through a lush countryside and "spying" birds, bees, clouds, flowers, and other delights of a summer day out of doors. As they head back home, a stream of questions inspired by their observations flows from Sarah. "Why do squirrels have bushy tails?" and "Why do bees buzz?" she asks. Mother patiently and intelligently answers Sarah's questions. She admits when she does not know the answers and asks Sarah what she thinks. When they arrive home and Mom tires of the continuing flow of questions, she suggests that they ask Grandpa, who, in the last picture, appears to have taken up the challenge of answering Sarah's questions. Both characters provide good models for adults who know how to nurture a child's curiosity. Bonners's lush impressionistic illustrations capture the dappled summer light.

■ **Ziefert, Harriet. UNDER THE WATER. Illus. by Suzy Mandel. Viking, 1990. Unp. (0-670-83198-0) SERIES: Hello Reading! Nonfiction. Interest Level: Ages 3−8**
Here is a book for preschoolers and beginning readers that will pique their interest in what is beneath the water—ocean water. With short simple sentences and bright pictures, *Under the Water* takes readers on a snorkeling tour of typical marine plants and animals in and around a coral reef. Ziefert

takes care to point out similarities and differences and introduces some ecological concepts. She also encourages respect for the environment as she reminds snorkeler's not to take shells with living creatures or to litter. "Take only photos; leave only bubbles, is the snorkeler's motto," says Ziefert. For children who are not likely to go snorkeling, *Under the Water* is a good introduction to the richness and diversity of life under the sea.

Respect for All Living Things

■ Aragon, Jane Chelsea. WINTER HARVEST. Illus. by Leslie Baker. Little, 1988. Unp. (LB 0-316-04937-9) Fiction. Interest Level: Ages 3–7
A family's custom of feeding deer in the winter is transformed in this story told from a young girl's point of view. A family of deer gather at the edge of a woods on a cold and snowy winter night watching the house in the distance. Every evening in the winter when the deer cannot find anything to eat, the young girl and her father bring them food. After eating, the young deer romp and play in the snow and then bed down under the pines. In the morning the deer pass by the house, pausing to look in the window at the girl and her younger brother. Baker alternates outdoor scenes of the cold, snowy winter night with illustrations of a cozy, caring family who take the time to think of the wildlife that surrounds them. Her watercolors are soft and gentle. In *Salt Hands* (Dutton, 1989), Aragon tells a related story of a magical encounter between a young girl and a deer.

■ Baker, Keith. WHO IS THE BEAST? Illus. by author. Harcourt, 1990. Unp. (0-15-296057-0) Fiction. Interest Level: Ages 2–5
In a thick, lush forest, animals scatter and hide to escape the beast, a tiger making his way through the jungle. When the tiger sees his reflection in a pond, he realizes that the animals think *he* is the beast. He then goes back through the jungle showing the animals how they are similar—the tiger and the snake both have green, round eyes; the tiger and the monkey both have tails that swing from side to side, and so on. In the final spread all the animals appear, and the tiger declares: "Who is the beast? Now I see. We all are beasts—you and me." The brief, rhyming text, one line per page, is simple and will hold the interest of young children. The bold, acrylic illustrations on two-page spreads make this suitable for a story hour as well as for sharing one-to-one. *Who Is the Beast* offers a subtle environmental lesson on the value of all "beasts" in the jungle and fosters an attitude of coexistence rather than confrontation.

■ Brinckloe, Julie. FIREFLIES! Illus. by author. Macmillan, 1985. Unp. (LB 0-02-713310-9) Fiction. Interest Level: Ages 5–9

Brinckloe captures perfectly those magical summer evenings when fireflies are out and excited children are drawn to them like moths are to street-lights. In *Fireflies!* she shows the distress a young boy feels when the fireflies he has so proudly caught and placed in a jar ("I caught hundreds!" he keeps telling his parents) stop glowing. His distress turns into empathy for the insects, which are beating their wings against the jar and falling to the bottom. He lets the fireflies out of the jar, and they "pour out into the night . . . blinking on, blinking off . . . like stars dancing." Brinckloe tells the story from the point of view of the boy, whose actions and feelings ring true. Her pencil sketches accurately reflect the boy's excitement, pride, wonder, and sadness. She portrays a sensitive story that may help children develop respect for living things.

■ **Burns, Diane L. ARBOR DAY. Illus. by Kathy Rogers. Carolrhoda, 1989. 48pp. (LB 0-87614-346-X)** SERIES: **On My Own. Nonfiction. Interest Level: Ages 6–10**
In an easy-to-read style, Burns weaves a lot of information on trees and their role in the environment into her narrative on the origins of Arbor Day and on various efforts to plant and conserve trees in America. Along with J. Sterling Morton, a Nebraskan known as the Father of Arbor Day, Burns mentions the efforts of John Chapman, also known as Johnny Appleseed, Theodore Roosevelt, who set aside millions of acres of national forest land, and Gifford Pinchot, the first head of the U.S. Forest Service. She also mentions how children have been involved with Arbor Day. An afterword explains how to plant your own tree for Arbor Day. The watercolor illustrations, which alternate with black line drawings, add to the appeal of this book for young readers. There is bibliography or index.

■ **Carrick, Donald. THE TREE. Illus. by author. Macmillan, 1971. Unp. o.p. Fiction. Interest Level: Ages 3–8**
When a favorite tree next to Erik's house has grown too large, it must be cut down, leaving an empty spot in the yard and an empty feeling in Erik. But he and his father find a way to remember the tree and to replace it as well. First, they go to the sawmill and watch the tree being cut up. They ask the worker at the sawmill to save some of the wood, and, in the spring when the boards are dry, they make a chair for Erik. Then they plant another tree in an open spot away from the house. Carrick is sensitive to Erik's sense of loss when the tree is cut down, and his watercolor illustrations in shades of brown effectively show Erik's feelings about the tree.

■ **Caseley, Judith. GRANDPA'S GARDEN LUNCH. Illus. by author. Green-willow, 1990. Unp. (LB 0-688-08817-1) Fiction. Interest Level: Ages 3–6**

A child would be lucky to have a grandfather like Sarah's, who nurtures her love of gardening. Together they plant vegetable and flower seeds, water plants, go to the nursery, plant seedlings, and, when the harvest is ready, they enjoy a lunch made with the vegetables and herbs from the garden. Caseley's short, matter-of-fact sentences are illustrated with cheerful water-colors, many with decorative borders. In this family, Grandpa not only gardens and teaches his granddaughter, but he also helps with the cooking and serves Grandma and Sarah their garden lunch.

■ Cazet, Denys. A FISH IN HIS POCKET. Illus. by author. Orchard, 1987. Unp. (LB 0-531-08313-6) Fiction. Interest Level: Ages 3–8
Russell is a small bear with a big heart in this funny and touching story. On his way to school, Russell stops by a pond and breaks the morning ice. While looking at a school of little fish, a book slips out of his backpack and falls into the pond. He retrieves the soggy book but, when he arrives at school, discovers that a small fish had gotten caught in the book. The teacher tells him that she can help him take care of the book but that she does not know what to do about the fish. Russell does not know what to do about the fish either, so he puts it in his pocket. For the rest of the day, he cannot keep his mind off it. During art class he finds a way to give the fish a fitting good-bye by making a paper boat that he names *Take Care*. After school he heads back to the pond, places the fish in the boat, sets it on the water, and watches it sail away. "Take care," he says. Russell's struggle to deal with his accidental killing of another creature is endearing and praiseworthy. As the characters do in Brinckloe's *Fireflies!* (Macmillan, 1985) and Johnson's *A Visit to the Country* (Harper, 1989), Russell decides on his own how to solve a problem. Cazet's watercolors add a light touch to the story.

■ Cooney, Barbara. MISS RUMPHIUS. Illus. by author. Viking, 1982. Unp. (0-670-47958-6) Fiction. Interest Level: Ages 4–8
As a small child, Alice helps her artist grandfather while listening to his stories of faraway places. These stories inspire her to tell her grandfather that she also wants to travel around the world and then return to live by the sea when she is old. Alice's grandfather gently reminds her of a third thing that she must do during her lifetime: to make the world a little more beautiful. Alice grows up and, just as she had hoped, journeys to a tropical island, climbs tall mountains, and explore jungles and deserts. One day, she accidentally falls off a camel and hurts her back. She decides it is time to return home and buy a house near the sea. There she plants a small garden of blue, purple, and rose-colored lupines. The next spring, much to her delight, the flowers bloom. Although she would like to plant more lupines, her bad back keeps her bedridden. During the following year, the wind and

the birds spread the seeds for her, and lupines begin to appear in many unexpected places. Alice's health improves and she orders five bushels of lupine seeds "from the very best seed house." Like Johnny Appleseed, Alice wanders through the countryside scattering flower seeds, much to the amusement of the local townspeople who dub her That Crazy Old Lady. As the beautiful lupines burst into bloom year after year, Alice becomes known as the Lupine Lady. Now very old, Alice, like her grandfather, gathers the children around her to tell them stories of her adventures and to pass onto them her legacy "to make the world a more beautiful place."

In Miss Rumphius, past and present, art and life are inextricably woven together into a unique picture book. Barbara Cooney's vibrant illustrations, painted in acrylics with colored-pencil accents, give her story a peaceful, old-fashioned quality. The inspiring story of Alice Rumphius reminds us that an individual can make a difference and that each of us has a responsibility to make the world in which we live a better, more beautiful place.

Awards: American Book Award, 1983; NSSB, 1982

■ Fife, Dale H. THE EMPTY LOT. Illus. by Jim Arnosky. Little, 1991. Unp. (LB 0-316-28167-0) Fiction. Interest Level: Ages 5–8
We often say a piece of land is empty when nothing has been built on it. Fife offers readers a fresh look at an "empty" lot in this story about a man who visits the vacant lot he owns before selling it. There he discovers that it is a habitat for birds, small mammals, insects, assorted trees, shrubs, and flowers. As he walks about he sees that the lot is quite occupied by typical city wildlife and that it also serves as a play area for neighborhood kids. He decides that rather than sell the land to someone who would use it for a parking lot or a factory, he will leave it just as it is. Fife's preservation message is presented lightly, and Arnosky's pencil and watercolor drawings are done in a similar spirit.

■ Johnson, Herschel. A VISIT TO THE COUNTRY. Illus. by Romare Bearden. Harper, 1989. Unp. (LB 0-06-022854-7) Fiction. Interest Level: Ages 4–8
While staying with his grandparents in the country, Mike finds an injured baby cardinal. He lovingly nurses the young bird to health. When the bird learns to fly, his grandfather finds a cage to keep it in, but before long it becomes clear that "Max" is not happy as a pet in a cage. Mike's grandparents let him handle this dilemma, and he makes the difficult decision to free the bird. Although he misses Max, Mike understands that he has made the right decision. The themes of kindness to animals and respect for wildlife are developed naturally, without didacticism. Romare Bearden's unusual watercolors are bright in color and primitive in design.

■ Kalas, Sybille. THE GOOSE FAMILY BOOK. Trans. by Patricia Crampton. Photos by author. Picture Book, 1986. Unp. (0-88708-019-7) Nonfiction. Interest Level: Ages 4–8
Appealing photographs of naturalist Kalas and her preschool-age son on their European goose farm illustrate this book about a family of geese on a farm. Mother (and son) observe the geese while Kalas describes in a conversational tone how eggs are incubated and hatched and how the young geese mature and find their place in the goose family and in the flock. The pictures and the narrative show the care and respect Kalas has for geese; it is clear that the Kalas family and the geese are comfortable with each other. Many of the colored photographs provide a close-up look at the eggs and the young goslings. In the preface Konrad Lorenz emphasizes the importance of introducing children to the beauty and harmony of nature, saying that a person's emotional response to an animal increases his or her awareness and respect. This book makes an attractive introduction for both preschool and primary nature awareness units. Other books by Kalas include *The Beaver Family Book* (Picture Book, 1987) and *The Wild Horse Family Book* (Picture Book, 1989).

Award: OSTB, 1986

■ Lapp, Eleanor. THE BLUEBERRY BEARS. Illus. by Margot Apple. Whitman, 1983. Unp. o.p. Fiction. Interest Level: Ages 4–7
This story pokes fun at Bessie Allen, a woman whose greed for the wild blueberries outside her cabin causes her to harvest more than she can use. Once she has picked every ripe berry in sight and has made every blueberry recipe imaginable (she even feeds them to her cat and dog), she still has a cabin full of blueberries. When the local bears (which also love blueberries) arrive to find the patch picked clean, they raid Bessie's cabin and rid her of all her extra blueberries, making a blue mess of things. Bessie vows to leave some of the berries for the bears next year. Although the story could have been told with greater effect, the black line drawings washed with touches of blue are humorous and have appeal. The message that one should take only what one needs from the earth's bounty is lightly conveyed.

■ Le Tord, Bijou. RABBIT SEEDS. Illus. by author. Macmillan, 1984. Unp. (0-590-07797-X) Fiction. Interest Level: Ages 2–6
With simple line drawings, Le Tord celebrates a gardener's annual cycle of growing. Her diligent and patient rabbit gardener prepares the soil, plans the garden, plants seeds, waters, weeds, harvests, and finally puts away his tools. Black line drawings against a white background are framed on each page with pastel washes in this small picture book that introduces young children to the gardener's year.

■ Newton, Patricia Montgomery. THE FIVE SPARROWS. Illus. by author. Atheneum, 1982. Unp. o.p. Fiction. Interest Level: Ages 6–10
Adapted from a Japanese folktale, *The Five Sparrows* tells of a kind old woman who tends a wounded sparrow back to health, in spite of ridicule from her family and friends. Her kindness is rewarded when the sparrow brings back a magic seed that produces an abundance of food for the family. When a jealous neighbor deliberately wounds four sparrows in order to "nurse" them back to health and reap even greater rewards, the neighbor and her family meet with misfortune. The story is told well and can be used in discussions on respect for wildlife and on how and why we value wildlife.

Award: NSSB, 1982

■ Paterson, Katherine. THE TALE OF THE MANDARIN DUCKS. Illus. by Leo Dillon and Diane Dillon. Dutton, 1990. Unp. (LB 0-525-67283-4) Fiction. Interest Level: Ages 6–9
Compassion for one's fellow creatures is one of the themes expressed in Paterson's retelling of a Japanese folktale about a wealthy lord driven to possess beautiful things to adorn his house and garden. In the story, the lord captures and cages a handsome mandarin duck. Kept in captivity and separated from his mate, the duck languishes. The chief steward suggests that the duck should be released, but the lord refuses. The kitchen maid pities the duck and sets him free. The lord first blames the steward who had tried to get the duck released but eventually blames the kitchen maid as well when he sees she and the steward have fallen in love. He sentences them both to death, but they are saved by two messengers who lead them through the forest to a house where the couple live in peace. The Dillon's subtle, stylized paintings are reminiscent of Japanese woodcuts. *The Tale of the Manderin Ducks* is a handsome, beautifully told story.

Awards: ALA Notable Children's Book, 1990; NSSB, 1990

■ Pedersen, Judy. THE TINY PATIENT. Illus. by author. Knopf, 1989. Unp. (LB 0-394-90170-3) Fiction. Interest Level: Ages 3–6
Pedersen's story of caring for an injured bird is told with simple matter-of-factness in this picture book. A young girl and her grandmother find an injured sparrow in their yard. They feed her, make a nest for her, and put her next to the window so that she can feel close to her friends and the trees. When her wing is mended and she is well enough to fly, they let her go. The girl does not try to make the bird into a pet, nor is she reluctant to let her go. Kindness and tenderness are evoked both through the text and the soft

but somewhat stiff illustrations. The simplicity of the message and the format make this a good choice for young children.

Award: OSTB, 1989

■ **Peet, Bill. THE GNATS OF KNOTTY PINE. Illus. by author. Houghton, 1975. 46pp. (0-395-21405-X) Fiction. Interest Level: Ages 4–8**
Bill Peet has written for young children on a number of environmental themes, and in *The Gnats of Knotty Pine* he takes aim at hunting. As he says in his dedication: "To my young friends who love toy guns with the hope that you won't grow up to love real guns with real bullets that kill real things." The story is told from the point of view of the animals of Knotty Pine Forest who gather together before hunting season to try to devise a plan to save themselves. They do not come up with a plan, but they shoo away the local swarm of gnats that offer to help. Nevertheless, when hunting season begins, the gnats save the day (and the animals) by swarming the hunters who quickly leave. Peet's antihunting position is obvious. *The Gnats of Knotty Pine* has a place on the shelves for readers who enjoy his good storytelling and sense of humor, and who share his attitude on hunting.

■ **Pike, Norman. THE PEACH TREE. Illus. by Robin DeWitt and Patricia DeWitt. Stemmer, 1983. Unp. (0-88045-014-2) Fiction. Interest Level: Ages 4–8**
Everyone in the Pomeroy family enjoys the new peach tree in their orchard and they look forward to ripe peaches. But when aphids attack, the leaves of the tree begin to wilt. Mr. Pomeroy takes advantage of a natural pest control by bringing in a horde of ladybugs, which devour the aphids and save the tree. Although some readers may find *The Peach Tree* somewhat on the sweet side, Pike effectively introduces the concept of the food chain to young readers in an attractively illustrated picture book that emphasizes the interdependence of all creatures. Organic gardeners will appreciate this story, which shows how pests can be controlled without chemicals.

■ **Pittman, Helena Clare. THE GIFT OF THE WILLOWS. Illus. by author. Carolrhoda, 1988. Unp. (LB 0-87614-354-0) Fiction. Interest Level: Ages 6–9**
Set in Japan, this romantic tale about a potter and his wife tells of their close affinity with nature and of how they are rewarded for their care of two willow trees. The childless couple live near a river. Over the years the potter takes great pleasure in watching two willow trees struggle to grow along the banks of the river where he comes for the clay he uses to make pots. The

trees provide shade and a place to rest. Fearing the trees will die during a drought, the potter and his wife water them and see them through the hard conditions. Soon they learn they are to have a child. But shortly after their son is born, a great winter storm floods the river and threatens their home. When one of the willows, now full grown, is knocked down during the storm, it forms a bridge that allows the family to cross the river to safety. *The Gift of the Willows* is a love story on two levels; of the couple for each other and of their love of nature. Graceful illustrations accentuate the drama and romance.

■ **Ryder, Joanne. LIZARD IN THE SUN. Illus. by Michael Rothman. Morrow, 1990. Unp. (LB 0-688-07173-2)** SERIES: **Just for a Day. Fiction. Interest Level: Ages 5–8**
In her Just for a Day series, Ryder takes young readers on an imaginary journey in which they are transformed into an animal "just for a day." The text of *Lizard in the Sun* is simple and poetic, emphasizing what it feels like to be an anole, a kind of lizard, as it changes color, hunts, is hunted, and warms itself in the sun. Rothman's bold acrylic paintings span the pages providing close-up, often dramatic views of the lizard and its world. Ryder's ability to get readers to imagine being a wild creature encourages their empathy and respect. Companion titles are *White Bear, Ice Bear* (Morrow, 1989) and *Catching the Wind* (Morrow, 1989).

■ **Say, Allen. RIVER DREAM. Illus. by author. Houghton, 1988. 32pp. (0-395-48294-1) Fiction. Interest Level: Ages 5–8**
When Uncle Scott sends Mark, who is sick, a small box for trout flies, it brings back memories of their first fishing trip together. When he opens the box, a cloud of mayflies flutter up and out the window, taking him into a river dream. He follows the mayflies out his window and finds a rowboat on a river, where in the hushed predawn hours he meets his uncle fly-fishing. Mark wants nothing more than to catch a trout and bring it home to show his parents. When his uncle catches one and lets it go, Mark is puzzled, but Uncle Scott says, "I like to leave the river the way I found it. It's like cutting trees, Mark. You keep cutting trees and soon you're going to have bald mountains." When Mark catches his trout, he too decides to let it go. Although Say's point of view is quite clear in *River Dream*, the story develops naturally and is not overwhelmed by that point of view. Discussions of why people fish may be sparked, however, and children may ask how the caught-and-released fish fare back in the water. The closeness between uncle and nephew and the magic of their very early morning fishing adventure is captured in Say's full-page watercolor illustrations.

■ Steele, Mary Q. ANNA'S GARDEN SONGS. Illus. by Lena Anderson. Green-willow, 1989. 32pp. (LB 0-688-08218-1) Nonfiction. Interest Level: Ages 5–9

Anna narrates these 14 poems about the tomatoes, the cherries, the cabbages, the herbs, and the other things growing in her garden. Both water-color illustrations and poems have a touch of whimsy. Anna is shown with a white rabbit and various friends among vegetables that at times become animated or grow to gigantic proportions. Anna contemplates picking them, eating or not eating them, selling them, and at the end of summer, remembering the fun of having a garden. This book is a slim but joyful collection of nature poems.

■ Takeichi, Yasoo, retold by. THE MIGHTY PRINCE. Illus. by Yoshimasa Sejima. Crown, 1971. Unp. o.p. Fiction. Interest Level: Ages 4–8

Adapted from a Japanese folktale, this story is a timely reminder that happiness comes from nurturing life, not from waging war. A warrior prince rules over his people with an iron fist, instigating wars and inspiring fear and hate. When a young child gives the prince a gift of seeds, he plants them, only because there are no battles to fight at the moment. As he works the soil and tends the garden, he has less time to fight, and his people think he has gone mad. When spring comes, the garden bursts forth with color, and the prince begins to think about the meaning of happiness. The child reminds him, "Look, my prince, look with all your heart. Instead of fighting, you have made things grow and people laugh and birds sing. They have all been waiting for this day. Aren't they beautiful?" Simple black-and-white drawings illustrate all but the final page, which, like the garden, bursts forth in color.

■ Titherington, Jeanne. PUMPKIN PUMPKIN. Illus. by author. Greenwil-low, 1986. 24pp. (LB 0-688-05696-2) Fiction. Interest Level: Ages 2–6

Titherington captures the joy and sense of accomplishment a young child has in planting and growing something in *Pumpkin Pumpkin*. Jamie plants a pumpkin seed and over the summer watches it grow into a huge pumpkin. In the fall, he picks it, scoops out the pulp, and carves a face in it for Halloween, but he saves six pumpkin seeds for planting next spring. Titherington's choice of a pumpkin will appeal to children. Her soft colored-pencil illustrations effectively show the enjoyment Jamie gets from watching the pumpkin grow, while in the background his grandfather gardens, and various animals wander through the scene. The simple cumulative text in large print make this a pleasure for very young children as well as for beginning readers (about Jamie's age). *Pumpkin Pumpkin* is a worthy successor to Krauss's *The Carrot Seed* (Harper, 1945).

Award: OSTB, 1986

■ **Udry, Janice May. A TREE IS NICE. Illus. by Marc Simont. Harper, 1956. Unp. (LB 0-06-026156-0) Fiction. Interest Level: Ages 3–8**
Winner of the Caldecott Medal in 1956, *A Tree Is Nice* describes the many ways we enjoy trees and benefit from them. Simont's watercolors show children playing around, climbing in, swinging from, and picnicking under trees. Udry also shows how trees shade people and houses. She ends by saying, "A tree is nice to plant. . . . Every day for years and YEARS you watch the little tree grow. You say to people, 'I planted that tree.' They wish they had one so they go home and plant a tree too." Although Udry focuses on how people benefit from trees and enjoy them, rather than on how trees play a role in providing food and shelter for animals, *A Tree Is Nice* captures the countless ways in which people enjoy trees. The simple text and fresh, colorful pictures (which alternate with black and white drawings) have held up well over the years. Her final encouragement to plant a tree is one that will continue to be taken to heart by families reading this book.

Award: Caldecott Medal, 1956

■ **Waterton, Betty. A SALMON FOR SIMON. Illus. by Ann Blades. Salem House, 1987. Unp. (paper 0-88899-036-7) Fiction. Interest Level: Ages 5–8**
Set off the western coast of Canada, this story tells of Simon, a young native boy who longs to catch a salmon. After a luckless summer of fishing, he gets a salmon unexpectedly when an eagle is startled into dropping its catch into a clam pool Simon had dug. But Simon finds that instead of joy, he feels sorry for the fish caught in the little pool. He decides to free it and digs a channel through the sand so the salmon can swim free. The book is not an antifishing story but one that gently conveys compassion for another creature. Simon is pleased with his actions, but he thinks ahead to tomorrow when he may fish again, although not for salmon. Full-page watercolors illustrate this picture book.

■ **Williams, Vera B. CHERRIES AND CHERRY PITS. Illus. by author. Greenwillow, 1986. Unp. (LB 0-688-05146-4) Fiction. Interest Level: Ages 3–8**
The joys of planting, growing, and reaping the fruits of one's labors to share with others is an underlying theme in this exuberant book about storytelling. The narrator writes about her neighbor and friend, Bidemmi, who has

a talent for making up stories to go with the pictures she draws. She tells and draws four stories that all revolve around cherries. The final story is about Bidemmi herself, who buys a bag of cherries and eats them, saving the pits to plant in her yard. She waters and weeds and watches as the pits grow, until the whole yard is filled with cherry trees and cherries, enough for the neighborhood, and "even for their friends from Nairobi and Brooklyn, Toronto and St. Paul." And the pits from all these eaten cherries "start to grow until there is a whole forest of cherry trees right on our block." Bright watercolors are interspersed with felt-tip-marker drawings in this imaginative and colorful picture book.

Award: ALA Notable Children's Book, 1986

The Web of Life

O ne of the most important aspects of children's environmental education is the study of ecology. This branch of science examines how living things interact with each other and their physical environment. If children gain a basic knowledge of ecology and its principles, they will be better equipped to understand environmental issues and problems like pesticide use, rain forest destruction, oil spills, global warming, and acid rain.

The first section includes books on ecological relationships: symbiosis in Margery Facklam's *Partners for Life,* food chains in Laurence Pringle's *Chains, Webs, and Pyramids* and some general ecology books like Norsgaard's *Nature's Great Balancing Act.* Several fine titles that appear in chapter two are, unfortunately, currently out of print.

Each ensuing section includes books that look at the ecological relationships found in habitats and ecosystems, from Arthur Dorros's appealing *Rain Forest Secrets* and Barbara Bash's excellent *Desert Giant* for younger readers to Bruce Hiscock's *Tundra* and Lynn Stone's *Wetlands* for middle or upper-level students.

General Ecology

■ Butcher, Julia. THE SHEEP AND THE ROWAN TREE. Illus. by author. Holt, 1984. Unp. o.p. Fiction. Interest Level: Ages 3–8
The familiar theme, "the grass is always greener" is used to tell a simple ecology lesson in this picture book. The protagonist is a rowan tree that shelters a flock of sheep in a beautiful grassy field. It longs to be able to move about like the sheep and see new sights. When an exotic migrating bird is blown off-course in a storm and lands on the tree, it tells the tree

about its far-off home and many other lands. Author-illustrator Butcher shows the personified tree languishing in several different habitats—desert, polar region, coral island, and so forth—as the bird explains how each would be unsuitable for the rowan tree. The desert is too hot and dry, the polar regions are too cold, and the coral islands are too windy and too close to salty seawater.

In the end the tree understands that it needs to live in its own habitat. The bordered and somewhat stylized illustrations are colorful and appealing. The illustrations of the anthropomorphized tree with its berry eyes and cheeks and twig nose and mouth are charming. *The Sheep and the Rowan Tree* makes an unusual introduction to habitats for young children.

■ Facklam, Margery. PARTNERS FOR LIFE: THE MYSTERIES OF ANIMAL SYMBIOSIS. Illus. by Pamela Johnson. Sierra Club, 1989. 48pp. (LB 0-316-25983-7) SERIES: A Lucas Evans Book. Nonfiction. Interest Level: Ages 9–12

Symbiotic relationships exist between animals, between plants, and between plants and animals. In *Partners for Life*, science writer Margery Facklam describes several of the unique relationships between animal species. In an introductory chapter Facklam explains three different kinds of symbiotic relationships—mutualism, commensalism, and parasitism. Subsequent chapters highlight colorful examples of partnerships between insects and partnerships between marine life and birds. She also gives examples of microscopic partners and parasitic partners. In a well-written final chapter Facklam puts symbiosis into an ecological perspective. Well-organized, clear writing, and an attention-getting topic will serve both interested young people and report writers. The book is nicely designed and illustrated with pencil drawings, and it includes an index. Sussman and James' *Big Friend, Little Friend* (Houghton, 1989) is not as thorough, but has a good selection of colored photographs.

Award: OSTB, 1989

■ Feltwell, John. ANIMALS AND WHERE THEY LIVE. Putnam, 1988. 64pp. (0-448-19218-7) SERIES: Windows on the World. Nonfiction. Interest Level: Ages 10 up

This attractive book on animal habitats is a good basic source of information for students who are doing research or who are just interested in the topic. Feltwell aims to discuss animals in relation to their habitats, noting that animals are adapted to particular terrains and climates. A picture map at the beginning of the book divides the world into various regions (polar, mountain, coral reef, ocean, desert), which provide the basis for his descriptions.

For each region he describes how animals have adapted to their surroundings and shows typical animals in attractive color illustrations. For each habitat he focuses on a particular geographic area—African savannahs in the section on grasslands, the North American desert for the section on deserts. Feltwell strays from his habitat approach, however, and interspersed among the sections on regions, he includes sections titled: "The Largest Animals," "Life on the Wing," "The Smallest Animals," and "Hunters and the Hunted," without making any connection between these animals and their habitats. Sections on cities as habitats and on endangered wildlife round out this overview. The book includes a chart defining major divisions in the animal world and an index.

■ **Gamlin, Linda. LIFE ON EARTH. Watts, 1988. 36pp. (LB 0-531-17120-5)** SERIES: **Today's World. Nonfiction. Interest Level: Ages 11 up**
Very broad in scope, high in visuals, and short on text, this overview of life on earth, like an encyclopedia, touches on a bit of everything. Divided into three sections—"What is Life?" "Living Communities," and "Habitats,"—*Life on Earth* covers topics such as growth and development, food webs, populations, conservation, endangered species, and wildlife preservation. The book is divided into two-page chapters with lots of photographs, boxed insert;, and illustrations. An extinction chart is appended, which includes several dozen currently endangered species. In her introduction, Gamlin stresses the delicate balance of nature and the often harmful effects people have on the environment. There is an underlying emphasis on environmental problems throughout the text. Because it tries to cover so much, *Life on Earth* sometimes oversimplifies. Although the text is well-written and short, the reading level is more difficult than the book's appearance suggests.

■ **Hughey, Pat. SCAVENGERS AND DECOMPOSERS: THE CLEANUP CREW. Illus. by Bruce Hiscock. Macmillan, 1984. 56pp. (0-689-31032-3) Nonfiction. Interest Level: Ages 9–14**
For most of us, garbage disposal means placing our trash in a can to be picked up and taken away to a landfill. But what happens to nature's "garbage," the wastes animals produce as well as the remains of plants and animals? In *Scavengers and Decomposers* Pat Hughey writes about nature's efficient partners, the animal scavengers who eat dead plants and animals and the decomposers who break down organic waste, producing nutrients for other living things. Explaining the important role these animals and organisms play in returning nutrients to the soil, she describes the habits of birds, mammals, ocean and freshwater animals, small insect and soil scavengers, molds, fungi, and bacteria. Respect for nature's cycles and

greater understanding and sensitivity to our effect on the environment are the topics of the final chapter. The chapters are short, and Hughey's writing is clear and readable. *Scavengers and Decomposers* will enrich both ecology and recycling units. The book includes a glossary and an index and is illustrated with pen-and-ink drawings.

Award: OSTB, 1984

■ Jacobs, Una. EARTH CALENDAR. Trans. by Jane Sutton. Illus. by author. Silver Burdett, 1986. 38pp. (paper 0-382-09219-8) Nonfiction. Interest Level: Ages 8–10
In *Earth Calendar,* Jacobs combines a broad look at the earth and the interconnections of life on it with picture-book illustrations. Beginning with the earth's place in the solar system, the author narrows her focus as she talks about the earth's crust, then about climate, soil, and plant and animal communities of the temperate zone. Natural habitats, adaptation, and food chains are described in the context of the changes from season to season. Soft, detailed ilustrations are keyed to the text. *Earth Calendar* is an imaginative and attractive presentation that can introduce readers to ecological concepts. Two others in the series, translated from German, are *Sun Calendar* and *Fish Calendar,* both published by Silver Burdett.

■ Lambert, David. VEGETATION. Bookwright, 1984. 48pp. (LB 0-531-03804-1) SERIES: Planet Earth. Nonfiction. Interest Level: Ages 9–12
This book presents a well-organized and attractive look at plants and their adaptations to different habitats. A beginning chapter on the development of plant life is followed by a discussion of vegetation in fresh water and oceans, polar regions, temperate and tropical forests, grasslands, and deserts. The emphasis is on how plants adapt to climate and terrain. A final section includes statistics and other kinds of information about plants. A glossary, a bibliography, and an index are included.

■ LIVING ON THE EARTH. National Geographic, 1988. 320pp. (LB 0-87044-736-X) Nonfiction. Interest Level: Ages 12 up
No study of habitats can be complete without exploring the human factor. National Geographic makes a fine contribution to the study of human ecology in *Living on the Earth.* Experts look at eight habitats—arid lands, arctic regions, islands, forests, grasslands, rivers, highlands, and coasts—examining the land and the various ways people have adapted to the particular conditions each offers. The writers are all experts in their field, and, while the writing style and format of this work is demanding, a wealth of informa-

tion is presented. Many striking, captioned photographs and a map accompany each chapter. The authors pay special attention to changes affecting the people and land in each habitat. Problems brought about by population growth, technology, climate change, and politics are addressed. The book includes a bibliography and an index.

■ Mazer, Anne. THE SALAMANDER ROOM. Illus. by Steve Johnson. Knopf, 1991. Unp. (LB 0-394-92945-4) Fiction. Interest Level: Ages 3–7
This striking picture book combines a young child's love of wild creatures (and desire to own them) with an introduction to the concept of habitat. A young boy, about six years old, finds an orange salamander on the forest floor and takes it home. As his mother asks him a series of questions on how he will take care of it, the boy describes the changes he will make to his room. As the illustrations show, the changes that the boy imagines transform his room bit by bit into a place where the salamander will feel at home. They show the boy bringing in leaves and moss for the salamander to sleep on, tree stumps and boulders for it to climb on, crickets and bullfrogs to keep it company, salamander friends to play with, and so on until the room finally becomes part of a forest environment. Only the sleeping boy and his bed remains, illuminated by moonlight. Johnson's paintings are rich with light and shadow and have a surrealistic touch that is in keeping with this imaginative story. Teachers introducing ecology to young children, parents looking for an imaginative book on caring for pets, and librarians seeking an unusual story-hour book with an ecological theme will all find this a satisfying story.

■ Norsgaard, E. Jaediker. NATURE'S GREAT BALANCING ACT: IN OUR OWN BACKYARD. Photos by Campbell Norsgaard. Dutton, 1990. 64pp. (0-525-65028-8) Nonfiction. Interest Level: Ages 9–12
There are no recently published general ecology books for young readers as attractive as this one. By using their own partially wild backyard to show how the balance of nature works, the Norsgaards can feature many plants and animals their readers will be familiar with. After brief conversational chapters on food chains and the balance of nature, the Norsgaards discuss the interrelationships of birds, insects, and mammals in their backyard. Insects, the most abundant inhabitants of a backyard environment, get the greatest emphasis. The sharply focused, color photographs that generously illustrate each two-page spread include many closeups of plants, insects, and other animals. This book will make an appealing supplement to an ecology unit, and should encourage readers to observe the balancing act in their own backyards. It includes a glossary and an index.

Award: OSTB, 1990

■ Pomerantz, Charlotte. THE DAY THEY PARACHUTED CATS ON BORNEO: A DRAMA OF ECOLOGY. Illus. by Jose Aruego. Addison, 1971. Unp. o.p. SERIES: Young Scott Books. Nonfiction. Interest Level: Ages 8 up

Based on a true incident, this inspired play conveys, as well as any book has since, the complex interrelationships of living things on the planet and the often unanticipated consequences of our solutions to environmental problems. Years ago on the island of Borneo, DDT was sprayed on the farmers' huts to rid the island of malaria-spreading mosquitoes. But the application of the chemical killed more than mosquitoes and brought on a series of troubles for the people of Borneo. Pomerantz tells the story through a drama that children can perform. The players in the drama—the island, the disease malaria, the chemical DDT, mosquitoes, cockroaches, caterpillars, lizards, cats, rivers, rats, helicopters, parapussycats, roof beams, the farmer, and the ecologist—tell their story in verse. Aruego's whimsical watercolors add humor to the ecological lesson and offer some ideas for costumes and props as well. DDT is now banned in the United States and several other countries, but it is still used in many developing countries. Pesticides are still a threat around the world. The lessons of this now out-of-print book are still timely.

■ Pringle, Laurence. CHAINS, WEBS, AND PYRAMIDS: THE FLOW OF ENERGY IN NATURE. Illus. by Jan Adkins. Harper, 1975. 34pp. (0-690-00562-8) Nonfiction. Interest Level: Ages 10–12

This older book on food chains remains a good basic title for most collections. Pringle explains how the process of photosynthesis enables plants to produce food energy, which in turn is used by other living things. The author also discusses the ways scientists study food chains in the laboratory and the field, other ecological models such as food webs and pyramids, and the impact of the world's growing population on the world food supply. Adkins's black-and-white illustrations and diagrams appear on most pages and enhance the text. The book's attractive cover and clean design keep it from looking dated. An index is included.

Award: OSTB, 1975

■ Pringle, Laurence. DEATH IS NATURAL. Morrow, 1991 (repr. of 1977 ed.). 64pp. (LB 0-688-10467-3) Nonfiction. Interest Level: Ages 8–12

"By learning about the deaths of many kinds of living things, we may accept more easily this natural and necessary part of the history of each living thing," says science writer Laurence Pringle. *Death Is Natural* is a thoughtful and reassuring book about the role death plays in the plant and animal world. Pringle begins by looking at the death of an individual animal. He shows what happens when a rabbit dies—how its body decomposes, becomes part of the soil, and nourishes other living things. He also looks at the role of death in balancing, or regulating, animal and plant populations, in evolution, and in the extinction of species. He notes with concern the accelerated pace of extinction of many species because of human interference, suggesting that humans may unwittingly be endangering their own future by their actions. The book is illustrated with black-and-white photographs, and it includes a glossary and an index.

Awards: ALA Notable Children's Book, 1977; OSTB, 1977

■ Pringle, Laurence. HOME: HOW ANIMALS FIND COMFORT AND SAFETY. Macmillan, 1987. 71pp. (0-684-18526-1) Nonfiction. Interest Level: Ages 9–14
"Anyone who cares about saving the earth's rich variety of animal life must also care about all of the diverse places that are animal homes," says Pringle in this book about the extraordinary variety of animal homes found in North America. Looking at burrows, webs, nests, shells, community homes, homes on other animals, and home territories, among others, Pringle describes how they are made and their importance to the animals' survival. Some animal homes are especially vulnerable at certain times, such as during an animal's breeding season, and their destruction at those times can threaten the whole population. Pringle includes as examples bluebirds, monarch butterflies, and hermit crabs. Instructions for making a bluebird nesting box are given. The book has a bibliography and an index, and it is illustrated with black-and-white photographs.

■ SECRETS OF ANIMAL SURVIVAL. National Geographic, 1983. 104pp. (LB 087044-431-X) SERIES: Books for World Explorers. Nonfiction. Interest Level: Ages 9 up
How animals adapt to and survive in their environments is the focus of *Secrets of Animal Survival.* The book is divided into five sections describing different biomes, or specific kinds of environments: polar regions, deserts, rain forests, savannas, and mountains. A brief overview of the features of each biome and a map begin each section. The authors describe many of the animals that make their home in each region, describing both physical and behavioral adaptations of the animals. Colorful photographs and drawings illustrate every page and help readers visualize each kind of adaptation. A picture of an arctic fox in its summer brown-and-white coat is placed next to a picture of one in its characteristic winter white. The white color helps it approach prey without being spotted. The authors point out that some distantly related animals live far apart from each other, for example, the

jerboa of Africa and Asia and the kangaroo rat of North America. They have adapted to desert life in similar ways. The book includes an index and a bibliography. *Secrets of Animal Survival* is more cohesive and more informative than Feltwell's *Animals and Where They Live* (Putnam, 1988), but it covers fewer habitats.

■ Seddon, Tony, and Jill Bailey. THE LIVING WORLD. Illus. with photos and diagrams. Doubleday, 1987. 160pp. (0-385-23754-5) Nonfiction. Interest Level: Ages 9 up
This enjoyable compendium of the living world covers a lot of ground. Well written, with many of boxed inserts and questions with answers at the back, *The Living World* covers topics that range from the animal and the plant kingdoms to life cycles, adaptations, behavior, food chains, symbiosis, and life in various habitats including rain forests, deserts, ponds, and streams. Also included are chapters on endangered species, conservation, nature photography, nature study, and art. A book list, wildlife quiz, glossary, and index round out the book. Each page is illustrated with color photographs and drawings. Most pages indicate where to find more about the subject elsewhere in the book. The eye-catching cover will attract readers. For those who like to absorb their information in bits and pieces, this will fill the bill.

■ Van Soelen, Philip. CRICKET IN THE GRASS AND OTHER STORIES. Illus. by author. Sierra Club, 1979. 128pp. o.p. Nonfiction. Interest Level: Ages 6 up
Five stories that explain ecological concepts are told with pen and ink drawings in a visually interesting format. Each story is set in a different habitat—grassland, oak log, plant, stream, and salt marsh. In the title story, "Cricket in the Grass," the food chain is the concept explained through a series of drawings in which a cricket is eaten by a frog, which is eaten by a snake, which is eaten by a hawk. Because the stories are wordless, they are sometimes challenging to figure out, and without prior knowledge, the stories may befuddle some readers. However, a final section explains each story, providing some basic information on the habitats and plant and animal activities within each. The book's unique visual approach will appeal to some teachers and children.

Forests

■ Arnosky, Jim. IN THE FOREST: A PORTFOLIO OF PAINTINGS. Illus. by author. Lothrop, 1989. Unp. (LB 0-688-09138-5) Nonfiction. Interest Level: Ages 9–12

Arnosky has a different approach to forest ecology, though his book is one that has a place in the classroom or library. His portfolio of 11 oil paintings shows various scenes in an eastern deciduous forest during fall and winter. Arnosky describes the setting for each of his paintings: when and where he painted each, what plants and animals are common to the area, and what changes have occurred there over the years. His knowledge of and respect for the forest is obvious, and the book may inspire both young artists and nature lovers.

Award: OSTB, 1989

■ **Bellamy, David. THE FOREST. Illus. by Jill Dow. Crown, 1988. Unp. (0-517-56800-4) SERIES: Our Changing World. Nonfiction. Interest Level: Ages 6–10**
In each of the titles in the excellent and accessible British series, Our Changing World, ecologist David Bellamy describes a specific habitat, the interdependence of the plants and animals there, and the changes that occur when people disturb the habitat. In *The Forest* he introduces the varied and busy life in a British forest, centering on a giant oak tree. Then Bellamy notes, "People are busy in the forest, too, and the foresters' saws can be heard in the distance." Without further ado, this section of the forest is cut down, and fast-growing conifers are planted for a future harvest. With their habitat disrupted, most animals flee.

As time goes on, other creatures who are better suited to the new open environment move in, and Bellamy allows that the foresters have made some attempts to compensate for the lumbering activity. But he points out that the balance has been disturbed, and that when the foresters use pesticides to protect the conifers from insects, some helpful insects, such as ladybugs, are destroyed. The endpapers show a bird's-eye view of the forest with a patchwork of old growth and new conifers. Jill Dow's detailed watercolor illustrations, with some cutaways to show life underground, enhance the somewhat restrained text. Because it is a British forest, readers will note some variations in animals. This does not detract from a balanced look at the effects of change on a forest community.

■ **Craig, Janet. WONDERS OF THE RAIN FOREST. Illus. by S.D. Schindler. Troll, 1990. 32pp. (LB 0-8167-1763-X) Nonfiction. Interest Level: Ages 7–10**
This simple text describes for young children the plant and animal life in a South American rain forest. Craig clearly explains the difference between tropical rain forests and forests in cooler climates, the great diversity of life in the rain forest, the difference between jungles and rain forests, the distinct levels of plant and animal habitats, and the interdependence of life.

Other topics are the people who live in the rain forest, the importance of rain forests, and the threats to the rain forests' survival. Like Arthur Dorros's *Rain Forest Secrets* (Scholastic, 1990), this book is a good introduction to rain forests for children in the primary grades, although its illustrations are not quite as appealing as Dorros's. The book does not have an index.

■ **Dorros, Arthur. RAIN FOREST SECRETS. Illus. by author. Scholastic, 1990. unp. (0-590-43369-5) Nonfiction. Interest Level: Ages 8–10**
Dorros captures the essence of both tropical and temperate rain forests in this attractive picture-book introduction for young readers. His excellent text emphasizes the interconnections of animal, plant, and human life, the importance of the rain forest ecosystem, and the consequences of its destruction. Many plants and animals are identified in the softly colored pen-and-wash illustrations, which include a map of rain forests around the world, and a picture of forest layers: canopy, understory, and forest floor. A list of 16 organizations that are concerned about rain forests is included. While the format suggests a younger audience, Dorros has an engaging writing style that integrates a great deal of information about his subject. Students will find enough information in this book for reports, and teachers may use it to introduce students to an endangered ecosystem.

■ **EXPLORE A TROPICAL FOREST. Illus. by Barbara Gibson. National Geographic, 1989. Unp. (0-87044-757-2) SERIES: National Geographic Action Book. Nonfiction. Interest Level: Ages 6–8**
Librarians may think twice about including a pop-up book in their collection. However, for those willing to risk it, *Explore a Tropical Jungle* is an interesting introduction to an endangered habitat, and it is one that will certainly involve readers. Each of the six two-page multidimensional spreads is filled with colorful animals and plants native to a South American rain forest. The text accompanying each spread provides a brief look at the forest layers and the organisms that live there. It ends with this plea: "Today, forests like this are disappearing fast as people clear the land for farming and for places to live. Animals of the rain forests need our help to save their homes." The book is not useful for reports, but it provides a good beginning for learning about rain forests.

■ **Forsyth, Adrian. JOURNEY THROUGH A TROPICAL JUNGLE. Simon and Schuster, 1988. 80pp. (0-671-66262-7) Nonfiction. Interest Level: Ages 10 up**
Forsyth is a biologist whose first-person account of his exploration of the Monteverde Cloud Forest Reserve in Costa Rica shows his enthusiasm and respect for the diversity of life in the rain forest ecosystem. This is a

particularly handsome book. It is illustrated with stunning photographs, some taken by the author, of tropical rain forest life. Many photographs are close-ups of birds, insects, and other animals encountered in the rain forest. Middle- and upper-level students will enjoy the journal style employed by the author. After a painful bite by an army ant, Forsyth says, "I didn't appreciate the sting. But the ant was part of a great spectacle, and seeing it was worth the pain. Today I had seen yet again how the relationships among different plants and animals were vital strands woven together in a living forest." His account ends with an argument for protecting the rain forests. This would make a good book for reading aloud and a good complement to more scientific books on the tropical rain forest such as those by Martin Banks and James D. Nations. See also Forsyth's collection of thoughtful essays, *Portraits of the Rainforest* (Camden House, 1990), celebrating the richness of rain forest ecosystems.

Award: OSTB, 1989

■ George, Jean Craighead. ONE DAY IN THE TROPICAL RAIN FOREST. Illus. by Gary Allen. Harper, 1990. 56pp. (LB 0-690-04769-X) Nonfiction. Interest Level: Ages 9–12
George continues her series of excellent ecology books that explore varying habitats by illuminating the events of one day in this easy-to-read drama. In *One Day in the Tropical Rain Forest*, the drama revolves around the search for a rare, as yet unnamed butterfly. If Tepui, a young Indian boy, can find it for scientist Dr. Juan Rivero, a wealthy industrialist will name the butterfly for his daughter and buy this Venezuelan rain forest, saving it from destruction. George effortlessly weaves details of rain forest ecology and the importance of saving this threatened habitat into her story. The book is illustrated with pencil sketches and includes a list of books for further reading and an index. It is a good book for reading aloud.

Award: OSTB, 1990

■ George, Jean Craighead. ONE DAY IN THE WOODS. Illus. by Gary Allen. Harper, 1988. 42pp. (LB 0-690-04724-X) Nonfiction. Interest Level: Ages 9–12
A young girl spends a day exploring a nearby woods in search of an ovenbird, which her naturalist uncle tells her is the "wizard of the woods." In this addition to her series on different biotic communities, Jean George provides a wealth of detail about the forest community in a narrative that brings out the mystery and wonder of the natural world. Readers who enjoy George's fictionalized style will find the girl Rebecca a good role model. She is a good observer, is comfortable by herself in the woods, and spends a whole day completely absorbed in her search for a particular bird. As she

explores different levels of the forest, she discovers much that is wizardry to her, including a flying squirrel, wood ducks, white-tailed deer, and a skunk. At day's end she discovers the ovenbird and what his special wizardry is. The book is illustrated with black and white pencil drawings. It includes a bibliography and an index.

Award: OSTB, 1990

■ **Hirschi, Ron. WHO LIVES IN . . . THE FOREST? Photos by Galen Burrell. Putnam, 1987. Unp. o.p.** SERIES: **Where Animals Live. Nonfiction. Interest Level: Ages 3–6**
This book is a charming introduction to forest animals for the very young. The crisp, colorful photographs and clean simple design of this small, square-shaped book will appeal to young children. The endpapers show a stand of aspen and provide a nice frame to the pictures inside, which show several birds and mammals common to one of three types of northern forests in the United States. Photographs are accompanied by a brief text that identifies the animals shown by some of the sounds they make and by their behavior or homes. An afterword suggests where one might look for each of the animals featured. The photographs were taken in different types of forests. Although the afterword explains this, some readers may be under the impression that all the animals come from one type of forest. The book, therefore, presents adults with an opportunity to explain that each kind of forest provides a home to different kinds of animals.

Award: OSTB, 1987

■ **Jaspersohn, William. HOW THE FOREST GREW. Illus. by Chuck Eckart. Greenwillow, 1980. 56pp. (LB 0-688-84232-X)** SERIES: **Read-Alone Books. Nonfiction. Interest Level: Ages 8–10**
Jaspersohn covers 200 years in this easy reader, showing the changes that take place as a cleared field becomes a magnificent hardwood forest. Jaspersohn has a knack for simple, moving prose. He describes the interrelationships of the plants and animals that thrive during each stage of the forest's succession. The book ends with a short section of suggestions for observing while in a forest and some "rules of the forest." *How the Forest Grew* is illustrated with pen-and-ink drawings that capture the stages of forest growth better than photographs would. Do not overlook this simple well-written explanation of one aspect of forest ecology.

Award: OSTB, 1980

■ **Landau, Elaine. TROPICAL RAIN FORESTS AROUND THE WORLD. Watts, 1990. 64pp. (0-531-10896-1)** SERIES: **First Book. Nonfiction. Interest Level: Ages 9–12**

An attractive format and straightforward writing are strengths in Landau's book on tropical rain forests. Nine short chapters explain rain forest structure; the animals, plants, and people who live there; the importance of rain forests; and some of the threats to them. The chapter on people of the rain forests is very skimpy. The captioned photographs are excellent, although photograph spreads occasionally interrupt the text. The map showing distribution of rain forests worldwide is shaded subtly, and it does not name individual countries. The book includes a glossary, an index, and a list of books for further reading. It is current, basic, introductory coverage.

■ Lauber, Patricia. SUMMER OF FIRE: YELLOWSTONE 1988. Orchard, 1991. 64pp. (LB 0-531-08543-0) Nonfiction. Interest Level: Ages 10 up
A few years have passed since fires raged through Yellowstone National Park in the summer of 1988. Patricia Lauber recounts the story of the fires as they ignited in several parts of the park. She examines the changes they brought to the Yellowstone ecosystem showing how beneficial the fires were to many of the plants and animals at Yellowstone. The fires also provided scientists with a rare opportunity to study how life returns to fire-ravaged areas. Excellent color photographs in a well-designed large format book add to the appeal for both browsers and report-writers. A map, glossary, a good bibliography, and an index make this useful to student researchers.

■ Lerner, Carol. A FOREST YEAR. Illus. by author. Morrow, 1987. 48pp. (LB 0-688-06414-0) Nonfiction. Interest Level: Ages 9–12
Carol Lerner, a botanical illustrator and author, shows how forest plants and animals adapt to the seasons in this well-designed book. Young readers are taken briefly through the four seasons in an eastern deciduous forest and shown how plants and animals depend on each other for survival. Beginning with winter, each season is divided into five two-page spreads in which typical plant, mammal, bird, reptile, amphibian, and insect behavior are described. A page of text is followed by a full-page watercolor illustration. Pictures of some of the smallest plants and animals are enlarged in insets and labeled, but readers must identify some of the more familiar species for themselves. A glossary and an index are included, but scientific names do not appear in either of these parts of the book.
Award: OSTB, 1987

■ Mabey, Richard. OAK & COMPANY. Illus. by Clare Roberts. Greenwillow, 1983. Unp. o.p. Nonfiction. Interest Level: Ages 9–12
British author Mabey writes with enthusiasm and drama of the nearly 300-year life span of an English oak and of the plants and animals living in

and around it. Like Barbara Bash's *Desert Giant* (Sierra Club, 1989), Mabey focuses on one member of a biotic community, showing the interrelationships of hundreds of plants and animals in the ecosystem. Starting with an acorn dropped by a blue jay, Mabey follows the sprouted seedling as it grows, matures, and eventually dies. He also shows how mosses, ferns, butterflies, woodpeckers, owls, rabbits, and countless other living things depend on the oak tree for food and shelter.

Clare Roberts's colorful illustrations, while not labeled, are beautiful, detailed pictures of the tree at various stages of growth and of the plants and animals that interact with it. Full page illustrations face the text. Smaller close-ups of plant and animal life decorate the margins. This is an attractive, readable book that would have been strengthened by the inclusion of an index or a glossary.

Awards: N.Y. Academy of Sciences, Children's Science Book Award, 1983; OSTB, 1983

■ Nations, James D. TROPICAL RAINFORESTS: ENDANGERED ENVIRONMENT. Watts, 1988. 143pp. (0-531-10604-7) Nonfiction. Interest Level: Ages 12 up

Older readers will find a thorough look at tropical rain forests around the world and a convincing argument for their protection from author James Nations, a scientist who specializes in the use of tropical resources. Nations cites many recent scientific studies in *Tropical Rainforests,* and he also includes a bibliography, an index, and a list of conservation organizations. The book is illustrated with black and white photographs, and its format is somewhat dated, considering its 1988 publication date. However, its message and well-documented information make it a good investment for schools and libraries who need upper-level material for student research.

■ Newton, James R. FOREST LOG. Illus. by Irene Brady. Harper, 1980. 26pp. o.p. Nonfiction. Interest Level: Ages 5–9

Newton focuses on the interrelationships of plants and animals in and around a fallen Douglas fir in a rain forest in the Pacific Northwest. The tree slowly decays, but it provides food and shelter for plants and animals of this forest community. It also acts as a nursery for several hemlock trees that have sprouted from the moss growing on the log. The log eventually decays, but the hemlocks, whose roots have formed over the log, survive and create a straight line of trees with a tunnel formed where the log once lay. Brady's black and white illustrations provide a close-up look at the busy life around the dead tree. The book's strength lies not in stunning graphics, but in an easy-to-read presentation of an aspect of the forest cycle. See also Newton's *A Forest is Reborn* (Harper, 1982) about ecological succession after a forest fire and *Rain Shadow* (Harper, 1983) about the dry environment on the leeward side of a mountain. Both are for a similar audience.

Award: OSTB, 1980

■ **Patent, Dorothy Hinshaw. YELLOWSTONE FIRES: FLAMES AND RE-BIRTH. Photos by William Munoz. Holiday, 1990. 40pp. (LB 0-8234-0807-8) Nonfiction. Interest Level: Ages 10–13**
The Yellowstone fires of 1988 and their aftermath serve as an ecology lesson in the hands of Dorothy Patent. Well-written and organized, Patent's narrative explains how conditions were right for such a devastating fire to start and spread, what efforts were made to control it, and how the fire affected the plant and animal life in the Yellowstone ecosystem. Patent emphasizes that, overall, the fires were beneficial and helped to open up meadows and provide habitat for a greater variety of wildlife. She also briefly explains the succession that will follow in the Yellowstone forests. The book has good color photographs of Yellowstone during and after the fires on every spread. The text is a bit more difficult than the format suggests. The good organization, the index, and the helpful statistics make this book useful for reports and for browsing. The book is for the same audience as Vogel and Goldner's *The Great Yellowstone Fire* (Sierra Club, 1990).

Award: OSTB, 1990

■ **Romanova, Natalia. ONCE THERE WAS A TREE. Illus. by Gennady Spirin. Dial, 1985. 24pp. (0-8037-0235-3) Fiction. Interest Level: Ages 5–9**
This ecological picture-book tale translated from Russian explores our relationship to nature. A forest tree is struck down by lightning, and a woodsman cuts the wood and takes it away. Author Romanova then follows the remaining stump through several seasons as various forest animals, such as a titmouse, a bark beetle, ants, a frog, a bear, an earwig (and a man), use the stump for food, protection, or rest, all "owning" the stump while they use it. Eventually the stump decays and a new tree grows in its place. Romanova rhetorically asks who really owns the stump and the new tree. Her answer is as follows: "The tree belongs to all, because it grows from the earth that is home for all." The story would be more successful if it were more open-ended, and Romanova's didacticism weakens this beautifully illustrated book. However, the illustrations—rich, earthy and detailed—will appeal to children and will show the interdependence of living things in the forest environment. Pair this book with Newton's *Forest Log* (Harper, 1980)

for a more detailed description of the plant and animal life surrounding a fallen log in a Pacific rain forest.

Award: OSTB, 1985

■ **Rowland-Entwistle, Theodore. JUNGLES AND RAINFORESTS. Silver Burdett, 1987. 48pp. (0-382-09500-6)** SERIES: **Our World. Nonfiction. Interest Level: Ages 10 up**
Clear writing, good organization, thorough coverage, and an appealing format combine to make this an excellent purchase for libraries and schools serving middle- and upper-level students. Rowland-Entwistle explains the difference between jungles and rain forests, and describes the structure, location, and variations in rain forest plants and animals around the world. The chapters on people and rain forests and rain forest resources are good as is the final chapter on rain forests in danger. The book includes color photographs and clearly marked diagrams and maps. A glossary, an index, and a list of books for further reading are appended.

■ **Schoonmaker, Peter K. THE LIVING FOREST. Enslow, 1990. 64pp. (LB 0-89490-270-9)** SERIES: **The Living World. Nonfiction. Interest Level: Ages 12 up**
For upper-level students, this book provides a thorough look at North American forests. It includes chapters on boreal, temperate coniferous, coniferous rain, and temperate deciduous forests; a chapter on the variety within the eastern deciduous forest; and a short chapter on the future of forests, in which the author calls for "a balance between timber harvesting and forest preservation." The book includes mediocre black-and-white photographs and some maps and diagrams. The type size is too small. A short but good glossary and index are appended. Schoonmaker does not write exciting prose, but his information is current and well organized. He mentions some current environmental issues facing these forests, including the possible effects of acid rain, logging, the fate of the northern spotted owl, and the greenhouse effect. A comprehensive but unexciting choice for student researchers.

■ **Schwartz, David M. THE HIDDEN LIFE OF THE FOREST. Photos by Dwight Kuhn. Crown, 1988. Unp. (LB 0-517-57058-0) Nonfiction. Interest Level: Ages 5 up**
Brilliant color photographs predominate in this seasonal walk through the woods. Close-up captioned pictures of plant and animal life common to a deciduous forest are accompanied by a text that briefly describes the behavior or life cycle of the animals and plants shown. This book, with its appeal-

ing photographs, is more useful for browsing than for its ecology lesson. David Bellamy's *The Forest* (Crown, 1988) does a better job of describing the interrelationships of life in a forest habitat for a similar audience. However, *The Hidden Life of the Forest*, along with Schwartz's *The Hidden Life of the Meadow* (Crown, 1988) and *The Hidden Life of the Pond* (Crown, 1988), are good choices for schools and libraries.

■ **Stone, Lynn M. RAIN FORESTS. Rourke, 1989. 48pp. (LB 0-86592-437-6)** SERIES: **Ecozones. Nonfiction. Interest Level: Ages 10 up**
Stone concentrates on rain forests of southern Mexico and Central America and differentiates between several types of rain forest in this addition to the Ecozones series. An attractive cover and excellent color photographs are strengths. However, the format is somewhat cramped, and the reading level is more difficult than Landau's *Tropical Rain Forests Around the World* (Watts, 1990), written for a similar audience. A glossary and an index are included, as are a list of rain forest sites and some suggested activities to learn more about the rain forest. A short list of conservation organizations that promote the protection of rain forests is also included. Stone's writing is less lucid in this book than it is in some of his other Ecozones titles; the vocabulary is also difficult.

■ **Tresselt, Alvin. THE DEAD TREE. Illus. by Charles Robinson. Parents Magazine Pr., 1972. Unp. o.p. Fiction. Interest Level: Ages 4–8**
A dying oak tree is the protagonist in this classic picture book. With dramatic prose, Tresselt shows how the tree, even after it dies, offers food and shelter for forest creatures. Over time the tree returns to the earth, enriching the soil so that new acorns can grow into oak trees. Robinson's soft, impressionistic illustrations provide a sense of drama and majesty to the oak and makes its decay seem a wonderful life-affirming event. This is an excellent introduction to forest ecology for young children.
Award: OSTB, 1972

■ **Vogel, Carole Garbuny, and Kathryn Allen Goldner. THE GREAT YEL-LOWSTONE FIRE. Sierra Club, 1990. 31pp. (LB 0-316-90522-4) Nonfiction. Interest Level: Ages 10 up**
Similar in size and format to Patent's *Yellowstone Fires* (Holiday, 1990), Vogel and Goldner's book also emphasizes the contribution of natural fires to the health of the forest and describes the effects of the fire on the Yellowstone ecosystem. The text is a short but vivid narrative without chapters, accompanied by exceptional photographs. Patent's book, with its chapters and index, may be easier for students writing reports, but Vogel

and Goldner's 31-page book is not hard to use. Both books would have benefited from a map. Ekey's *Fire! in Yellowstone* (Stevens, 1990) has less information and is written for younger readers.

Award: OSTB, 1990

Deserts

■ **Bash, Barbara. DESERT GIANT: THE WORLD OF THE SAGUARO CAC-TUS. Illus. by author. Sierra Club, 1989. Unp. (LB 0-316-08301-1)** SERIES: **Tree Tales. Nonfiction. Interest Level: Ages 7–11**
Readers will feel the life in and around the saguaro cactus in Bash's engaging book, which focuses on the ecology of this long-lived desert plant. Her narrative progresses naturally as she describes the animals and people (Tohono O'odham Indians) that depend on the cactus for food or shelter and the whole new set of creatures that take over and make use of the plant when it dies. By shifting to the second person on occasion, Bash brings the reader into the desert world of the saguaro as she describes what you will hear: the "tap . . . tap . . . tap of the Gila woodpecker, the hissssss . . . of the wind through the spines of the cactus, the flapping of the wings of the long-nosed bat." The colorful watercolor illustrations bleed off every page of this large-size picture book. Plants and animals are labeled where necessary. The text is printed in readable calligraphy. The book is a wonderful introduction to desert ecology for research or for pleasure. It does not have an index.

Award: OSTB, 1989

■ **Dewey, Jennifer Owings. A NIGHT AND DAY IN THE DESERT. Illus. by author. Little, 1991. Unp. (LB 0-316-18210-9) Nonfiction. Interest Level: Ages 7–10**
Throughout a night and day, naturalist Dewey follows the animals that inhabit a North American desert. She starts at sunset when most desert activity begins. It is then that coyotes, Mexican free-tail bats, great horned owls, and many other animals leave their shelter in search of food, water, or a mate. Dewey, a sharp observer of the desert landscape, introduces readers to some of the physical and behavioral adaptations and the life cycles of desert animals. As in her book *At the Edge of the Pond* (Little, 1987) readers may find themselves searching for illustrations of the animals described, as the text is descriptive of many more species than the softly colored pencil drawings actually depict. Dewey emphasizes the richness and diversity of life in the desert, often thought of as barren, but does not bring out the interdependence of plant and animal life in the desert habitat to the

extent that Jean George or Barbara Bash do in their books. This book, however, provides a good introduction to desert life.

■ **George, Jean Craighead. ONE DAY IN THE DESERT. Illus. by Fred Brenner. Harper, 1983. 48pp. (LB 0-690-04341-4) Nonfiction. Interest Level: Ages 9–12**
On a scorching hot July day in the Sonoran Desert of Arizona, the people, animals, and plants struggle to stay cool. A thunderstorm breaks the heat, but it also begins a chain of events that affect every living thing around the arroyo, or dry river bed, where George's dramatic story takes place. Naturalist George has a special talent for painting a vivid and informative picture of the interrelationships between living things and their environment.

Here, her story follows a wounded mountain lion seeking water and the life around the arroyo where he heads. George introduces a Papago Indian woman, her daughter, and the animals and plants common to this desert—including saguaro cacti, kangaroo rats, peccaries, road runners, tarantulas, coyotes, and elf owls—showing how they adapt to the harsh desert conditions and how they react to the flash flood caused by the thunderstorm. Many die in the flood, but the desert is also renewed by the rain. *One Day in the Desert* has the same format as others in George's series on different habitats. Fred Brenner's black and white line drawings illustrate every page. *One Day in the Desert* is an excellent introduction to desert ecology for students in the middle grades, and it is a good book for reading aloud, too. The book includes an index.

■ **Guiberson, Brenda Z. CACTUS HOTEL. Illus. by Megan Lloyd. Holt, 1991. Unp. (0-8050-1333-4) Nonfiction. Interest Level: Ages 5–10**
In an attractive picture book format, author Guiberson describes the long cycle of life of the saguaro cactus, which is found only in Arizona's Sonoran Desert. She follows a saguaro seed as it sprouts and slowly grows into a cactus, highlighting stages in its 200-year life span. She uses the analogy of a hotel to show how many desert creatures depend on the saguaro for food or shelter, and she effectively conveys the concept of the interdependence of life in the desert. An afterword offers more information, noting the Native American use of the cactus and recent threats to the saguaro by cactus "rustlers" who steal them for use in home landscaping. Lloyd's softly colored watercolor-and-pencil illustrations add to the appeal of the book. Like Barbara Bash's *Desert Giant* (Little, 1989) this is a good introduction to desert ecology for younger children.

■ **Holmes, Anita. THE 100-YEAR-OLD CACTUS. Illus. by Carol Lerner. Macmillan, 1983. Unp. o.p. Nonfiction. Interest Level: Ages 7–10**

Holmes incorporates a lot of information in this simple, easy-to-read picture book that, like Bash's *Desert Giant* (Sierra Club, 1989) describes the place of the saguaro cactus in the ecology of the desert. Lerner's stunning illustrations, line drawings with black, green, and yellow halftones, enhance this book. Holmes does not mention people's use of the cactus nor that even after it dies, the saguaro provides water, food, and shelter for other creatures, as Bash does, but she does provide more detail about the cactus and the animals that depend on it. The book makes a good introduction to desert ecology. For an in-depth look at cacti, see Holmes's *Cactus: the All-American Plant* (Macmillan, 1982).

Award: OSTB, 1983

■ **Hughes, Jill. A CLOSER LOOK AT DESERTS. Illus. by Roy Coombs and Maurice Wilson. Watts, 1987 (rev. ed.). 32pp. (LB 0-531-17037-3) SERIES: A Closer Look. Nonfiction. Interest Level: Ages 9 – 12**
Hughes writes clearly about hot deserts in this revised edition, which serves as an introduction to desert life for middle-grade readers. The emphasis here is on the ways in which plants and animals adapt to harsh desert conditions. Brief two-page chapters, so typical of series books now being published, are illustrated with colorful drawings or diagrams on every page. The chapter on desert people is as long as the one on how deserts are formed and the one on desert birds. Food chains and life cycles are mentioned. No mention is made of issues such as strip mining, drought, desertification, or conservation. An index is included.

■ **Lerner, Carol. A DESERT YEAR. Illus. by author. Morrow, 1991. 48pp. (LB 0-688-09383-3) Nonfiction. Interest Level: Ages 9 – 12**
The North American desert is the setting for author-illustrator Carol Lerner's seasonal exploration of plants and animals that make their home there. Utilizing the same format as she did in *A Forest Year* (Morrow, 1987), Lerner devotes five two-page spreads to each season. Four or five typical mammals, birds, reptiles, amphibians, arthropods, and plants of each season are described. Their behaviors and adaptations to the changing seasons of the harsh desert environment reveal the interdependence of life. Detailed watercolor illustrations show animals above and below ground. Pictures of some of the smaller animals and plants are enlarged in insets and labeled, but otherwise readers must identify for themselves. A brief glossary and list of books about desert life are appended. The index includes scientific names. *A Desert Year* lacks the drama of Bash's *Desert Giant* (Little, 1989) or George's *One Day in the Desert* (Harper, 1983), but it introduces readers to a wide variety of desert life and will make a good companion to these and other books about desert ecology.

■ Lye, Keith. DESERTS. Silver Burdett, 1987. 48pp. (LB 0-382-09501-4) SERIES: Our World. Nonfiction. Interest Level: Ages 10 up
Although the emphasis here is not on the ecology of deserts, Lye's clear writing and excellent organization earn his book's inclusion in this bibliography. Lye describes the differences in deserts and in desert plant and animal life. His chapters on human use of deserts emphasize how land reclamation, farming, mining, and other activities affect and often destroy the fragile balance of life in the desert. A final chapter covers desertification and conservation efforts. Color photographs, many clear diagrams and illustrations, and an attractive format make this book useful for middle- and upper-grade students. *Deserts* includes a glossary, an index, and a list of books for further reading.

■ Posell, Elsa. DESERTS. Childrens, 1982. 48pp. (LB 0-516-01613-X) SERIES: New True. Nonfiction. Interest Level: Ages 5–9
Large type, color photographs, and a short text that simply explains its subject characterize books in the New True series. In *Deserts* author Posell offers a simple introduction to hot deserts, explaining the conditions that form a desert and the animals and plants that are adapted to this environment. A final chapter on people and the desert mentions irrigation, mining, and adaptations North African nomads have made for life in the desert. For young students and beginning readers, this is an adequate introduction.

■ Pringle, Laurence. THE GENTLE DESERT: EXPLORING AN ECOSYS-TEM. Macmillan, 1977. 58pp. o.p. Nonfiction. Interest Level: Ages 10–14
Despite its older publication date, this book remains useful because of its ecological slant. Pringle writes about the North American desert, introducing several smaller ecosystems within it, such as arroyos and sand dunes, and the special plants and animals that thrive in each. He describes some of the adaptations desert plants and animals make to survive and the often complex interconnections between them. Some of the threats to the fragile desert ecosystem are covered, including the effects of off-road vehicle use and a growing population that puts a greater burden on the water resources of the area. He clearly sides with those who do not want to reclaim, improve, or change the desert, but to appreciate it as it is. The book is illustrated with black-and-white photographs on every spread and includes a map, a glossary, an index, and a list of books for further reading.
Award: OSTB, 1977

■ Sabin, Louis. WONDERS OF THE DESERT. Illus. by Pamela Baldwin Ford. Troll, 1982. 32pp. (LB 0-89375-574-5) Nonfiction. Interest Level: Ages 5–8

Sabin describes desert animals and plants in this picture book introduction to desert life. He focuses mostly on North American deserts, but inexplicably diverges near the end of the book to describe North African palm trees, camels, and nomads. Ford's very attractive watercolors add to the book's appeal. Sabin's simple, short text emphasizes the variety of life that makes its home in a harsh but beautiful environment. The book can be used as basic introductory material.

■ Wiewandt, Thomas. THE HIDDEN LIFE OF THE DESERT. Photos by author. Crown, 1990. Unp. (LB 0-517-57356-3) Nonfiction. Interest Level: Ages 6–12
Author-photographer Wiewandt's photo essay examines animal and plant life throughout *five* seasons—spring, dry summer, wet summer, autumn, and winter—in the Sonoran Desert of Arizona and southern California. Wiewandt describes how animals and plants adapt to the hot days and cool nights as well as to the changing seasons. An afterword provides more detail about desert conditions and desertification. Excellent photographs and a nice format will appeal to children. Although this and the other titles in the series (written by David Schwartz and photographed by Dwight Kuhn) are designed for browsing, they will make attractive additions to schools and libraries needing material on deserts.
Award: OSTB, 1990

Prairies and Grasslands

■ Bash, Barbara. TREE OF LIFE: THE WORLD OF THE AFRICAN BAOBAB. Illus. by author. Sierra Club, 1989. Unp. (LB 0-316-08305-4) SERIES: Tree Tales. Nonfiction. Interest Level: Ages 7–11
Barbara Bash explores the the importance of the baobab tree to the people and animals of the dry savannas of Africa. She begins with a myth from the !Kung tribe about the baobab and then follows the tree's annual cycle. Lush watercolor illustrations depict the tree both night and day throughout its seasonal cycle and the people and many animals who depend on it, including yellow-billed hornbills, longhorn beetles, Masonga caterpillars, bushbabies, baboons, and boomslang snakes. Without mentioning the word *ecosystem*, without a glossary or an index, Bash shows and tells the interdependence of the creatures in this habitat. A watercolor map on the end papers to show where the savannas of Africa are found would have been a helpful addition. The text, printed in Bash's clear calligraphy, may bother some, but it is not hard to read. Like her *Desert Giant* (Sierra Club, 1989), a book about the saguaro cactus, this is an outstanding introduction to the ecology of a region for lower- and middle-grade readers.

■ George, Jean Craighead. ONE DAY IN THE PRAIRIE. Illus. by Bob Mar-stall. Harper, 1986. 42pp. (LB 0-690-04566-2) Nonfiction. Interest Level: Ages 9–12

With drama and an amazing wealth of information seamlessly woven into her story, author George explores a day on a southwestern Oklahoma prairie in this addition to her series on various habitats. A boy spends hours attempting to photograph a prairie dog doing a back flip while George describes the prairie community and the activity of the wildlife, such as tarantulas, buffalo, elk, and coyote, in and around the prairie dog town. The boy is oblivious to a storm brewing throughout the day, a storm that develops into a tornado from which he narrowly escapes. Readers attracted to this easy-to-read fictionalized style will learn a lot about the prairie habitat. Black-and-white pencil drawings profusely illustrate this short book. *One Day in the Prairie* is good for reading aloud. The book includes an index.

Award: OSTB, 1986

■ Hess, Lilo. SECRETS IN THE MEADOW. Photos by author. Macmillan, 1986. 64pp. (0-684-18525-3) Nonfiction. Interest Level: Ages 10 up

Author-photographer Lilo Hess takes a look at the animals common to a meadow in this informative book on meadow ecology. She examines both daytime and nocturnal animals, paying special attention to smaller crea-tures, such as the spittlebug, the praying mantis, the earthworm, and the paper wasp. Life cycles, adaptations, and behavior are covered.

Although Hess provides more information on a greater number of ani-mals than Schwartz does in *The Hidden Life of the Meadow* (Crown, 1988), her black and white photographs are a little disappointing. Most are not captioned, and, although the text is closely coordinated with them, captions would have been helpful, especially with her series of photographs of ani-mals laying eggs, eating, and building homes. In some cases animals are only identified generically, as when she describes spiders and owls. People are introduced at the end, surveying the meadow where a housing develop-ment is being planned. Hess asks, "Where will the animals go? Will there be enough meadow left for all the small and large creatures to pursue their short and secret lives?" These questions are a gentle reminder that human progress and development affects the natural world around us.

■ Hirschi, Ron. WHO LIVES ON . . . THE PRAIRIE? Photos by Galen Burrell. Putnam, 1989. Unp. (0-399-21901-3) SERIES: Where Animals Live. Nonfiction. Interest Level: Ages 3–8

This small, beautifully designed addition to the Where Animals Live series introduces young children to animals of the North American prairies. The small, square book is well suited for young hands. Its outstanding color photographs of typical prairie animals like the prairie dog, meadowlark, and pronghorn deer are accompanied by a brief text in large print that conveys the activities of and interconnections between prairie animals and plants. The endpapers show a wide-angle view of a prairie in bloom, providing a nice frame for the many close-up photographs inside. An afterword for adults talks about the decline of many of these animals, without going into the reasons for their decline. Hirschi ends the afterword with the hope that "this introduction to prairie wildlife will encourage you to learn more about the prairie and the urgent needs of many vanishing prairie animals." The book provides an attractive, basic introduction for the youngest.

■ Lambert, David. GRASSLANDS. Silver Burdett, 1988. 48pp. (LB 0-382-09789-0) SERIES: Our World. Nonfiction. Interest Level: Ages 10 up
Lambert gives thorough coverage of grasslands around the world for middle- and upper-level students. Silver Burdett's Our World series, of which this is a part, is characterized by an attractive large-size format, excellent color photographs, good organization, and clear writing. While *Grasslands* does not approach the subject strictly from an ecological point of view, it provides good basic information on temperate and tropical grasslands around the world. The chapters on human use of grasslands over time, the fragility of the soil, the misuse of grasslands, and the methods for their conservation make this book useful for reports and provides an environmental focus. Read Bash's *Tree of Life* (Sierra Club, 1989) for an ecological look at the baobab tree from the African savanna, George's *One Day in the Prairie* (Harper, 1986) for an ecological approach to the North American prairie. *Grasslands* includes a glossary, an index and a list of books for further reading.

■ Lerner, Carol. SEASONS OF THE TALLGRASS PRAIRIE. Illus. by author. Morrow, 1980. 48pp. o.p. Nonfiction. Interest Level: Ages 9–12
With her focus on plants, Lerner's smoothly written book explains prairie ecology and the role prairie fires take in preserving this fragile habitat. Beginning with a brief overview of America's tallgrass prairie, much of which has been lost to farming and grazing, Lerner describes typical tall-grass prairie plants of each season. She discusses the great variety of perennial grasses and forbs and their features and adapatations to the dry prairie environment. Detailed black-and-white line drawings show fascinating cutaways of plants with often deep and extensive root systems. Drawings are labeled with common names; scientific names are included in an appendix. The seasonal approach makes this useful in conjunction with field study, especially if supplemented with a field guide with color photographs.
Awards: ALA Notable Children's Book, 1980; OSTB, 1980

■ Rowan, James P. PRAIRIES AND GRASSLANDS. Childrens, 1983. 48pp. (LB 0-516-01706-3) SERIES: New True. Nonfiction. Interest Level: Ages 7– 10
There is nothing fancy in this introduction to prairies and grasslands, an addition to Children's Press's New True series. Rowan describes characteristics of prairies in simple terms in large print. Some animals typical of prairies in North America, South America, Australia, and Africa are described. He concludes with a look at people and prairies and the loss of prairie land through farming and cattle grazing, noting that national parks and wildlife sanctuaries help protect some of these habitats. Sometimes oversimplified to the point of inaccuracy (for example, Rowan says that fires are bad when they burn forests), nevertheless, the book serves as a brief factual look at prairie and grassland ecosystems for young readers. *Prairies and Grasslands* includes color photographs, a glossary, and an index.

■ Schwartz, David M. THE HIDDEN LIFE OF THE MEADOW. Photos by Dwight Kuhn. Crown, 1988. Unp. (LB 0-517-57059-9) Nonfiction. Interest Level: Ages 6–12
This book presents a beautiful photo essay on the life in a meadow community. Author Schwartz and photographer Kuhn take the reader through the seasons, with spring and summer given the most coverage. The many captioned close-up photographs of plants and animals common to a meadow make this a good introductory book, one to share before a meadow walk. Schwartz provides information on habits of the animals and on the animals' interrelationships, but his basic intent is to encourage appreciation of the life in this community. The book is similar to his two other titles, *The Hidden Life of the Forest* (Crown, 1988) and *The Hidden Life of the Pond* (Crown, 1988).
Award: OSTB, 1988

■ Stone, Lynn M. PRAIRIES. Rourke, 1989. 48pp. (LB 0-86592-446-5) SERIES: Ecozones. Nonfiction. Interest Level: Ages 9–12
Stone's addition to the Ecozones series is a basic, serviceable look at North American prairies. Following the same format as others in the series, Stone describes different types of prairies, tall grass, mixed grass, and short grass; their formation; and the plant and animal communities found there. A chapter titled "The Flow of Energy" discusses the prairie as a community, the process of photosynthesis, and the food chain. In a final chapter on prairie conservation, Stone explains how settlement and agriculture have destroyed much of the prairie and the plant and animal communities that live there. This is a slim, attractive book with color photographs, a glossary,

an index, a list of prairie sites in the United States and Canada, and a list of activities for middle- and upper-grade students. Although the book is well organized and fairly brief, readers will find Stone's vocabulary and writing style a challenge.

Mountains, Tundra, and Polar Regions

■ George, Jean Craighead. ONE DAY IN THE ALPINE TUNDRA. Illus. by Walter Gaffney-Kessell. Harper, 1984. 44pp. (LB 0-690-04326-0) Nonfiction. Interest Level: Ages 9–12
The community of plants and animals in the alpine tundra are the stars in George's exploration of alpine ecology on Rendezvous Mountain in Wyoming's Teton Range. In *One Day in the Alpine Tundra*, Johnny Moore has camped in an alpine meadow and will head down the mountain later that day to meet his forest ranger dad. George weaves details of ecology into her narrative, describing typical tundra plants like lichens and mosses, and animals like pikas, pocket gophers, and marmots as they prepare for winter. Middle-grade readers who like George's style will want to read the others in her series of ecology tales set in varying habitats. Black-and-white drawings illustrate nearly every page. An index and a bibliography is included.

Award: OSTB, 1984

■ Hirschi, Ron. ONE DAY ON PIKA'S PEAK. Photos by Galen Burrell. Dodd, 1986. 48pp. (0-396-08778-7) Nonfiction. Interest Level: Ages 6–10
Author Ron Hirschi and photographer Galen Burrell join together again to present a day in the life of a weasel family and the animals they share "Pika's Peak" within the Rocky Mountains. This book is similar to their Who Lives in . . . series published by Putnam, but it has a longer text and more photographs. Simple, clear text accompanies close-up color photographs of the weasel family, marmots, pikas, a water pipit, a vole, and a deer mouse. The action focuses on the mother weasel as she hunts for food for her litter of nine. An appendix provides more information on the habits of the animals introduced in the story. An index makes this a candidate for primary grade researchers, studying mountain communities or food chains. The book also makes a good read-aloud for this age group and for even younger children. Its attractive cover will keep it from sitting on the shelf.

■ Hirschi, Ron. WHO LIVES IN . . . THE MOUNTAINS? Photos by Galen Burrell. Putnam, 1989. Unp. (0-399-21900-5) SERIES: Where Animals Live. Nonfiction. Interest Level: Ages 3–8

Another book in the beautifully designed Where Animals Live series, *Who Lives in . . . the Mountains?* introduces young children to animals living in mountain meadows, forests, and along streams. Its small, square format is a nice size for young hands. The minimal text and wonderful photographs with ample white space introduce readers to mountain goats, ptarmigans, pikas, weasels, juncos, black bears, and otters. Endpapers show a lake with surrounding mountain peaks, a nice frame for the close-up colorful photographs inside of the alpine animals. An afterword for older readers and adults provides more information about observing mountain animals.

■ **Hiscock, Bruce. TUNDRA: THE ARCTIC LAND. Illus. by author. Macmillan, 1986. 135pp. (0-689-31219-0) Nonfiction. Interest Level: Ages 10 up**
Hiscock's narrative of his trip to "the barren lands," an area of arctic tundra in Canada west of Hudson Bay, is a thorough and authoritative look at tundra ecology that middle- and upper-grade readers can use for research. With a guide, Hiscock joined an expedition to the tundra for several weeks of canoeing and camping. His personal story is secondary to the well-written account of the plant, animal, and human inhabitants of this region and their interrelationships. Readers will learn about lemmings, musk-oxen, ground squirrels, caribou, foxes, bears, snowy owls, and many other plants and animals that make the tundra their home. Hiscock's subtle black and white watercolors are helpful but not eyecatching in an informational book for this age group. However, the cover is attractive, and a glossary, an index and a bibliography add to the book's usefulness.

Award: OSTB, 1986

■ **Hughes, Jill. ARCTIC LANDS. Illus. by R. Coombs, D. Cordery, and M. Wilson. Gloucester, 1987. 32pp. (LB 0-531-17036-5) SERIES: A Closer Look. Nonfiction. Interest Level: Ages 9–12**
After briefly describing the formation and physical features of arctic regions (a map is included), Hughes discusses the plant and animal life there throughout the year, paying special attention to the ways plants and animals adapt to the often harsh conditions. She briefly mentions the Inuit, a people native to these regions, but does not address any current environmental concerns. *Arctic Lands* is a slim book, with attractive illustrations, that will introduce readers to the ecology of arctic regions. The book includes a short glossary and an index.

■ **Lambert, David. POLAR REGIONS. Silver Burdett, 1988. 48pp. (LB 0-382-09502-2) SERIES: Our World. Nonfiction. Interest Level: Ages 10 up**
Lambert's addition to the excellent Our World series provides broad coverage of polar regions. He discusses geology, geography, natural resources,

people, exploration, and plant and animal life. A final chapter discusses environmental concerns, such as overhunting and overfishing, pollution from oil, radioactive contamination from Chernobyl, and even disturbance of habitats from tourism. He mentions some of the efforts made by nations and environmental groups to preserve and protect these lands. The book includes attractive photographs, diagrams, a list of books for further reading, and an index. It is a good resource for school reports.

■ **Stone, Lynn M. ARCTIC TUNDRA. Rourke, 1989. 48pp. (LB 0-86592-436-8)** SERIES: **Ecozones. Nonfiction. Interest Level: Ages 9–12**
Attractive and up-to-date, Stone's addition to the Ecozones series describes the arctic tundra, explaining different types of tundra, how tundra is formed, and the plant and animal life there. A chapter is devoted to the tundra as an ecosystem and the relationships among plants, animals, and land. Another chapter briefly discusses conservation. Each book in this series ends with a glossary, a list of sites (in this case, places in Canada and the United States where tundra is found), a brief list of activities, and an index. Stone's writing style and vocabulary are more difficult than what one might expect in a 48 page book with lots of photographs. But the book is well organized and, although brief, it will be useful for students studying this region.

■ **Stone, Lynn M. MOUNTAINS. Childrens, 1983. 48pp. (LB 0-516-01698-9)** SERIES: **New True. Nonfiction. Interest Level: Ages 6–9**
Stone describes how mountains are formed, emphasizing the differences in mountains around the world. He gives examples of the variety of plants and animals that live on mountains, depending on where the mountain is located, the climate of the region, the amount of rainfall, and the elevation. Stone also mentions how people use mountains both for pleasure and for their livelihood and describes the damage that can occur with too much mining and woodcutting.

Part of the New True series for young readers, *Mountains* is characterized by large type, simple vocabulary, and colorful photographs. Stone does a credible job of introducing young readers to mountain ecology. The book includes a glossary and an index. See also Stone's *The Arctic* (Childrens 1985), which introduces children to arctic regions.

Wetlands, Rivers, and Inland Waters

■ **Cristini, Ermanno, and Luigi Puricelli. IN THE POND. Illus. by authors. Picture Book, 1984. Unp. (0-907234-43-7) Nonfiction. Interest Level: Ages 3–8**
A wordless picture book introduction to pond life shows young children many of the creatures in and around a pond. The watercolor illustrations are

simply executed, with a side view, showing activity above and below the water's surface. The reader sees the birds, insects, amphibians, reptiles, plants, and a muskrat, which live together in this habitat. The animals come in and out of view on the two-page spreads, giving a sense of movement and purpose. As in their other wordless picture books, *In the Woods* (Picture Book, 1985) and *In My Garden* (Picture Book, 1985), Cristini and Puricelli offer children the opportunity to scrutinize the pictures carefully on their own. On the last page, numbered pictures identify each of the plants and animals illustrated.

■ **Cutchins, Judy, and Ginny Johnston. SCOOTS THE BOG TURTLE. Illus. by Frances Smith. Macmillan, 1989. 32pp. (0-689-31440-X) Nonfiction. Interest Level: Ages 7–10**
This is a charming introduction to a unique animal and its habitat. The authors, who are science educators, follow a young bog turtle throughout a year in Duck Potato Bog, a fictional bog based on those found in the mountains of North Carolina. Their story approach is effective; it helps the reader see and feel what living in the bog is like for a turtle, and they do a good job of describing the varied activity in this environment as animals struggle to survive. Readers will learn what bog turtles eat, where they sleep and hibernate, and who their enemies are. The realistic, detailed illustrations enhance the text, but are a bit flat. An introduction describes how bogs are formed and how they are important for many living things. The authors say, "If bogs are not protected from human disturbance, they will soon disappear—and so will the plants and animals that live there." An index is included. Fans of Jean George's books on various ecosystems may also enjoy *Scoots the Bog Turtle*. For older readers, Lorus J. and Margery Milnes' *Mystery of the Bog Forest* (Dodd, 1984) will provide more in-depth information.
Award: OSTB, 1989

■ **Dewey, Jennifer Owings. AT THE EDGE OF THE POND. Illus. by author. Little, 1987. Unp. (LB 0-316-18208-7) Nonfiction. Interest Level: Ages 7–10**
In author-artist Jennifer Dewey's poetic exploration of pond life between daybreak and nightfall, she looks at life on the surface, on the shoreline, in deep water, and at the bottom of the pond. Longer and more detailed than Williams's similar approach to pond ecology in *Between Cattails* (Macmillan, 1985), Dewey's book is filled with sensory language. She evokes sounds: "Chirps, buzzes, hums, croaks, and splashes—sounds from the pond grow lusty and strong as the day begins." The book is also filled with minute

observations: "A water strider slips between two stems and skims out over the water's mirror surface, its six legs reflected beneath it." In fact, the detail, while fascinating, is almost overwhelming for one reading. Her softly colored pencil illustrations are charming, but they do not reflect all that is in the text, sometimes leaving the reader searching for an illustration of something described. Nevertheless, she captures the life cycles and complex relationships of pond life in an appealing picture book.

■ **Freschet, Berniece. YEAR ON MUSKRAT MARSH. Illus. by Peter Parnall. Scribner, 1974. Unp. o.p. Nonfiction. Interest Level: Ages 7–10**
Berniece Freschet follows several animals throughout a year in a northern Minnesota marsh. Her very readable narrative portrays the drama that surrounds the day-to-day struggle for food and life for muskrats, a bullfrog, a water snake, a mink, wood ducks, and many other animals that inhabit or use the marsh. Like Jean George, Freschet smoothly integrates aspects of ecology into an interesting narrative. Peter Parnall's pen-and-ink drawings, without added color, reflect the tone of Freschet's prose. These drawings are more realistic than others he has done. Readers will also enjoy Cutchins and Johnston's *Scoots the Bog Turtle* (Macmillan, 1989) and George's series of books on different ecosystems.

Award: OSTB, 1974

■ **Hirschi, Ron. WHO LIVES IN . . . ALLIGATOR SWAMP? Photos by Galen Burrell. Putnam, 1987. Unp. o.p. SERIES: Where Animals Live. Nonfiction. Interest Level: Ages 3–8**
This is another book in the beautifully designed series Where Animals Live by Ron Hirschi, with photographs by Galen Burrell. These chunky, square-shaped books that introduce animals of a particular habitat should be well received by young children. In *Alligator Swamp,* readers are taken on a tour of a swamp in the southeastern part of the United States. A simple, lively text accompanies wonderful color photographs of a swamp rabbit, alligators, and many birds (anhinga, blue heron, spoonbill, gallinule). An afterword for parents or for older readers describes the near extinction of American alligators and crocodiles in the swamp and encourages readers to "care for the future of these special places." The book makes an attractive introduction for the youngest.

■ **Lavies, Bianca. LILY PAD POND. Photos by author. Dutton, 1989. Unp. (0-525-44483-1) Nonfiction. Interest Level: Ages 4–8**
This story and photo essay by Bianca Lavies centers on the life cycle of a bullfrog as it grows from a tadpole to a frog. The amphibian's pond neigh-

bors, both friend and foe, are described: a snapping turtle, a dragonfly nymph, a newt, a water strider and a fisher spider. Lavies's simple text emphasizes the pond food chain. The colorful enlarged photos and the story organized around the tadpole's growth make this book very appropriate for preschoolers and primary students. A note at the front of the book indicates approximate enlargements for each of the animals photographed. Lavies' *Tree Trunk Traffic* (Dutton, 1989), which centers around a squirrel family in a maple tree, has a similar format.

Award: OSTB, 1989

■ Michels, Tilde. AT THE FROG POND. Trans. by Nina Ignatowicz. Illus. by Reinhard Michl. Harper, 1989. Unp. (LB 0-397-32315-8) Nonfiction. **Interest Level: Ages 6–9**

Michels invites readers to experience the life around a small pond in this simple picture book. "Did you ever stumble onto a secluded spot where you could see and hear the wondrous ways of nature? . . ." With a simple, evocative text and muted watercolor illustrations, Michels introduces readers to a pond environment in the spring, when frogs mate and tadpoles hatch, and continues through the summer with twilit nights and a thunderstorm followed by a "grand frog concert." She touches on life cycles, the food chain, and hibernation, but her main intent is to convey a sense of the wonder and the beauty of the pond. The illustrations enhance the text. Included are pictures of the pond and its inhabitants at night, the pond during and after a storm, and some kinds of underwater life. Michels ends with an encouragement to quietly observe a pond saying, "And for a little while you will be a part of things that live and grow around this small frog pond."

Award: OSTB, 1989

■ Milne, Lorus J., and Margery Milne. THE MYSTERY OF THE BOG FOREST. Photos by Fred Bavendam. Dodd, 1984. 127pp. o.p. Nonfiction. **Interest Level: Ages 12 up**

This is a thorough, interesting, but wordy book on bogs by Lorus J. and Margery Milne. Topics that are covered here are how bogs differ from other wetlands, how they are formed, what plants and animals live in this unique habitat, and how cranberries, which thrive in bogs, are harvested. An appendix lists plants and animals common to North American peat bogs with their scientific names and habitat. The Milnes have a conversational but rambling style of writing. The captioned black-and-white photographs are helpful but not outstanding. An index is included.

Award: OSTB, 1984

■ Parker, Steve. POND & RIVER. Photos by Philip Dowell. Knopf, 1988. 64pp. (LB 0-394-99615-1) SERIES: Eyewitness Books. Nonfiction. Interest Level: Ages 10 up

Pond and River is one of the eye-catching *Eyewitness* series books published by Knopf. With its large format, superb photography, and aesthetically pleasing design, it will attract both children and adults. Each of the 28 sections, usually two pages long, includes a paragraph of text giving an overview of pond or river ecology. Pictures of plants and animals with captions and common name labels are set against a white background, making them seem to pop off each busy, picture-filled spread. The effect is visually striking and also reminiscent of the photography in some mail-order catalogs.

Beginning with a seasonal look at typical pond plants and animals, the book continues with descriptions of fish, fowl, reeds, waterside mammals, amphibians, insects, shells, and so on. The book ends with sections on life along the riverbank, the river's mouth, the salt marsh, and a section on the study of environments and conservation. While the brief text provides an ecological perspective, the individual photographs (in which everything is singled out) do not support the ecological perspective. The editor's decision to feature photographs of detached bird wings and other animal parts is also a little odd. Originally published in Great Britain, it may not be useful as a field guide. It has a bare-bones index and a short list of North American environmental organizations. It is a beautiful, browser's book.

■ Pringle, Laurence. ESTUARIES: WHERE RIVERS MEET THE SEA. Macmillan, 1973. 55pp. o.p. Nonfiction. Interest Level: Ages 9–12

For over 20 years Laurence Pringle has been writing about ecology and conservation. In this older title he introduces readers to the inhabitants of estuaries, "one of the most valuable ecosystems on earth." Pringle writes simply and clearly, explaining how estuaries provide homes for many plants and animals. People, too, benefit from estuaries. Pringle states that "two out of every three kinds of valuable food fish netted along the Atlantic coast spend part of their lives in estuaries. Half of the seafood harvested along the Pacific Coast also depends on estuaries." Cities often grow up around estuaries, which make good harbors. Many estuaries have been polluted and filled in, affecting the plant and animal life there and sometimes drastically reducing the amount of seafood harvested. Excellent black-and-white photographs illustrate the text. In spite of the older publication date and the now somewhat dated appearance of the book, it is an excellent source of information on estuaries for middle- and upper-grade readers. A glossary and an index are included.

Award: OSTB, 1973

■ Rockwell, Jane. ALL ABOUT PONDS. Illus. by Joseph Veno. Troll, 1984. 32pp. (LB 0-89375-971-6) SERIES: Question and Answer Book. Nonfiction. Interest Level: Ages 8–12
Rockwell's simple, clear explanations of pond succession in a question-and-answer format give readers basic information on pond ecology. Rockwell stresses that the pond is an ecosystem, a community of living things, and describes the plants and animals typical of each stage of a pond's existence; new, mature, aging, and old. The slightly cartoonish watercolor illustrations do not enhance the text. The book has no glossary or index.

■ Schwartz, David M. THE HIDDEN LIFE OF THE POND. Photos by Dwight Kuhn. Crown, 1988. Unp. (LB 0-517-57060-2) Nonfiction. Interest Level: Ages 6–10
Like their collaborations on forest and meadow life, David Schwartz and Dwight Kuhn's *The Hidden Life of the Pond* takes readers on a photographic journey observing animals and plants typically found in and around ponds and marshes. The emphasis of the book is on striking close-ups of mammals, birds, amphibians, reptiles, insects, and plants. Series of photographs show the life cycle of the mosquito, the spring peeper frog and the dragonfly. The photographs and the text follow the cycle of the seasons as well, and although interrelationships are not stressed, Schwartz covers the habits, life cycles, and adaptations these animals make in the pond habitat. Lavies's photographic look at *Lily Pad Pond* (Dutton, 1989) is similar, but that book follows a tadpole as it grows and focuses on the concept of the food chain.
Award: OSTB, 1988

■ Stone, Lynn M. POND LIFE. Childrens, 1983. 48pp. (LB 0-516-01705-5) SERIES: New True. Nonfiction. Interest Level: Ages 6–9
Stone begins by explaining various ways ponds are formed, both naturally and by people. He also describes the many ways people use or enjoy ponds. But the bulk of this book describes the plants and animals that use the pond or make it their home and the interrelationships between them. Without making a pitch for conservation, he stresses the importance of each member of the pond community in maintaining the health of the pond. Stone writes clearly in this beginner's book on pond ecology. The large type, easy vocabulary, and color photographs make this series inviting to young readers. The book includes a glossary and an index. *Marshes and Swamps* (Childrens, 1983), another New True book by Stone, takes a similar approach and includes information on various kinds of marshes and swamps.

■ Stone, Lynn M. WETLANDS. Photos by author. Rourke, 1989. 48pp. (LB 0-86592-447-3) SERIES: Ecozones. Nonfiction. Interest Level: Ages 10–12

Stone presents a good overview of wetlands in North America, explaining how wetlands are formed and describing what plants and animals inhabit them in this addition to the Ecozones series. In a chapter called "The Flow of Energy," he discusses wetlands as ecosystems, explaining the complexity of wetland food chains and the disruption of the balance of nature when exotic plants and animals are introduced or when an animal is removed. In a final chapter on conservation, he discusses the importance of wetlands to people as well as to wildlife. Wetlands help control flooding, filter pollutants, and add to the water table. Good color photographs and maps illustrate the text, although the captions on one set of photographs were switched. A glossary, an index, a list of wetland sites in ten states and three Canadian provinces, and a brief list of activities follows. *Wetlands* is more difficult to read than the size and format suggest.

■ **Williams, Terry Tempest. BETWEEN CATTAILS. Illus. by Peter Parnall. Macmillan, 1985. Unp. (0-684-18309-9) Nonfiction. Interest Level: Ages 6–10**
Terry Williams captures the vitality, fragility, and connectedness of marsh ecology in this tour of a marsh and of the plants and animals that make their home "between cattails." Using a free-verse poetic style, she gets readers to see and feel activity in the marsh while showing the roles animals and plants play and the interdependence of everything there. The blue herons are "sentries of the marsh," the muskrat is the "marsh specialist who builds islands," and marsh plants are "marsh producers, [which] make food from the sun, while becoming food for others." Parnall's characteristic ink drawings, awash with intense blues, greens, and yellows, create a stylized view of the marsh that complements Williams's poetic style. Like Dewey's *At the Edge of the Pond* (Little, 1987), this is nonfiction that, although informative, appeals to the senses. The book contains no index or glossary, but it is a visually appealing introduction to the marsh. For a straightforward look at wetlands, see Freschet's *Year on Muskrat Marsh* (Macmillan, 1974) and for photographic essays, see Lavies's *Lily Pad Pond* (Dutton, 1989) and Schwartz's *The Hidden Life of the Pond* (Crown, 1988).

Oceans, Coasts, Reefs, and Estuaries

■ **Arnold, Caroline. A WALK ON THE GREAT BARRIER REEF. Illus. by Arthur Arnold. Carolrhoda, 1988. 48pp. (LB 0-87614-285-4) SERIES: Carolrhoda Nature Watch Book. Nonfiction. Interest Level: Ages 8–12**
Caroline Arnold describes the varied and colorful plants and animals of the coral reef community in her look at the Great Barrier Reef off the northeast coast of Australia. Arnold explains the formation of reefs, different types of

coral, and the life in and around the reef, noting the delicate balance of life on the reef and the danger posed by human interference. Colorful photographs, a map, and diagrams enhance the text. A glossary further explains many scientific terms used in the text. An index is included. This book is a good source of information for middle-grade readers and report writers.

Award: OSTB, 1988

■ Arnosky, Jim. NEAR THE SEA: A PORTFOLIO OF PAINTINGS. Illus. by author. Lothrop, 1990. 32pp. (LB 0-688-09327-2) Nonfiction. Interest Level: Ages 9–12

Eleven oil paintings by the prolific artist-author Jim Arnosky depict places on an island off the coast of Maine. Each painting is accompanied by a page of text reflecting Arnosky's observations as he worked. The two combine to give readers both the naturalist's and the artist's view of the area. His interest in color and form seen in the paintings are balanced by his interest in the history, setting, and life of the seashore. A companion to his *In the Forest* (Lothrop, 1989), art students will see how this artist thinks and works; budding naturalists will see how much there is to observe in any habitat.

Award: OSTB, 1990

■ Bellamy, David. THE ROCK POOL. Illus. by Jill Dow. Crown, 1988. Unp. (0-517-56977-9) SERIES: Our Changing World. Nonfiction. Interest Level: Ages 8–10

In each of the titles in the excellent and accessible British picture-book series Our Changing World, ecologist David Bellamy describes a specific habitat, the interdependence of the plants and animals there, and the changes that occur when people disturb it. In *The Rock Pool*, Bellamy describes the seaweeds, kelps, jellyfish, starfish, sea anemones, crabs, and others who make their homes in the tide pool, explaining how they protect themselves and get food. When a tanker leaks oil during a storm, it spells disaster for much of the life in and along the seashore, including that in the tide pool. Only a few creatures escape.

But Bellamy's look at the rock pool a year later is optimistic (perhaps overly optimistic in light of recent oil spills). The oil slowly washes away, and he reminds readers that "it is the way of nature to cleanse, heal, and recolonize. Let us hope that the creatures that live here will never have to face such a disaster again." The book begins and ends with an aerial view of the beach where the rock pool is situated. Dow's detailed watercolors add to the simple text. Although numbered keys identify many species, the small numbers are hard to find in the illustrations, and at least one animal is mislabeled.

■ Bender, Lionel. LIFE ON A CORAL REEF. Illus. with photos. Watts, 1989. 32pp. (0-531-17163-9) SERIES: First Sight. Nonfiction. Interest Level: Ages 8–12
The large-size format, excellent colorful photographs and illustrations, and minimal text in the First Sight series will appeal to many children. In *Life on a Coral Reef,* Bender describes the rich wildlife community formed by reefs in short two-page chapters. Small insets show the relative size of the coral inhabitants to a human hand. The book includes a "survival file," in which Bender alerts readers to threats to coral reefs including oil exploration, tourism, and pollution from sewage, toxic waste, and even pesticides. The book ends with an identification chart of many of the animals found on coral reefs and suggests an art project as a follow-up activity. The author does not relate the art project to any science or ecological concept. An index is included.

■ Cole, Sheila. WHEN THE TIDE IS LOW. Illus. by Virginia Wright-Frierson. Lothrop, 1985. Unp. (LB 0-688-04067-5) Fiction. Interest Level: Ages 4–7
In this picture-book introduction to tides, tide pools, and beach life, an inquisitive young girl wants to go to the beach, which is now under water during high tide. Her mother explains to her the action of the tides, and they discuss the variety of animals (hermit crabs, sea anemones, clams, mussels) they will find in tide pools and along the beach when the tide is low. Illustrated with pleasant watercolors, this book is ideal for sharing before visiting the seashore. A glossary for adults further describes and illustrates the animals mentioned in the story. Older readers will prefer Bellamy's *The Rock Pool* (Crown, 1988) or Malnig's *Where the Waves Break* (Carolrhoda, 1985).
Award: OSTB, 1985

■ Gilbreath, Alice. THE GREAT BARRIER REEF: A TREASURE IN THE SEA. Illus. with photos. Dillon, 1986. 103pp. (LB 0-87518-300-X) SERIES: Ocean World Library. Nonfiction. Interest Level: Ages 9 up
The Great Barrier Reef is a unique series of coral reefs and shoals off the northeast coast of Australia. Gilbreath clearly describes and explains aspects of this unique ecosystem—its formation, its probable habitation by Australian Aborigines during the last ice age, its more recent discovery by Captain Cook of the *Endeavour,* the varied marine life above and below the water's surface, and the ecological problems the reef faces, including the invasion of crown-of-thorns starfish and damage from such pollutants as sewage, pesticides, and oil drilling. In a final chapter Gilbreath talks about exploring the reefs through reef walking and scuba diving. She notes that

a small part of the reef is now protected. Both color and black-and-white photographs illustrate the text in this informative book. The book includes an appendix with scientific names of sea animals, a glossary, a bibliography and an index.

This book is more thorough than Arnold's *A Walk on the Great Barrier Reef,* but is not as attractive. However, the Ocean World Library series is a sound investment. Three other titles of interest in the series are Gilbreath's *The Continental Shelf* (Dillon, 1986), which stresses the dangers of pollution to the shelf and the efforts to preserve it; Sibbald's *Homes in the Sea* (Dillon, 1986), which describes animals that live in various habitats in the sea; and Daegling's *Monster Seaweed* (Dillon, 1986), which examines the ecology of giant kelps. All are useful for middle- and upper-grade students studying the ecology of ocean and marine life.

■ **Lye, Keith. COASTS. Silver Burdett, 1988. 48pp. (LB 0-382-09790-4) SERIES: Our World. Nonfiction. Interest Level: Ages 10 up**
Lye's addition to the excellent Our World series looks at coasts around the world. This book is an overview of many aspects of coasts: climate, plant and animal life, human use, coastal resources, pollution, and conservation. It is well written and organized with clearly captioned color photographs, maps, and diagrams. A glossary and an index is included. *Coasts* is a useful book for middle- and upper-grade students.

■ **Malnig, Anita. WHERE THE WAVES BREAK: LIFE AT THE EDGE OF THE SEA. Photos by Jeff Rotman, et al. Carolrhoda, 1985. 48pp. (LB 0-87614-226-9) SERIES: Carolrhoda Nature Watch Book. Nonfiction. Interest Level: Ages 8 – 12**
After explaining high and low tides, Malnig describes many of the plants and animals found in tide pools such as starfish, snails, periwinkles, and sea cucumbers. Malnig writes engagingly about marine life, noting places where one is likely to find particular animals and plants, discussing their physical features, and, to some extent, explaining the ways they adapt to their environment. Numerous captioned color photographs provide many close-up views of marine life. No mention is made of threats to tide pool life such as oil spills, but this is an attractive introduction to life along the shore. The book includes an explanation of scientific classification and an index.

Award: OSTB, 1985

■ **Parker, Steve. SEASHORE. Photos by Dave King. Knopf, 1989. 64pp. (LB 0-394-92254-9) SERIES: Eyewitness Books. Nonfiction. Interest Level: Ages 10 up**

Ideal for browsing, this addition to the Eyewitness Books series introduces readers to the life along the seashore and the adaptations various plants and animals make to the changing conditions there. Its large format, stunning color photographs, and attractive design are strengths. Parker begins by describing how coasts are shaped and what effects water and wind have on different kinds of rock. Then in two-page spreads with brief text and numerous captioned photographs and diagrams, he looks at plants, shells, tide pools, and marine animals including birds and mammals to be found along the shore. Sections on beachcombing and seashore preservation follow, although the author could have made more of problems of pollution and overcollecting along the shore.

■ Sabin, Louis. WONDERS OF THE SEA. Illus. by Bert Dodson. Troll, 1982. 32pp. (LB 0-89375-578-8) Nonfiction. Interest Level: Ages 7–9
Lush blues and greens predominate in the watercolors depicting marine life in this picture-book introduction to plants and animals of the sea. With a simple text, Sabin describes a variety of underwater life, from one-celled plants and animals to the much larger sea kelps, mackerel, tuna, and whales. He shows how various animals are adapted to their watery life and how they move. He also explains the ocean food chain, taking into account the part people play in the chain. Sabin makes no mention of pollution or the fragility of the ocean environment. *Wonders of the Sea* works as an attractive but basic introduction to marine ecology. The book has no index.

■ Silverstein, Alvin, and Virginia Silverstein. LIFE IN A TIDAL POOL. Illus. by Pamela Carroll and Walter Carroll. Little, 1990. 60pp. (LB 0-316-79120-2) Nonfiction. Interest Level: Ages 10–14
In their introductory chapter, veteran science writers Al and Virginia Silverstein do an excellent job of explaining the dynamics of tide pool ecology, showing how important it is for tide pool creatures to adapt to the changing and fragile conditions of the pool. In following chapters they describe the variety of life found in the tide pool—plankton, algae, seaweed, kelp, barnacles, starfish, sea cucumbers, and many others. A final chapter on observing the life in tide pools stresses respect for the life there. The Silversteins caution that in some coastal areas, many tide pool communities have been wiped out by overeager collectors. The black-and-white line drawings washed with gray are detailed and attractive, but would be much more appealing with color. Two complements to this book are Malnig's *Where the Waves Break* (Carolrhoda, 1985), which has colorful close-up photographs, and Bellamy's *The Rock Pool* (Crown, 1988), which shows the effects of an oil spill on the life in a tide pool. *Life in a Tidal Pool* includes a glossary, but the book's usefulness for both re-

searchers and browsers would have been enhanced with the inclusion of an index. Its omission is a mystery.

■ Tayntor, Elizabeth, Paul Erickson, and Les Kaufman. DIVE TO THE CORAL REEFS. Crown, 1986. Unp. (0-517-56311-8) SERIES: New England Aquarium Book. Nonfiction. Interest Level: Ages 6 up
This brief but inviting and informative introduction to coral reefs takes readers on a dive with a team of scientists to two reefs off the coast of Jamaica in the Caribbean. The authors emphasize the interdependence of animals and plants on coral reefs and mention both natural and human threats to their existence, including hurricanes, souvenir collectors, oil spills, and coastline development. The book's attractive design and outstanding photographs will appeal to children and adults. There is no index or glossary, but this book is a browser's delight.

Award: OSTB, 1986

Urban and Other Unique Habitats

■ Bash, Barbara. URBAN ROOSTS. Illus. by author. Sierra Club, 1990. Unp. (LB 0316-08306-2) Nonfiction. Interest Level: Ages 6–10
"All across the country, as their natural habitats have been destroyed, birds have moved to town. The ones that have been able to adapt are thriving in the heart of the city." So begins Bash's informative look at 13 birds who make their homes in urban areas. Bash tracks down pigeons roosting under highway overpasses, sparrows and finches in the metal casings surrounding traffic lights, nighthawks who may hatch their young on the flat, graveled roofs of buildings, and snowy owls who sometimes winter at airports in northern cities. Bash's watercolors are stunning and offer detailed, close-up views of these urban dwellers and some bird's-eye views of the city, as in the cover illustration. A good read-alone or read-aloud book, *Urban Roosts* makes an excellent addition to any study of urban ecology and a prerequisite to a city bird-watching walk.

Award: OSTB, 1990

■ Dethier, Vincent G. THE ECOLOGY OF A SUMMER HOUSE. Univ. of Mass. Pr., 1984. 133pp. (LB 0-87023-421-8) Nonfiction. Interest Level: Ages 12 up
Zoologist Vincent Dethier could make the most inveterate bug hater appreciate insects in this engaging look at the ecology of a home. With humor, insight, and a sense of wonder, this keen observer writes about the nonhu-

man residents from chimney to root cellar sharing his summer home on the coast of Maine. Birds, wasps, spiders, crickets, a bat, wood mice, and red squirrels "share" the home with the Dethier family, each inhabiting a spot best suited for its survival, often adapting to the particular human-made niche it chooses. In one chapter he observes a paper wasp building a nest off a side porch, noting in irony that "the creatures that invented paper were never destined to write upon it."

The book is filled with details on the life cycles, habits, and interrelationships of its mostly summer residents. For junior-high readers, the book is an inspiration to the study of household ecosystems as well as an inspiration to the further study of ecology and natural science. Dethier has an endearing respect for these small creatures he is willing to share his home with, and his book offers another avenue for ecological discussion.

■ Dunrea, Olivier. DEEP DOWN UNDERGROUND. Illus. by author. Macmillan, 1989. Unp. (0-02-732861-9) Fiction. Interest Level: Ages 3–8
Young children will be delighted to discover all the activity beneath their feet in Dunrea's clever counting book, which introduces 10 animals that make their homes underground. While a counting book is not the most ordinary way of beginning ecology studies, this clever, whimsical book does provide a simple lesson on soil habitats. Dunrea's pen-and-ink and watercolor cutaways follow "one wee moudiewort" (the Scottish word for mole) as it digs underground past other under-the-soil creatures: beetles, earthworms, caterpillars, spiders, toads, mice, snakes, sow bugs, and ants. Also shown is underground debris—bones, skeletons, a button, a key, and a screw. The alliterative, rhythmical prose combines nicely with the earthtoned illustrations to produce a picture book that children will enjoy listening to as they search out and count animals common to this underground habitat.

Award: OSTB, 1989

■ Lavies, Bianca. TREE TRUNK TRAFFIC. Photos by author. Dutton, 1989. Unp. (0-525-44495-5) Nonfiction. Interest Level: Ages 4–8
A backyard maple with a family of squirrels and other living things in and around the tree are featured in this photo essay by Bianca Lavies, a National Geographic photographer. Lavies builds the story around the squirrel family during one spring and summer. Young children will find this book appealing and will be encouraged to begin observing wildlife in their backyards, too. Sharp color photographs of katydids, tree crickets, spiders, birds, butterflies, and raccoons, all making use of the tree, show the variety of life and

some of the relationships between the living things. The book has a catchy title and catchy photographs. See also Lavies' *Lily Pad Pond* (Dutton, 1989) for a similar approach to pond ecology.

■ **McLaughlin, Molly. EARTHWORMS, DIRT, AND ROTTEN LEAVES: AN EXPLORATION IN ECOLOGY. Illus. by Robert Shetterly. Macmillan, 1986. 86pp. (0-689-31215-6) Nonfiction. Interest Level: Ages 9–14**
"What's so interesting about a slimy creature that lives in the dirt and eats dead leaves?" asks Molly McLaughlin in this thorough and engaging introduction to earthworms and the important role they play in soil ecology. McLaughlin treats her subject with respect and with a light touch. In addition to describing the anatomy of earthworms and their adaptations to their environment, McLaughlin shows how earthworms have an important ecological role; they have a place in the food web and an important function in decomposing dead leaves, putting nutrients back into the soil so that plants can make use of them. Incorporated into each well-written chapter are activities and experiments to increase the reader's knowledge of earthworms' physical characteristics and behavior. McLaughlin stresses the importance of treating earthworms humanely while conducting experiments. The book is a winning combination of attention to scientific method with an ecological perspective. For a more wide-ranging but less engaging look at soil ecology, see the Milnes' *A Shovelful of Earth* (Holt, 1987). *Earthworms, Dirt, and Rotten Leaves* is illustrated with pencil drawings and diagrams. It includes a glossary, a bibliography, and an index.

Awards: ALA Notable Children's Book, 1986; OSTB, 1986

■ **Milne, Lorus J., and Margery Milne. A SHOVELFUL OF EARTH. Illus. by Margaret La Farge. Holt, 1987. 114pp. (0-8050-0028-3) Nonfiction. Interest Level: Ages 10 up**
Lorus J. and Margery Milne introduce young people to soil ecology in this informative but wordy book. After explaining soil composition and layers, they describe life in the litter layer, topsoil layer, and subsoil layer, discussing ground beetles, land snails, earthworms, yellow jackets, cicadas, shrews, star-nosed moles, and other animals. They also compare soil in evergreen forests, tropical forests, grasslands, deserts, and arctic and alpine areas. Suggestions for observing soil are interspersed throughout the beginning chapters. There is no question that the Milnes' are knowledgeable and enthusiastic. However, their writing, which incorporates a lot of historical anecdotes and results of research studies, at times seems inappropriate for a young audience, and children may have difficulty getting through the

book. McLaughlin's *Earthworms, Dirt, and Rotten Leaves* (Macmillan, 1986) is narrower in scope but far more engaging. *A Shovelful of Earth* includes a glossary, a bibliography, and an index.

■ **Parnall, Peter. APPLE TREE. Illus. by author. Macmillan, 1987. Unp. (LB 0-02-770160-3) Nonfiction. Interest Level: Ages 6–10**
Parnall combines an ecology lesson with his love of nature in *Apple Tree*. Delicate pencil-and-watercolor illustrations in his characteristic style enhance this tribute to a lone apple tree, once part of a nearby orchard. While Parnall did not set out to write a science book, his prose incorporates information about the interdependence of the tree with various animals and plants throughout the year: bees, beetles, flies, yellow jackets, lichens, birds, raccoons, mice, and deer. A good observer and a tree climber as well, the narrator also becomes a part of this small community. Parnall's personal response to this small habitat is appealing. It may encourage children to observe, appreciate, and understand the ecology of a place special to them.

■ **Parnall, Peter. WINTER BARN. Illus. by author. Macmillan, 1986. Unp. (0-02-770170-0) Fiction. Interest Level: Ages 5–8**
The varied creatures who take shelter in a barn during a long and snowy Maine winter form a unique community in *Winter Barn*. Wild animals find nooks and crannies there among the domestic cats, horses, chickens, and sheep. Some hibernate, others feed on spilled grain or cat food, but all get along during the long winter. Parnall shows feeling for all the creatures, wild and tame, who take refuge in the barn. His charcoal drawings are washed with brown and a touch of red on a white background. The book presents an understated lesson in the peaceful coexistence of all creatures.

Awards: OSTB, 1986; NSSB, 1986

■ **Parnall, Peter. WOODPILE. Illus. by author. Macmillan, 1990. Unp. (0-02-770155-7) Nonfiction. Interest Level: Ages 6–9**
Teachers who are looking for a small community with a variety of animals to show students may enjoy using *Woodpile*. The woodpile in Parnall's book, including soil underneath and space around it, serves as a home or a resting place to a whole community of animals. A worm, a mole, a mouse, a weasel, a chipmunk, a bat, a wasp, a spider, a moth, a frog, a mosquito, a fly—all make use of it. Parnall's lyrical first-person narration muses about the animals living there as well as the many kinds of wood that make up the pile—ash, oak, poplar, birch—and the various ways in which the wood has been used. Parnall's flowing pen-and-ink drawings are washed with soft

browns, greens, and yellows. They show the woodpile from various angles with its inhabitants coming in and out. Taking a close look at a small community can make it easier to understand the larger ones.

Award: OSTB, 1990

■ Smith, Howard Everett, Jr. SMALL WORLDS: COMMUNITIES OF LIVING THINGS. Illus. by author. Macmillan, 1987. 180pp. (0-684-18723-X) Nonfiction. Interest Level: Ages 12 up
Smith describes 11 small and unique ecosystems, including an old house, a sand dune, a milkweed plant, a tide pool, an old wooden barn, a tree, a vacant lot, a waterfall spray area, a fence line on the prairie, roadsides, and cliffs and boulders. Smith includes much information, incorporating scientific terms into his narrative.

One or more of these small communities should be accessible to anyone in urban or rural areas, and the small size of the habitats makes them useful and interesting for individual or class study. Each chapter is introduced by a black-and-white line drawing and the chapter itself is illustrated with individual drawings of plants or animals. Smith's informative book is not for a quick browse. His style is not as engaging as Jean George's or Laurence Pringle's, but for the serious naturalist, it fills a niche of its own. A glossary and an index are included.

■ Waters, John F. NEIGHBORHOOD PUDDLE. Illus. by Kazue Mizumura. Warne, 1971. 40pp. o.p. Nonfiction. Interest Level: Ages 7–10
Waters's look at a seasonal pond that forms in a vacant lot after the spring rains gives readers another small ecosystem to explore. How life comes to this "neighborhood puddle" and survives after the pond dries up is as interesting as the life cycles, habits, and interrelationships of the plants and animals that inhabit it. By looking at a pond next to a town, Waters also incorporates human interaction with the pond—children play around it, build a model raft, and collect tadpoles there. However, unlike Jorg Müller's *The Changing Countryside* (Macmillan, 1977), which depicts the devastating effects of human encroachment on the rural landscape, the pond in *Neighborhood Puddle* is not yet threatened. By understanding the richness and complexity of this ordinary pond, children can perhaps better appreciate the loss of rain forests in faraway places as well as the loss of these small habitats. Greens predominate in Mizumura's soft watercolor illustrations, which alternate with black and white washes. *Neighborhood Puddle* is an older title, but it is one that remains useful and appropriate for young children.

 **3**

At Issue

Many books on current events and issues are produced quickly and are short-lived. The issues themselves rise and fall in popularity, information soon becomes dated, and events cast new light on a subject. But children need access to current information on environmental issues written at their level. Some of the books that follow serve simply as quick overviews or introductions to broad subjects like energy or pollution. Others explore environmental problems in more depth.

Since authors and publishers of varying viewpoints are interested in environmental issues, readers will find books written from different perspectives in Chapter Three. Some authors focus on human-interest aspects, as Roland Smith does in *Sea Otter Rescue*. Others explore the economic, social, and political context of an issue as Laurence Pringle does in *Nuclear Energy: Troubled Past, Uncertain Future* and as Roy Gallant does in *The Peopling of Planet Earth*. Others go straight to the heart as in John Christopher Fine's *The Hunger Road* or as in Lynn Cherry's picture book for younger readers, *The Great Kapok Tree*. Environmental issues find their way into fiction, too: James Lincoln Collier describes pollution in *When the Stars Begin to Fall* and Gibbs Davis speaks of endangered manatees in *Fishman and Charly*, for example.

The interconnectedness of environmental issues makes it difficult to pigeon-hole "issue" books. Many of the books included in one section could easily have been placed in another and many of the ecology books in Chapter Two address environmental concerns. Not surprisingly, more books are published on some very current topics like acid rain, global warming, rain forests, and endangered species than there are on alternative energy resources, land use, pesticides, and recycling. Of course, that will change as new information or new theories emerge and public interest in the issues changes.

General

■ Dudley, William. THE ENVIRONMENT: DISTINGUISHING BETWEEN FACT AND OPINION. Greenhaven, 1989. 32pp. (LB 0-89908-603-9) SERIES: Opposing Viewpoints Juniors. Nonfiction. Interest Level: Ages 10–14

The environment is one of the "Opposing Viewpoints Juniors" series by Greenhaven Press. The series is designed to develop critical thinking skills and this title helps readers learn to distinguish between fact and opinion. In separate chapters the author examines four environmental issues: "Is there an environmental crisis?"; Does the U.S. have a garbage crisis?"; "Is acid rain a serious problem?"; and, "Is the earth running out of resources?" Two viewpoints are given for each issue. The author interjects several questions to help readers analyze the arguments and each chapter concludes with activities to practice distinguishing fact and opinion. This will be useful to debate students as well as anyone preparing an oral or written report on environmental issues. Older students will find *The Environmental Crisis* (Greenhaven, 1991), one of the "Opposing Viewpoints" series a more in-depth resource.

■ Hecht, Jeff. SHIFTING SHORES: RISING SEAS, RETREATING COAST-LINES. Macmillan, 1990. 151pp. (0-684-19087-7) Nonfiction. Interest Level: Ages 12 up

"About three-quarters of the people in the United States live within 50 miles of an ocean or one of the Great Lakes," says Hecht, who takes a close look at both natural and human forces that have shaped coasts, including weather, erosion, rising sea levels, and human development. He provides a history of coastal development (both geological and human), but the thrust of the book is on the potentially catastrophic effects of erosion and rising sea levels to the land and to human populations along coasts. He discusses various strategies for protecting our shorelines. How these areas are threatened as ecosystems is not a point that is emphasized, but there is ample discussion of global warming. The book includes black-and-white photographs, charts, diagrams, and an index.

■ Herda, D.J. ENVIRONMENTAL AMERICA: THE NORTH CENTRAL STATES. Illus. by Renee Graef. Millbrook, 1991. 64pp. (LB 1-878841-08-4) SERIES: The American Scene. Nonfiction. Interest Level: Ages 10–14

This is one of a series of six books that focuses on the ecology and environmental problems of different geographic regions of the United States. In *The North Central States,* (covering North and South Dakota, Nebraska, Minnesota, Iowa, Wisconsin, Illinois, Michigan, Indiana, and Ohio) Herda traces the development of agriculture on the prairies and the effects of agricultural practices on the land and wildlife: soil erosion, water pollution from chemical runoff, pesticides that kill beneficial plants and animals, and irrigation that results in high concentations of salt in the topsoil. He looks at other problems specific to the upper midwest as well as efforts to protect the environment. Each book in the series includes numerous general suggestions for readers and several toll-free telephone numbers of groups such as the Superfund Hotline and the Asbestos Hotline. Bibliographies and lists of organizations to contact are tailored to each title. Chapter notes, glossary and index are included in an attractive design with colored photographs, maps, and some charts. Other regions covered include: The Northeastern States, The Northwestern States, The Southeastern States, The South Central States, and The Southwestern States.

■ **Hoover, H.M. ORVIS. Viking, 1987. 188pp. (0-670-81117-3) Fiction. Interest Level: Ages 10–14**
In this engaging futuristic novel, Earth has recovered from the effects of global warming, which forced people into domed cities and eventually sent them to seek life in space colonies. Earth is now recovering but is sparsely populated; people who do live there rarely venture into "the Empty," the wild areas outside cities. In fact, most people prefer life off Earth in the space colonies. Just as Earth has been abandoned, so have twelve-year-old Toby West and her friend Thaddeus, who attend a prestigious boarding school for children of "ex-terrans" who want a character-building experience for their children. Toby and Thaddeus befriend Orvis, an obsolete robot headed for the junkyard. In an effort to save Orvis from the junk heap, they set off on an adventure which strands them in "the Empty." and, with Orvis's help, they eventually find a home for the robot and for themselves. Hoover's vision of Earth as an abandoned home, along with her endearing characters, human-robot friendship, and a fast-moving plot, make this a readable science fiction novel that sparks speculation on the consequences of the destruction of the environment.

■ **Leinwand, Gerald. THE ENVIRONMENT. Facts on File, 1990. 122pp. (0-8160-2099-X) SERIES: American Issues. Nonfiction. Interest Level: Ages 12 up**
The Environment is a useful book for upper-level students researching environmental issues. Leinwand begins with a historical overview of American attitudes toward the environment. He follows up with chapters on land pollution, water pollution, air pollution, and energy, summarizing current problems and efforts to solve them. In later chapters Leinwand discusses the politics of environmental protection; the development of our national parks; and the role of federal and state governments in cleaning up the environ-

ment. Although the emphasis is on environmental problems in the United States, Leinwand stresses the need for a global approach to these problems. This book includes a bibliography and an index.

■ **Lowery, Linda. EARTH DAY. Illus. by Mary Bergherr. Carolrhoda, 1991. 48pp. (LB 0-87614-662-0)** SERIES: **On My Own. Nonfiction. Interest Level: Ages 5–9**
In an easy-reader format Lowery tells the story of Earth Day, April 22, 1970, the idea of then U.S. Senator Gaylord Nelson (who wrote the foreword to the book). Through the efforts of Nelson, Denis Hayes, and thousands of volunteers, millions of people across the country participated in classes, speeches, rallies, marches, nature walks, and other activities to learn more about taking care of the environment. Lowery briefly assesses the impact of Earth Day, which spearheaded political and legislative efforts to clean up the environment. A decade later both the public and the government had become lax, and environmental problems continued to mount. On April 22, 1990, a second, even bigger Earth Day celebration was held, and this time more than 140 countries participated. Lowery includes simple suggestions for students on ways to conserve and recycle and gives a brief list of environmental organizations. The book's illustrations are colorful. This book will be useful for planning Earth Day activities and for supplementing units on environmental protection.

■ **McCoy, J.J. HOW SAFE IS OUR FOOD SUPPLY? Watts, 1990. 160pp. (LB 0-531-10935-6)** SERIES: **An Impact Book. Nonfiction. Interest Level: Ages 12 up**
McCoy's timely look at the food industry and the host of threats to safe, wholesome food will be useful to middle- and upper-level student researchers. McCoy starts with a brief history of food preservation and the history and growth of a multibillion-dollar industry that produces, processes, and distributes food. He then outlines legislative efforts to regulate and protect food, noting criticism of testing methods and questions about the effectiveness of the Food and Drug Administration. He covers environmental issues surrounding production, preservation, and packaging of food in separate chapters on additives, pesticides, hormones and antibiotics, artificial sweeteners, and food irradiation. Chapters include examples of controversies such as those surrounding the use of Alar and bovine growth hormone. A bibliography and an index are included.

■ **Markham, Adam. THE ENVIRONMENT. Rourke, 1988. 48pp. (LB 0-86592-286-1)** SERIES: **World Issues. Nonfiction. Interest Level: Ages 10 up**

Well written and organized, *The Environment* presents an overview of worldwide environmental issues, emphasizing their global nature and the influence of humanity on the quality of the environment in the past as well as the present. Markham covers air and water pollution, global warming, the destruction of the ozone layer, deforestation, the draining of wetlands, desertification, endangered species, and other issues, discussing some of the reasons for the problems as well as possible solutions. A chapter on environmental policy discusses the costs of protecting the environment and describes some international conservation efforts. A final chapter suggests ways an individual can make a difference. Coverage of the topics is brief, however, the book is still timely and useful for students studying environmental issues. *The Environment* is illustrated with color photographs. It does not have a bibliography, but it does include a glossary and an index.

■ **Middleton, Nick. ATLAS OF ENVIRONMENTAL ISSUES. Facts on File, 1989. 63pp. (0-8160-2023-x) Nonfiction. Interest Level: Ages 12 up**
Twenty-eight current environmental issues are highlighted in this global overview. Each two-page spread briefly describes an issue with maps, photographs, and diagrams providing more information and examples. Many of the issues, modern agriculture, soil erosion, desertification, deforestation, genetic engineering, and irrigation, for example, are related, and there is some cross-referencing between topics. Middleton's global perspective is welcome, and a chapter on war as an environmental issue is timely. An introduction to put all these issues and facts in context would have been helpful, but the book as it is will be useful to students looking for ideas for reports and to those who are just browsing. An index is included.

■ **Peckham, Alexander. CHANGING LANDSCAPES. Watts, 1991. 36pp. (LB 0-531-17289-9) SERIES: Green Issues. Nonfiction. Interest Level: Ages 10– 14**
Peckham looks at human activities that have contributed to environmental damage in this smoothly written, well-organized addition to the Green Issues series, which offers overviews of current environmental issues for middle- and upper-level students. Peckham points to "technological progress, the growing population and overexploitation of resources and farmland" as prime factors in worldwide environmental degradation. He contrasts the relatively slow rate of change to the earth from natural processes with the alarming rate of change brought about by humans, particularly since the Industrial Revolution. He argues that the rate of change is often too rapid for living things to adapt, resulting in the loss of species and habitats, the destruction of farmland, and pollution. He also notes that some scientists believe environmental damage has contributed to the demise of

civilizations in the past. Population control, conservation, and less destructive farming methods are three areas he discusses as solutions to the earth's environmental woes. This book has an attractive design, good photographs, a glossary, and an index. See also Peckham's *Resources Control* (Watts, 1990), another title in the Green Issues series.

■ Pringle, Laurence. LIVING IN A RISKY WORLD. Morrow, 1989. 105pp. (0-688-04326-7) Nonfiction. Interest Level: Ages 12 up
By approaching a broad range of environmental hazards including pollution, earthquakes, pesticides, and nuclear power from the standpoint of risk assessment, Pringle offers readers another way of looking at issues surrounding environmental health and safety. He shows how perceptions of risk often differ from the actual risk involved and how those perceptions may affect public opinion and policy. Pringle explains how scientists study and assess risk with examples of how regulatory agencies like the FDA and EPA determine the safety of food additives and pesticides. He ends with several suggestions. He advises readers to be informed, to be aware of how they perceive risks, to change what they can in their lives, and finally, to take political action. A list of regulatory agencies, a glossary, and an index is appended. Pringle's now out-of-print *Lives at Stake: The Science and Politics of Environmental Health* (Macmillan, 1980) examines political, economic, and social factors affecting environmental health and discusses the role of the government, of industry, and of consumers in creating and solving environmental problems.

■ Pringle, Laurence. WATER: THE NEXT GREAT RESOURCE BATTLE. Macmillan, 1982. 144pp. (0-02-775400-6) Nonfiction. Interest Level: Age 12 up
Is water a renewable resource? Yes, but our taken-for-granted water supply is in trouble on a number of fronts, according to Pringle, a veteran science writer. In his characteristic style, Pringle explores the economic, political, and historical factors that have made water into an environmental issue. He discusses water use, supply, contamination, treatment, protection, management, and planning practices, citing numerous federal and state policies and projects, many of which are shortsighted and wasteful. In a final chapter he cites a number of possible solutions, including more efficient irrigation systems, higher water prices, treatment of waste water, household reduction of water use, and dual water systems. The book includes a glossary and an index. It is illustrated with black and white photographs. In spite of its 1982 publication date, this book still fills a need for material on the subject and will be useful to upper-level research-

ers. See also Edward Dolan's *Drought: The Past, Present and Future Enemy* (Watts, 1990).

Award: OSTB, 1982

■ **Sanders, Scott Russell. THE ENGINEER OF BEASTS. Watts, 1988. 258pp. (LB 0-531-08383-7) Fiction. Interest Level: Ages 12 up**
This imaginative fantasy incorporates several environmental themes. It is set in a future when rising oceans, poisoned air and water, exhausted soil, and radioactive dumps have driven people into floating cities enclosed in plastic bubbles. Life in the city is regimented and mechanized. People have no contact with the natural world. "Those younger than fifty had lived all their days inside the Enclosure. Trees and birds and sharks and bears, no less than dragons, had become for them the stuff of legend." Spunky thirteen-year-old Mooch is an orphan who needs some connection with nature and wildness in her life. She meets and goes to work for Orlando, the engineer of beasts, at a "disney," a mechanical zoo that serves as an amusement park. Mooch is a whiz at mechanics and soon begins tinkering with the mechanical animals to make them more realistic and wild. This leads to some funny happenings, but it also brings about the eventual destruction of the disney and Mooch's expulsion from the domed city to a "refarmatory." From there she is sent to the outside, where she undertakes a spiritual quest in the wilderness. The novel's strength lies in Sanders's imaginative description of life in the domed city, a Disney World/EPCOT Center creation, taken a few steps farther, and in his vision of a future earth suffering from severe environmental damage with its people alienated from nature.

■ **Seidenberg, Steven. ECOLOGY AND CONSERVATION. Stevens, 1989. 64pp. (LB 0-8368-0005-2) SERIES: Gareth Stevens Information Library. Nonfiction. Interest Level: Ages 10–12**
This book is really an overview of environmental issues. Seidenberg looks at three regions of the biosphere—land, air, and water, then examines two biomes—deserts and forests, and ends with a chapter on wildlife. For each chapter, he introduces the topic, offers a brief look at problems such as pollution, erosion, and deforestation, and then suggests conservation measures as solutions to the problems. The coverage is basic. Some of the information that should be part of the text is put into boxed insets. Each heavily illustrated chapter includes a "Facts and Feats" inset with facts such as "The world's longest river is the Nile at 4,160 miles." Facts relating to environmental problems or solutions would have been more helpful. The

book includes a glossary and an index. Paula Hogan's *Ecology: Our Living Planet* (Stevens, 1990) is an adaptation of this book for children in primary grades.

■ Whitfield, Philip. CAN THE WHALES BE SAVED? Viking, 1989. 96pp. (0-670-82753-3) Nonfiction. Interest Level: Ages 9–12
This book offers a browsing treat and a quick source of information on ecological concepts and current environmental issues. Utilizing a question-and-answer format, it covers subjects like animal survival, ecosystems, genetic diversity, endangered animals, acid rain, pollution, recycling, and preservation. The book's large format with both black-and-white and full-color photographs, drawings, and maps will appeal to middle graders. Access to information through the table of contents, which lists each question, and the index, which includes references to the many illustrations, make this book useful. Although the 119 questions are answered by the "National History Museum," no information on the author or which natural history museum he is affiliated with is included. A glossary is included.

Fragile Habitat

■ Baker, Jeannie. WHERE THE FOREST MEETS THE SEA. Illus. by author. Greenwillow, 1987. Unp. (LB 0-688-06364-0) Fiction. Interest Level: Ages 6 up
Past, present, and future meet in this unusual and effective picture book about changes to the tropical rain forest on the coast of Australia. In the story a father and his son take their small motorboat over to an isolated beach on the edge of the rain forest. The boy's father tells him what the forest was like years ago, and, when the boy wanders into the forest, he pretends he is back in prehistoric times. As he explores the woods, images from the past appear: a dinosaur, an Aboriginal boy from long ago, and an extinct mammal. Baker's relief collages are constructed from clay, paper, paint, and other materials, and they successfully create the feel of the rain forest. As they leave, the father says they will return some day. The boy asks, "But will the forest still be here when we come back?" In the final spread, a shadowy vision of a future with cars, hotels, and boats along the coast is superimposed on the still-pristine setting. An afterword includes a map showing the location of the rain forest and text in which Baker voices her concern for the future of the largest remaining undisturbed area of rain forest in Australia.

■ Banks, Martin. CONSERVING RAIN FORESTS. Steck-Vaughn, 1990. 48pp. (LB 0-8114-2387-5) SERIES: Conserving Our World. Nonfiction. Interest Level: Ages 10 up

Excellent, captioned color photographs and numerous boxed insets help create an attractive, up-to-date, but brief look at the state of tropical rain forests around the world. Banks writes about the structure of rain forests, the diversity of animal and plant life within them, the people inhabiting rain forests, and the effect of modern technology on their lives. Consequences of rain forest destruction are discussed, and a final chapter highlights conservation efforts by government, industry, and conservation organizations. Lists of organizations, places to visit, and books for further reading are appended, as is a glossary and an index. While the reading level will make this useful mainly for older students, the well-designed graphic format with numerous illustrations and insets will make it usable for a somewhat wider audience.

■ Bond, Nancy. THE VOYAGE BEGUN. Macmillan, 1981. 319pp. (0-689-50204-4) Fiction. Interest Level: Ages 12 up
Set sometime in the 21st century in a world suffering the consequences of depletion of energy resources, pollution, and global warming, Bond's compelling novel is about several inhabitants of a small Cape Cod community. The characters include Paul, a sixteen-year-old son of a research scientist recently transferred to the town; Mickey Cafferty, the eleven-year-old daughter of the local grocer; Maggie Rudd, the local game warden and a conservationist in a land with little left to conserve; and Walter Jepson, a retired boat builder who tries to maintain his independence in a world that no longer has use for fishing boats. Strong characterizations within a believable although sketchy setting portray a wounded earth, a declining culture, and a blind government looking for technological solutions to get them through what they call "transitional periods" of severe economic, social, and environmental crises. The environmental message is not forced in *The Voyage Begun,* but it offers readers a vision of a future that could be theirs.

■ Cherry, Lynne. THE GREAT KAPOK TREE: A TALE OF THE AMAZON RAIN FOREST. Illus. by author. Harcourt, 1990. Unp. (LB 0-15-200520-X) Fiction. Interest Level: Ages 5–10
While a worker rests from chopping down a huge kapok tree in the Amazon rain forest, he falls asleep and has a dream. In the dream a young Indian boy and several animals approach one by one and tell him how important the tree is. It is home and a source of food to many animals. Its roots hold the soil in place, and its leaves give off oxygen. The animals also tell him of the tree's beauty and voice their concern for the future if this tree and others are destroyed. When the man awakes, he pauses, then leaves the tree and forest intact.
Cherry's lush, detailed watercolor and pencil illustrations convey the

richness of rain forest life. The endpapers depict a world map that shows the extent of original and current tropical rain forests and an illustration of the layers of forest growth with appropriate animals in each layer. The map is bordered with labeled illustrations of animals common to the Amazon rain forest. Although Cherry's message is a bit heavy, *The Great Kapok Tree* is beautifully illustrated and it introduces young children to the richness, complexity, and fragility of this threatened habitat.

Award: OSTB, 1990

■ **Cook, David. ENVIRONMENT. Crown, 1985. 30pp. (paper 0-517-55428-3)**
SERIES: **Our Endangered Earth. Nonfiction. Interest Level: Ages 9–12**
This is a short overview of ecosystems and the threats to them by human encroachment. Says Cook, "We have become so powerful that we can control what grows in fertile land, and we can change or destroy habitats in most areas of the world." He discusses several ecosystems—temperate forests and rain forests, grasslands and savannas, deserts, mountains, and inland waters—briefly describing the plants and animals that have adapted to each and their interrelationships. He then explores some of the threats to each area, from mining, agricultural practices, urbanization, and so forth. The book concludes with an argument for conservation. *Environment* is illustrated with colored drawings and diagrams. It has an index. Also in the Endangered Earth series are *Birds, Land Animals,* and *Ocean Life.*

Award: OSTB, 1985

■ **Cowcher, Helen. ANTARCTICA. Illus. by author. Farrar, 1990. Unp. (0-374-30368-1) Fiction. Interest Level: Ages 6–9**
A stunning book, *Antarctica,* like Cowcher's *Rain Forest* (Farrar, 1988), is a picture-book story about an environmental problem, habitat loss. The threat to Antarctica's penguin and Weddell seal populations from human encroachment is the story here, told with a spare text. Cowcher's illustrations are exquisite. The stylized emperor penguins, the smaller Adélie penguins, and the Weddell seals stand out against the whites, grays, and blues of the polar landscape.

Although the penguins and the Weddell seals live with natural enemies in a harsh environment, the human intruders pose a new threat, one the animals may not be able to tolerate. Children will have questions that are not answered by the story. Who are the people in the ships and the helicopter, and what are they doing? Why are the skuas eating the penguin eggs? A brief afterword providing more information for children or for adults reading to them would have been helpful.

Award: OSTB, 1990

■ Cowcher, Helen. RAIN FOREST. Illus. by author. Farrar, 1988. Unp. (LB 0-374-36167-3) Fiction. Interest Level: Ages 6–9
Lush watercolors illustrate this fable about rain forest destruction. The story is told from the point of view of the forest animals who flee to higher ground as bulldozers destroy their homes. The animals get a reprieve when the denuded river banks erode and cause a flood, which sweeps away the bulldozer—and driver! Young children will want and need further explanation than Cowcher provides; nevertheless, she dramatically captures some of the consequences of extensive logging in this fragile habitat. See also Lynne Cheery's *The Great Kapok Tree* (Harcourt, 1990) and Jeannie Baker's *Where the Forest Meets the Sea* (Greenwillow, 1988) for different approaches to this subject.

Awards: NSSB, 1988; OSTB, 1988

■ Fine, John Christopher. OCEANS IN PERIL. Photos by author. Macmillan, 1987. 141pp. (0-689-31328-4) Nonfiction. Interest Level: Ages 12 up
Fine's varied background, experiences, and idealism come together in this book on marine ecology that makes a plea for protection of this much abused, but valuable resource. Educated in biology and law, Fine is also an expert scuba diver and underwater photographer. He also worked for the State Department reporting on drought and famine in Cambodia and in Africa. These experiences come together in his exploration of the many threats to oceans from pollution, development, human carelessness, and destruction of habitats. In his view, conservation and wise management of the oceans is essential, for the oceans are and will continue to be a major source of food for the world's growing population. Fine looks at the destruction of coral reefs, the killing and capturing of endangered marine animals, the sport killing of sharks, ocean dumping of toxic wastes, and the environmental damage wrought by coastal development. In the final chapter on developing ocean resources, Fine calls for the reader's commitment: "protecting these marine resources will mean the difference between life and death for millions of people." Black-and-white photographs do not do justice to the subject, but Fine's knowledge of and reverence for marine life and his commitment to this issue should be an inspiration to readers of all ages. A bibliography and an index are included.

■ Foreman, Michael. ONE WORLD. Illus. by author. Little, 1990. Unp. (1-55970-108-0) Fiction. Interest Level: Ages 6–9
A beachcombing boy and girl discover a tide pool rich with beauty and life, marred only by a small blob of oil, a rusty tin can, and two feathers. Slowly they transfer the things of beauty they find there into their own bucket,

recreating another "world" but destroying the one they have taken from. Eventually they realize what they have done—"The pool that had reminded the children of the beauty of the world now showed how easily it could be spoiled. It reminded them of the larger world they knew, where forests were disappearing in clouds of smoke and people were poisoning the land and the seas." They restore the tide pool, removing only the oil, the can, and the feathers and decide to enlist the help of other children to help keep the beach and pools clean. An overly earnest tone mars this beautifully illustrated picture book. David Bellamy's *The Rock Pool* (Crown, 1988) matter-of-factly shows the effects of an oil spill on a tide pool and its slow recovery.

■ **Geisel, Theodore. THE LORAX. Illus. by author. Random, 1971. Unp. (LB 0-394-92337-5) Fiction. Interest Level: Ages 4–8**
Dr. Seuss brings two things to this environmental tale that some more recent environmental stories are lacking: humor and child appeal. In this zany, rhyming story, published in 1971, a creature known as a "once-ler" explains how this once fertile land filled with colorful truffula trees was destroyed by greed and pollution. When the once-ler discovered he could make "thneeds" out of truffula trees and sell them, he chopped down trees and built factories. In spite of warnings from the Lorax, spokesman for all the wildlife, the land and the water became polluted, the animals left, the last truffula tree was chopped down, and the Lorax disappeared. But Dr. Seuss leaves his young readers with hope. One truffula seed remains. Says the once-ler: "Plant a new Truffula. Treat it with care. Give it clean water. And feed it fresh air. Grow a forest. Protect it from axes that hack. Then the Lorax and all of his friends may come back."

■ **Graham, Ada, and Frank Graham. THE CHANGING DESERT. Illus. by Robert Shetterly. Sierra Club, 1981. 90pp. o.p. Nonfiction. Interest Level: Ages 10–14**
Authors Ada and Frank Graham show how people have changed—and threatened—the fragile ecosystem of the North American desert. They alert readers to several threats: wild burros that are not native to the desert but who thrive there and destroy habitat for the native bighorn sheep; desert motorcycle racing, which destroys plant life; cactus rustlers who steal mature saguaros and sell them for a profit; population growth and farming, which have depleted the water table; and overgrazing of cattle, which contributes to desertification—the change from grassland to desert. The Grahams also describe efforts of scientists in finding native desert plants that are beneficial and in helping farmers find better ways to farm or use the land. The book is well documented, but not tightly organized; the authors sometimes include more anecdotes and commentary than necessary. However, the

emphasis on threats to the North American desert make this now out-of-print title worth keeping in a collection. It includes a bibliography and an index.

■ Hare, Tony. RAINFOREST DESTRUCTION. Illus. by Ian Moores. Watts, 1990. 32pp. (LB 0-531-17248-1) SERIES: Save Our Earth. Nonfiction. Interest Level: Ages 12 up
This slim book has attractive color photographs, maps, and diagrams that support the brief, but to the point text. The author, Tony Hare, describes the conditions that create rain forests, the richness and diversity of life there, and the rainforests' importance. He cites two main reasons for their destruction, money and survival, and the consequences of their destruction, including the extinction of species, global warming, erosion, and the loss of habitat for people who make the rain forest their home. A few suggestions for individual or school projects is included with addresses of four environmental organizations. The information in the appended "fact files" could easily have been incorporated into the text. The book provides a brief introduction to a fragile habitat. A glossary and an index are included.

■ Herda, D.J., and Margaret L. Madden. LAND USE AND ABUSE. Watts, 1990. 143pp. (LB 0-531-10953-4) SERIES: Science, Technology & Society. Nonfiction. Interest Level: Ages 13 up
Worldwide land use is a broad topic and there is not a lot published on it for children. Herda and Madden begin their overview with a quick world history of land use, abuse, and the early conservation movement. Subsequent chapters show how careless, greedy, and improper use of the land, coupled with population growth and urbanization, results in such problems as erosion, deforestation, and desertification and contributes to loss of agricultural land and plant and animal life. The authors strike a preachy tone and oversimplify some issues. For example, they cite greed as one of the principal reasons for the destruction of the rain forests but they do not mention an equally important reason: survival. Nevertheless, *Land Use and Abuse* covers a lot of ground and upper-level researchers may find this up-to-date and useful. Pringle's *What Shall We Do with the Land?* (Crowell, 1981) is out of print but better. *Land Use and Abuse* is illustrated with black-and-white photographs. It includes a glossary, a bibliography, and a too-short index.

■ Johnson, Annabel. I AM LEAPER. Illus. by Stella Ormai. Scholastic, 1990. 106pp. (0-590-43400-4) Fiction. Interest Level: Ages 9–12
A talking kangaroo rat, a mystery monster, two ambitious scientists and a twelve-year-old boy are the characters in this science fiction story with an

ecological theme. Leaper, the kangaroo rat, has developed the ability to communicate with humans, but the scientists who discover her are not interested in her strange call for help. She enlists the aid of Julian, who helps out in the lab after school, to get rid of the monster that has been terrorizing her desert home. Julian finds out more about the marvelous desert and finally learns the "awful" truth—the monster Leaper fears is the dirt bike, and he owns one. Johnson provides enough mystery and action to keep younger readers interested without being too heavy-handed in her environmental message. Older readers may guess the nature of the monster sooner, or wish the story was longer. *I Am Leaper* makes a good class read-aloud book. With lots of detail on desert life, it is a good introduction to the fragile desert ecosystem.

■ Lawrence, Louise. THE WARRIORS OF TAAN. Harper, 1988. 249pp. (LB 0-06-023737-6) Fiction. Interest Level: Ages 12 up
"And the mess and despair they had made of their own world they would make of Taan, as if they had learned nothing from their history." So begins Lawrence's fine fantasy novel with an ecological theme. The story takes place on a planet colonized by earthlings. The people of Taan, or New Earth, as the colonizers call it, have been moved to reservations in less habitable regions of the planet. The Outworlders, with superior technology, plunder the planet for its resources. The story follows two segments of Taan society who oppose the Outworlders: the male Warriors and the Sisterhood, a group of women who seek a peaceful solution to the destruction their world and society faces. There are parallels to the Native American experience, lots of action, strong characters, and even a another life form to thicken the plot.

■ Mendoza, George. WERE YOU A WILD DUCK, WHERE WOULD YOU GO? Illus. by Jane Osborn-Smith. Stewart, Tabori & Chang, 1990. 32pp. (1-55670-136-5) Fiction. Interest Level: Ages 8 up
In rich and poetic language a mallard duck chronicles the changes to the land from human activity and the resulting loss of nesting grounds. It recalls "once-upon-a-time when North America was a bird's fairy tale" and makes a plea for saving and restoring habitat. Mendoza puts readers into the mind of the mallard so that they can empathize with the duck's predicament, essentially, the loss of if its home. This loss is something children will relate to, if they can make it through the challenging language and imagery. Osborne-Smith's graceful, delicate watercolors portray the fragility of the duck's circumstances. This environmental tale may have difficulty finding an audience in spite of its attractive design and sincere message. The book may find a home with creative writing or art teachers who wish to infuse environmental themes into their classes.

■ Miller, Christina G., and Louise A. Berry. JUNGLE RESCUE: SAVING THE
NEW WORLD TROPICAL RAIN FOREST. Macmillan, 1991. 118pp.
(0-689-31487-6) Nonfiction. Interest Level: Ages 10–14
"By understanding the ecology of the rain forest and the reasons for its
destruction, you can become part of the worldwide jungle rescue presently
underway" say Christina Miller and Louise Berry in this relatively detailed
look at Central and South American rain forests. Written in a conversational
tone that encourages reader involvement, they describe the ecology and
wealth of resources in the rain forest and the effects of logging, mining, and
converting the forest into range and farm land on wildlife, native people,
and climate. They argue for finding a balance between "utilization and
preservation" of rain forests. Conservation and research efforts are described throughout the book. A glossary, further sources of information,
suggested books and magazine articles, and an index are appended. The
book's attractive cover gives way to primarily black and white photographs
that do not do justice to the subject.

■ Mutel, Cornelia Fleischer, and Mary M. Rodgers. OUR ENDANGERED
PLANET: RAIN FORESTS. Lerner, 1991. 64pp. (LB 0-8225-2503-8)
SERIES: Our Endangered Planet. Nonfiction. Interest Level: Ages 9–12
In a well-organized and presented text, the authors first describe the physical features and the ecology of tropical rain forests around the world. Then
they describe the many ways people benefit from the uniqueness and variety
of life in the tropical rain forest. Other chapters describe how rain forests
are being destroyed and provide current information on the state of rain
forests around the world and the progress of conservation efforts. A final
chapter suggests ways individuals and groups can become involved in efforts to save rain forests.
    The authors, Mutel and Rodgers, state that "by understanding the ways
that rain forests support our planet's well-being, we can become strong
activists in saving them." Maps, diagrams, and color photographs, including
pictures of native peoples are well chosen. The book includes a brief list of
environmental organizations, a glossary, and an index.

■ Newton, David E. LAND USE A–Z. Enslow, 1991. 128pp. (LB 0-89490-
260-1) SERIES: Environment Reference. Nonfiction. Interest Level: Ages 12
up
What do the words *urban planning, reclamation, desertification, clear-
cutting, leapfrog development,* and *green revolution* have in common? They
are all land use terms defined in Newton's dictionary reference guide for
young researchers. A brief introduction that highlights some of the questions to be considered by people who make land use decisions is followed
by a list of general terms used in the field and a brief review of laws and

regulations pertaining to land use. The bulk of the book is a dictionary list of terms and definitions with ample cross-references. Definitions range from a sentence or two for terms like *arable land* and *greenway* to a page or more for *conservation* and *highway congestion*. A list of agencies and organizations brings together about two dozen sources to write or call for further information. *Land Use A–Z* does not offer enough information on any one topic for a student report, but it does show how broad and complex land use issues are. Students may find this book helpful as they are defining or refining their topics and as they write papers. A bibliography is included.

■ Orr, Katherine. MY GRANDPA AND THE SEA. Illus. by author. Carolrhoda, 1990. Unp. (LB 0-87614-409-1) Fiction. Interest Level: Ages 5–8
My Grandpa and the Sea is a quiet picture book with colorful folk-style illustrations that sends an understated ecological message. On the island of Saint Lucia in the Caribbean, an old small-time fisherman loses his way of life because big commercial ships have depleted the supply of fish in the area. With nothing to keep him occupied, he becomes despondent until he comes up with an inspired idea that keeps him by the sea where his heart is. He builds special rafts on which he grows sea moss (a popular local food, which is also becoming scarce) just offshore, then sells it locally. The story, told by his granddaughter, and the pictures reflect the color and pace of life in the Caribbean.

■ Park, Ruth. MY SISTER SIF. Viking, 1991. 180pp. (0-670-83924-8) Fiction. Interest Level: Ages 10 up
Park has created an original fantasy with a strong environmental message. The story is narrated by fourteen-year-old Erika Magnus, part sea person, or mermaid, who tells the story of her and her sister's life when they return to the island of Rongo in the South Pacific where they were born. A whole community of sea people live in an underwater city not too far off the island. Initially Erika's greatest fear is that she will either lose her sister, Sif, to a visiting young scientist, who is attracted to the beautiful girl, or that he will discover their "family secret." But she finds out that there are greater concerns she faces. Ocean dumping, nuclear testing in the South Pacific, air pollution, and mining on the ocean floor have damaged the ocean ecosystem. The sea people, led by Erika and Sif's mother, are forced to leave their underwater city near the island for cleaner waters far across the globe. The strong environmental message that Park expands particularly at the end of the novel is matched by an intriguing premise, a lush setting, an imaginative cast of characters, and a story line that will keep readers turning pages.

■ Parnall, Peter. THE MOUNTAIN. Illus. by author. Doubleday, 1971. Unp. o.p. Fiction. Interest Level: Ages 5–10

The Mountain is an irreverent picture-book look at the down side of parks and preservation. In a cumulative style, Parnall introduces readers to a mountain in the west and the plants and animals that live in harmony there. When a family discovers the mountain on a nature walk, they want to keep it just the way it is, and eventually, Congress passes a law making the mountain a national park. Then a road, parking lots, toilets, drinking fountains, and food stands are built, making it possible for hordes of people to visit this "natural" setting. None appear to have any interest in the mountain or in the natural beauty the park was created to preserve. The deep color washing Parnall's line drawings begins to fade in the pictures showing more and more people visiting the park, and the last two spreads are just black line drawings with one colored flower poking out of a pile of trash. Parnall has a talent for caricature, not usually seen in his work for children. The people in *The Mountain* are cartoon characters, and they look out of place among the graceful lines of tree and mountainside. They emphasize his point that people can thoughtlessly destroy what they mean to cherish. This is a book to include with classroom units on preservation or in discussions about trash.

■ Pringle, Laurence. RESTORING OUR EARTH. Enslow, 1987. 64pp. (LB 0-89490-143-5) Nonfiction. Interest Level: Ages 12 up
Our attention is often directed to environmental problems rather than solutions. In *Restoring Our Earth,* noted author Laurence Pringle writes about efforts being made on behalf of the land. In the relatively new scientific field called ecological restoration, damaged land is restored to conditions close to the original. Restorers attempt to remove exotic species and bring back native plants and animals. In separate chapters, Pringle looks at efforts to restore marshes, grasslands, woodlands, rivers and lakes, and land that has been strip-mined. He includes many examples of efforts on public and private land throughout North America. Pringle notes that although most restoration projects are planned and managed by botanists, ecologists, and other professionals, many restorations succeed "only because of the volunteer efforts of ordinary people, both young and old." He offers suggestions for potential volunteers on where to inquire about restoration projects. A glossary, an index, and adult sources for further reading are appended. The book is illustrated with black and white photographs.
Award: OSTB, 1987

■ Pringle, Laurence. WHAT SHALL WE DO WITH THE LAND? CHOICES FOR AMERICA. Harper, 1981. 152pp. o.p. Nonfiction. Interest Level: Ages 11 up
Land use is a broad and complex topic. Laurence Pringle looks at it from a historical perspective as he explores "some of the conflicts between our

need to use the land for today and our need to love and respect the land so that we will have it tomorrow." He concentrates on land use practices in North America, showing how decisions, both private and public, have harmed or destroyed the land. Separate chapters on farmlands, rangelands, forests, coasts, and wild areas detail the use of each kind of land and the problems each has faced. Pringle provides many examples in this well-researched book. In a final chapter, he looks at some state and federal efforts to regulate land use and discusses the concept of stewardship, the responsibility we all have of ensuring that the land will be there for future generations. Although *What Shall We Do With the Land?* is out of print, it is not out of date. The book will give the upper-level student an understanding of the issues and choices regarding land use. It is illustrated with black-and-white photographs, and it includes a bibliography and an index.

Award: NSSB, 1981

■ Service, Pamela F. WINTER OF MAGIC'S RETURN. Macmillan, 1985. 192pp. o.p. Fiction. Interest Level: Ages 10–14
Five hundred years after a nuclear war, Britain still suffers from the effects of a nuclear winter. Society is feudal, the countryside is bleak, many animals and plants are extinct, and mutant animals and humans rove the land. But the nuclear winter's effects are waning, days are warmer, and a new age is coming. The story is set in a boarding school for the children of the rich, where three misfits become friends. When one of them discovers he is a reincarnation of Merlin, the three friends are propelled on a dangerous journey across a desolate landscape to find Arthur, who they think may still live. In a fast-moving plot, Service weaves a fascinating tale of a future society in which magic rather than science and technology emerges as the moving force. "There used to be magic in the old, old days didn't there? Stories say so, before people learned how to do all that nonsense with science. Well, science took over, but it did no good in the end, did it? What's going to hold this old world together except magic, I'd like to know. Makes sense that does." Service paints a unique picture of an environment devastated 500 years earlier by nuclear war. Seeing snow melting, experiencing a sunny day, or hearing a bird sing is a rare event, but it is not uncommon to come across mutant animals or even humans in this story. By setting her story centuries after the war, she avoids much of the shock and horror found in other post-nuclear-war survival stories and concentrates on plot, character, and a vision of a new age.

■ Simon, Noel. VANISHING HABITATS. Watts, 1987. 32pp. (LB 0-531-17062-4) SERIES: Survival. Nonfiction. Interest Level: Ages 10 up

Population, pollution, and commercial exploitation are three reasons author Simon gives for the worldwide degradation of habitats resulting in the loss of plant and animal species. *Vanishing Habitats* looks at forests, deserts, grasslands, polar regions, wetlands, mountains, rivers, lakes, oceans, and islands, citing threats to each. In 32 heavily illustrated pages, Simon can only provide an overview of problems, but with its attractive format, large size, color photographs, maps, and diagrams, *Vanishing Habitats* pulls together information for middle- and upper-level students on a current issue.

■ **Strieber, Whitley. WOLF OF SHADOWS. Knopf, 1985. 105pp. (LB 0-394-97224-4) Fiction. Interest Level: Ages 12 up**
This thought-provoking post–nuclear war novel explores the war's effects on both humans and animals and describes how human relationships to animals could change. Told from the point of view of a wolf, this is the story of a wolf pack and an alliance the wolves form with a human mother (who has done field research on wolves) and her two daughters, who go to northern Minnesota after the war. Eventually they make their way south to escape the effects of the nuclear winter in hopes of finding food and other survivors. The journey is a horrifying one as they pass destroyed cities, evidence of looting, and violence among survivors. The few people they encounter are threatening. The novel ends on a hopeful note in that they make it to a warmer climate, the mother and one daughter and most of the pack are alive, and a new relationship between wolves and humans has emerged. The horror of the loss, devastation, and evidence of brutality could overshadow any hopefulness in the minds of readers. Nevertheless, for the right audience, *Wolf of Shadows* offers more than the shock, horror, and devastation of nuclear war.

Awards: NSSB, 1985; OSTB, 1985

■ **Young, Donald, and Cynthia Overbeck Bix. THE SIERRA CLUB BOOK OF OUR NATIONAL PARKS. Sierra Club, 1990. 64pp. (0-316-97744-6) Nonfiction. Interest Level: Ages 9–14**
An attractive format and an engaging writing style add to the value of this book, which introduces readers to our national parks and other nationally protected areas, such as national monuments, seashores, lakeshores, wild and scenic rivers, scenic trails, recreation areas, and historic sites. More than just a travel guide for young people, this book also briefly explains the history behind the development of these protected areas and mentions people who were instrumental in their preservation, such as John Muir and Theodore Roosevelt. Another chapter offers a tour of several parks, suggesting many kinds of activities and experiences the parks offer. The final

chapter discusses the ways in which human activity continues to threaten these preserved areas. The book includes a map of national parks in the United States and a brief guide to each park's size, features, and activities. The attractive color photographs and black-and-white historical photos, including one of John Muir at Yosemite, combine in an appealing format. An index is included.

Endangered Species

■ Ancona, George. TURTLE WATCH. Photos by author. Macmillan, 1987. Unp. (LB 0-02-700910-6) Nonfiction. Interest Level: Ages 7–10
The efforts of scientists to protect sea turtles off the northeast coast of Brazil are described in this photo essay by George Ancona. TAMAR is the name of the project coordinated by oceanographers Guy and Maria Angela Marcovaldi and their helpers. Black-and-white photographs, many taken at night when the turtles come ashore, show turtles laying eggs and scientists measuring and tagging them, then removing the eggs to be hatched in the safety of their laboratory. The newly hatched turtles are then released. Ancona also describes efforts to work with local fishermen, who have traditionally hunted the eggs and turtles. TAMAR pays them for eggs brought to them to be hatched, thus providing them with income they otherwise would make selling the eggs commercially. Two local children who find eggs in the sand and deliver them to TAMAR are also featured. *Turtle Watch* is not filled with statistics on the current status of endangered sea turtles; it documents rather the work of a particular conservation project. The book includes a map showing where sea turtles come ashore to lay eggs in the Western Hemisphere.

Awards: ALA Notable Children's Book, 1987; OSTB, 1987

■ Arnold, Caroline. SAVING THE PEREGRINE FALCON. Photos by Richard Hewett. Carolrhoda, 1985. 48pp. (LB 0-87614-225-0) SERIES: Carolrhoda Nature Watch Book. Nonfiction. Interest Level: Ages 8–12
With an attractive format and excellent pictures, Arnold's engaging account of a captive breeding program in California will interest young readers. The efforts of the Santa Cruz Predatory Bird Research Group (SCPBRG) to reintroduce peregrine falcons into the wild are followed in a very readable style. Richard Hewett's full-color photographs explain and dramatize these splendid birds and the work at SCPBRG. Although uncaptioned, most photographs are integrated with the text and do not need explanation. Arnold briefly describes the falcon's physical features and habits and how the use of DDT led to their near extinction. Text and pictures dramatize the

work at SCPBRG, showing how falcon eggs are collected and hatched and how the young birds are raised and later released in cities and wild areas. However, some questions are unanswered. The author does not make it clear to young readers that the use of DDT was banned in the United States or that the ban has had an effect on peregrine populations. Although the program appears successful, she provides no statistics. How many chicks have been hatched and successfully released? What is the current peregrine population? Are any efforts being made to halt DDT use in Central and South America where the birds that the peregrines prey on spend their winters? These omissions make the book less helpful to student researchers needing facts. However, Arnold's book will engage readers who may also enjoy other titles in the Carolrhoda Nature Watch series. Pair this with McNulty's *Peeping in the Shell* (Harper, 1986), which describes the hatching of a whooping crane chick at the International Crane Foundation.

Awards: ALA Notable Children's Book, 1985; OSTB, 1985

■ Bloyd, Sunni. ENDANGERED SPECIES. Lucent, 1989. 96pp. (1-56006-106-5) SERIES: Overview. Nonfiction. Interest Level: Ages 12 up
Endangered Species is a solid addition to any collection with a need for more information on this timely topic. Bloyd writes about several species (passenger pigeon, bison, black-footed ferret, tiger), some extinct, others that have made a comeback, and others that are still endangered, to illustrate the role humans have played in the destruction and recovery of species. She also includes chapters on the rain forest as an endangered environment; on legislation to protect wildlife such as the Endangered Species Act of 1973 and the Lacey Act; on organizations that help endangered wildlife; and on suggestions for individuals to get involved in the protection of endangered species. The book includes a glossary and an index, a list of books for further reading, and a list of organizations concerned with the protection of wildlife. The black-and-white photographs are a disappointment and do not enhance this book. Look to other titles for outstanding full-color photos.

■ Bright, Michael. MOUNTAIN GORILLA. Watts, 1989. 32pp. (LB 0-531-17179-5) SERIES: Project Wildlife. Nonfiction. Interest Level: Ages 8–12
In just 32 pages, Bright concisely describes the status of the mountain gorilla, the most threatened of the three subspecies of gorilla living in Africa. Habitat destruction is cited as one cause of the gorillas' dwindling numbers. Other causes include the slaughter of gorillas for food and the souvenir trade, and the capture of baby gorillas to sell to private collections, zoos, or for animal research. Bright describes the often insufficient an-

tipoaching efforts of the Rwandan government and also the Mountain Gorilla Project that works to save mountain gorillas from extinction. Other efforts mentioned include those of American researcher Dian Fossey, who was murdered in 1977. Gorilla-watching tours, besides bringing in money to the Rwandan government, increase public awareness of the gorilla's plight. An appended "fact file" offers information on the range, physical features, and behavior of gorillas. The focus of the titles in the Project Wildlife series is on the endangered status of the species. Other animals featured include giant pandas, eagles, tigers, humpback whales, elephants, koalas, alligators and crocodiles, seals, and polar bears. Well written and nicely designed, the books are ideal for students studying conservation issues or endangered species. Schlein's *Gorillas* (Macmillan, 1990), part of the Jane Goodall's Animal World series, is for younger readers. It emphasizes the natural history of the gorilla. McClung's *Gorilla* (Morrow, 1984) is an excellent fictional account of the plight of the mountain gorilla.

■ **Burningham, John. HEY! GET OFF OUR TRAIN. Illus. by author. Crown, 1989. Unp. (LB 0-517-57643-0) Fiction. Interest Level: Ages 4–9**
A little boy plays with his train set until his mother sends him to bed with his toy dog. As he falls asleep, an environmental fantasy unfolds. On this dream journey, boy and dog engineer the train, stopping to picnic and play on their travels. At each stop they are interrupted by an animal that tries to get on the train. And their response, "Hey! Get off our train," becomes the refrain throughout the book. Each rare or endangered animal (an elephant, a seal, a tiger, a crane, and a polar bear) pleads its case, explaining why it needs rescue (from poachers, hunters, pollution, and habitat loss), and each is allowed on the train, which becomes a modern day ark. With dry humor, Burningham ends with a mix of fantasy and reality in the story when the boy's mother wakes him the next morning and announces the presence of "lots of animals in the house." Children will enjoy shouting the refrain and possibly will derive a sense of power or satisfaction from seeing the animals rescued. Burningham's mixed media illustrations in muted tones are most effective with one-on-one sharing or reading in small groups. Teachers might consider staging *Hey! Get Off Our Train* to encourage awareness of endangered species and to lead in to discussions on environmental activities that children can do. Burningham dedicates the book to murdered rain forest activist Chico Mendez. Some may find Burningham's message in *Hey! Get Off Our Train* too heavy-handed.

■ **Clark, Margaret Goff. THE VANISHING MANATEE. Dutton, 1990. 64pp. (0-525-65024-5) Nonfiction. Interest Level: Ages 9–12**

An abundance of up-to-date information for the student researcher fills Clark's readable book on this endangered marine mammal. Although she describes the three species of manatee existing today, Clark writes mostly about the West Indian manatee, which in the United States makes its home in the coastal waters and rivers of Florida. She interweaves information on the manatee's physical features, habits, and behavior with the threats to their existence. In addition to their loss of habitat because of the development of coastal areas, manatees are particularly prone to injury and death from motorboat propellers. Clark cites research efforts to learn more about manatees and state and federal programs aimed to protect manatees and their habitats. A map showing manatee habitats and a list of manatee sanctuaries in Florida would have been helpful. A lengthy list of sources for more information on manatees is appended. *The Vanishing Manatee* is illustrated with color photographs. An index is included. Other books on the manatee for the same audience are Jean Sibbald's *The Manatee* (Dillon, 1990) and Gibbs Davis's *Fishman and Charly* (Houghton, 1983), a good companion novel.

Award: OSTB, 1990

■ Cutchins, Judy, and Ginny Johnston. THE CROCODILE AND THE CRANE: SURVIVING IN A CROWDED WORLD. Morrow, 1986. 54pp. (LB 0-688-06305-5) Nonfiction. Interest Level: Ages 9–12
With a growing world population and rapidly diminishing habitats for wildlife, the future for many species is uncertain. While preserving habitat is a major way conservationists work to protect species, captive breeding programs are another, perhaps less known, way. Authors Cutchins and Johnston look at six captive breeding programs for endangered species at zoos and environmental centers throughout the country. They note some of the goals of captive breeding: to raise animals that can be released in the wild to bolster dwindling populations, to supply zoos so that endangered animals will not be taken from the wild, and to study animals in order to improve captive breeding programs. With an engaging text and enough information for report writers, the authors briefly discuss captive breeding programs for the Morelet's crocodile, African wattled crane, Grevy's zebra, the cheetah, golden lion tamarin, and the Arabian oryx. The book is illustrated with black-and-white photographs, and it includes a glossary and an index. Irvine's *Protecting Endangered Species at the San Diego Zoo* (Simon and Schuster, 1990) has a more attractive format, but the book is limited to efforts made at the San Diego Zoo to protect several species.

Award: OSTB, 1986

■ Davis, Gibbs. FISHMAN AND CHARLY. Houghton, 1983. 166pp. (0-395-33882-4) Fiction. Interest Level: Ages 10–14
Protection of the manatee, a gentle marine mammal living in Florida coastal waters, is one of the themes in a heartwarming novel that will keep readers' interest and win their compassion for this endangered animal. The story centers around Tyler, also known as Fishman, and his older sister Charly, who acts as a mother as well as a sister to him, since their mother died four years earlier. Tyler and Charly become friends with their wealthy and eccentric neighbor, Byron, and his uncle Christian, who are trying to protect the manatees that live in their cove. Tyler, who loves animals, especially fish, is captivated by the mother manatee Piety and her infant, Bow. When Bow and other manatees are slaughtered by poachers, Tyler becomes instrumental in capturing them. Although some characters could have been developed more, the plot moves quickly. Davis handles the themes of love and respect in a natural way, and in *Fishman and Charly*, caring and concern for family and friends is extended to compassion for our fellow creatures.

■ Facklam, Howard, and Margery Facklam. PLANTS: EXTINCTION OR SURVIVAL? Enslow, 1990. 96pp. (0-89490-248-2) Nonfiction. Interest Level: Ages 12 up
Plants are not as popular a subject as animals. But plants are a source of food, medicine, and other products that we use. They also help to clean the air and give off oxygen. We are dependent upon plants for our existence. This book is all the more important because there has been so little written on plant conservation and extinction for young people. In a very readable style, Howard and Margery Facklam cover several aspects of the topic. They emphasize the importance of genetic diversity in plant crops, citing the potato famine in Ireland, in which over a million people died when the single strain of potato cultivated there was wiped out by a fungus. They maintain that dependence on a small number of plant strains for our food needs may be putting people at risk, and that because of the destruction of important habitats such as tropical rain forests, the world is losing major sources of genetic diversity. They also trace the history of scientific interest in plants, highlighting plant collectors, and plant breeders, and discuss the uses of plants in medicine and some of the current efforts of genetic engineers to produce new, hardier, disease-resistant plants for food. The book contains some difficult vocabulary and concepts, but it will be a good resource for upper-level students. The illustrations are black-and-white photographs. An index is included. Edward Ricciuti's *Plants in Danger* (Harper, 1979), also covers this topic with a less technical approach.

Award: OSTB, 1990

■ Facklam, Margery. AND THEN THERE WAS ONE: THE MYSTERIES OF EXTINCTION. Illus. by Pamela Johnson. Sierra Club, 1990. 56pp. (LB 0-316-25984-5) SERIES: Sierra Club Books for Children. Nonfiction. Interest Level: Ages 9–12

A thoughtful, well-written, and ultimately hopeful book that considers the many reasons animals have become extinct and are currently endangered. Facklam explains that extinction "is part of the slow process of evolution," giving several examples of the ways species have adapted to changes in the environment or have died out. She moves on to human causes of acceleration of extinction and endangerment—overhunting, destruction of habitat, pollution and garbage, acid rain. In a final chapter she discusses legislation and organizations that aim to preserve habitats and protect animals, including the Endangered Species Act and the role of zoos and wildlife refuges. Facklam concludes with a plea to stop polluting and destroying habitats: "All creatures large and small have the right to live because they share their home planet with us. We can do nothing about the way animals adapt to the changes in the environment, but we can do something about how the environment changes." Attractive design with pencil drawings complement the balanced text that will give readers a larger perspective on the issues of extinction and endangered species. The book includes an index.

■ Irvine, Georgeanne. PROTECTING ENDANGERED SPECIES AT THE SAN DIEGO ZOO. Simon and Schuster, 1990. 45pp. (LB 0-671-68776-X) Nonfiction. Interest Level: Ages 8–13

Georgeanne Irvine is the public relations director for the San Diego Zoo and the editor of the zoo's Koala Cub News. Her appealing book introduces young readers to the different ways zoos work to save animals from extinction. Irvine tells the stories of six endangered animals at the San Diego Zoo and Wild Animal Park, where there is a center for the reproduction of endangered species. She features the clouded leopard, the Galapagos tortoise, the black rhinoceros, the Tahitian lory, the lion-tailed macaque, and the mhorr gazelle in an upbeat, readable fashion. Irvine includes information on the particulars of each animal's history and the status of each species. She concludes with suggestions for further reading and some general suggestions on conservation and wildlife protection for readers. The book has an attractive cover, excellent photographs and an inviting design, but there is no index. A companion book, Raising Gordy Gorilla at the San Diego Zoo (Simon and Schuster, 1990), tells the story of a gorilla born prematurely, raised by the zoo staff, and eventually released to live in a wildlife preserve. Cutchins and Johnston's The Crocodile and the Crane (Morrow, 1986) looks at captive breeding programs at six zoos and environmental centers around the country.

■ Johnson, Sylvia A., and Alice Aamodt. WOLF PACK: TRACKING WOLVES IN THE WILD. Lerner, 1985. 96pp. (LB 0-8225-1577-6) Nonfiction. Interest Level: Ages 10 up
This natural history of the wolf, an endangered species in most parts of the United States, is a well-written account that covers wolf social life and hierarchy, rearing of young, communication, and hunting. A chapter on the wolf in history and myth will help readers understand what led to the wolf's endangered status today. Johnson and Aamodt end with a chapter on biologists' efforts to study wolves in the wild. Fine color photographs, maps, and diagrams illustrate the text. A glossary and an index are appended. R.D. Lawrence's *Wolves* (Sierra Club 1990) has outstanding photographs and a smoothly written, engaging text. Anyone inspired to learn more about wolves should not miss Farley Mowat's classic *Never Cry Wolf* (Little, 1963), about his study of a wolf pack in the Canadian barren lands.
Awards: ALA Notable Children's Book, 1985; OSTB, 1985

■ Jonas, Ann. AARDVARKS, DISEMBARK! Illus. by author. Greenwillow, 1990. Unp. (LB 0-688-07207-0) Nonfiction. Interest Level: Ages 5–10
In retelling the biblical story of Noah's ark, Ann Jonas pays tribute to lesser known and endangered animals of the world, while offering a book with multiple dimensions. In Jonas's version, there are still a lot of animals left on the ark after Noah has called forth all those whose names he knows. So he calls upon the others to disembark and heads down the mountain. What follows is a parade of unusual, rare, endangered, or now extinct animals who wind down the snow-covered mountain over a two-day period, zigzagging across the pages, which the reader tilts and reads vertically. The animals head down in reverse alphabetical order, each letter represented by at least one animal. As the pages turn, the animals appear larger, as if one were watching them get closer and closer. When they all reach the bottom they head off "to settle new lands in different parts of the world." A final page lists all the animals (with a pronunciation and a brief description of each), indicating which ones are extinct or currently in danger, a sobering afterword. *Aardvarks, Disembark!* is a picture book that older readers, familiar with the story of Noah's ark and with the concept of endangered species, will get more out of than the traditional picture-book audience.
Award: ALA Notable Children's Book, 1990

■ Lewin, Ted. TIGER TREK. Illus. by author. Macmillan, 1990. Unp. (0-02-757381-8) Nonfiction. Interest Level: Ages 6–10
Ted Lewin takes readers on a trek through two national parks in India, where, riding on top of an elephant, he observes the hunting behavior of a

mother tiger and the other animals that inhabit these protected areas. The environmental message is implicit in *Tiger Trek*. In a short preface, Lewin simply explains that "without these protected islands of habitat, these magnificent creatures would have no place left on earth." What follows is a lushly-illustrated picture book that gives readers a chance to see and hopefully appreciate this magnificent predator in its natural surroundings. For older readers, Robert McClung's *Rajpur: Last of the Bengal Tigers* (Morrow, o.p.) shows the threats to this endangered species in a story format.

Award: OSTB, 1990

■ McClung, Robert. GORILLA. Illus. by Irene Brady. Morrow, 1984. 92pp. (LB 0-688-03876-X) Nonfiction. Interest Level: Ages 9–12
Nature writer Robert McClung successfully combines fact and fiction in this story of a band of mountain gorillas from the Virunga Mountains in central Africa. The story, which makes a good read-aloud for classes studying endangered species, follows the band over several months describing their daily habits and experiences and the birth of two gorillas. Their peaceful life is shattered when poachers ambush and kill several of the adult gorillas and capture the two youngest, Beni and Coco. Beni and Coco are eventually freed from their captors and accepted by another band of gorillas, a happy ending to a sad story that is based on the research and writings of George Schaller and Dian Fossey. In an afterword McClung summarizes the history of the now endangered gorilla, the human threats to its existence, and the work of researchers like Dian Fossey (who was murdered since this book was written). A bibliography of primarily adult books and magazine articles is included. The book is illustrated with black-and-white line drawings. Other titles about endangered species with a story format by McClung include *Lili: A Giant Panda of Sichuan* (Morrow, 1988) and *Rajpur: Last of the Bengal Tigers* (Morrow, o.p.).

Award: OSTB, 1984

■ McCoy, J.J. THE PLIGHT OF THE WHALES. Watts, 1989. 144pp. (LB 0-531-10778-7) SERIES: An Impact Book. Nonfiction. Interest Level: Ages 12 up
McCoy takes a comprehensive look at the plight of this still-threatened species. He describes size, physical features, and status of various whales, and looks at threats to their existence. Separate chapters are devoted to the history of commercial whaling; the International Whaling Commission; pollution; the plight of dolphins, porpoises, and other whales caught in fishing nets; conservation efforts; and the possible threat of whale-watching tours

to whale migratory routes and feeding grounds. McCoy notes the major role that economics and politics continues to play in deciding the future of whales. Sources of information and an index are appended. The book has an attractive color photograph on the cover and black-and-white photos illustrating the text.

■ McGrath, Susan. SAVING OUR ANIMAL FRIENDS. National Geographic, 1986. 34pp. (LB 0-87044-640-1) SERIES: Books for Young Explorers. Non-fiction. Interest Level: Ages 7–10
National Geographic's excellent full-color photographs enhance this brief but informative book on wildlife conservation that has a reassuring and positive tone. *Saving Our Animal Friends* introduces younger readers to the various ways wildlife species are protected in the United States. Beginning with zoos and wildlife rehabilitators, McGrath goes on to talk about habitat protection, which she says is the best way to protect animals, and legislation that protects wildlife. She also mentions the danger trash and litter pose to wildlife and suggests ways young people can help (by not littering, by learning more about animals, and by feeding neighborhood birds and squirrels). An appended section has a map showing national wildlife refuges in the lower 48 states and has more information on threats to wildlife, the role of refuges, hunting, and captive breeding programs. The book is sold as one of the four-volume set number 13 in the Books for Young Explorers series.

■ McNulty, Faith. PEEPING IN THE SHELL: A WHOOPING CRANE IS HATCHED. Illus. by Irene Brady. Harper, 1986. 60pp. (LB 0-06-024135-7) Nonfiction. Interest Level: Ages 8–12
This dramatic story reveals the dedication of some scientists to the preservation of species. George Archibald, an ornithologist and the director of the International Crane Foundation in Baraboo, Wisconsin, did not want to waste the reproductive potential of Tex, a female whooping crane he brought to the center from a zoo. Because she had imprinted on humans, she would not mate with a crane. Archibald took the unheard-of step of "courting" her by imitating the mating dance of whooping cranes. The courtship worked; Tex was artificially inseminated and layed an egg that was hatched at the center. McNulty, a nature writer, visited the center and watched the egg hatch. She describes these huge birds, how they came to be endangered, and the efforts being made to increase their numbers. The drama of the courtship and the story of the incubation and hatching are filled with fascinating detail. McNulty's narrative style is easy to read, and words are explained in context. Although the cover design and type size make this book more appealing to younger children, the story will interest all ages. Read this aloud to a class studying endangered species. It may also

be used in conjunction with Patent's *The Whooping Crane: A Comeback Story* (Clarion, 1988). The book is illustrated with pencil drawings.

Awards: ALA Notable Children's Book, 1986; OSTB, 1986

■ Nickl, Peter. CROCODILE, CROCODILE. Trans. by Ebbitt Cutler. Illus. by Binette Schroeder. Interlink, 1989. Unp. (0-940793-33-4) Fiction. Interest Level: Ages 7–11

Sophisticated art and a satiric text combine in this reissue of a 1976 picture book in which a crocodile takes revenge on humans who have hunted his kind. Omar, a crocodile from the Nile, overhears some human tourists talk about a crocodile store in Paris. "A store for me? This is something I've got to see," he says. He travels to Paris only to find that the store sells things not *for* crocodiles, but *of* crocodiles—handbags, shoes, belts, and so on. Schroeder's surrealist art, with a dapper crocodile hero, may appeal to Teenage Mutant Ninja Turtle fans. This is a picture book that begs for an older audience. Try it with third or fourth graders studying endangered species.

■ Paladino, Catherine. OUR VANISHING FARM ANIMALS: SAVING AMERICA'S RARE BREEDS. Photos by author. Little, 1991. 32pp. (0-316-68891-6) Nonfiction. Interest Level: Ages 6–10

While headlines alert us to the plight of endangered wildlife all over the globe, it may come as a surprise to learn that many of our domestic breeds of farm animals could soon become extinct. Why should we care? Catherine Paladino argues that the traits that helped these breeds survive through the harsh conditions in the early days of our country may become valuable again. These breeds provide a "variety of genetic traits" that farmers may look for in the future. In a stunningly photographed and well-written book, Catherine Paladino opens young readers' eyes to the plight of eight rare breeds, including the Dutch Belted cow, the Gloucester Old Spot pig, the Guinea hog, the Navajo-Churro sheep, the American Mammoth jackstock, the Ancona and Black Australorp chickens, and the American Bashkir Curly horse. The photographs show the animals on the farms where they are being bred, often with the children who help care for them, adding to the appeal of the book for its intended audience. A list of farm animals currently in danger of extinction is appended. The book gives a fresh approach to the study of endangered species.

■ Patent, Dorothy Hinshaw. BUFFALO: THE AMERICAN BISON TODAY. Photos by William Munoz. Clarion, 1986. 73pp. o.p. Nonfiction. Interest Level: Ages 9–12

Although no longer endangered, the buffalo, or bison, has a story, like that of the now extinct passenger pigeon, that dramatically shows how a species can be affected by human encroachment. Once numbering in the millions and ranging widely throughout the United States and Canada, fewer than 100,000 now live on preserves and private ranches. Dorothy Patent, a zoologist and science writer, takes readers through the history of the bison, describing how westward expansion and relentless hunting nearly wiped them out. But most of the book is about the bison today. She describes their physical features, their adaptations to life on the plains, their behavior, and the role they play (or had played) in their environment. Because bison live in restricted areas, current policy is to carefully manage, or control, their numbers, so herds are culled annually. The numbers of other large animals on these preserves are also controlled to keep these artificial habitats in balance.

Patent writes without emotion about the bison. The information on bison management practices is quite fascinating. This book will be useful in discussions on endangered species and wildlife management, as well as for natural history studies. Black-and-white photographs illustrate most pages. A useful list of state and national parks where buffalo herds can be seen is appended. An index is included.

Award: OSTB, 1986

■ Patent, Dorothy Hinshaw. THE WHOOPING CRANE: A COMEBACK STORY. Photos by William Munoz. Clarion, 1988. 88pp. (0-89919-455-9) Nonfiction. Interest Level: Ages 9-12
In 1988 the worldwide whooping crane population was estimated at 195. This tiny number is the basis for Patent's amazing and hopeful comeback story about a species that in 1941 was on the brink of extinction with only 21 birds known to exist. She describes the whooping crane's physical features, migration patterns, and nesting and mating behavior, showing how westward expansion and hunting contributed to the whooper's decline in North America. Her focus however, is on the sometimes extraordinary efforts made to build up the whooping crane population. Although the summer and winter grounds of the major flock are protected, scientists have been creative in finding ways to increase crane numbers. Patent describes the captive breeding program at the Patuxent Wildlife Research Center in Laurel, Maryland, a U.S. Fish and Wildlife Service experiment in cooperation with the Canadian Wildlife Service to start a new flock, and various management and educational efforts designed to protect migrating birds. Excellent color and black and white photographs illustrate this informative and upbeat book about a still-threatened North American species. The book

includes an index. Use in conjunction with Peter and Connie Roop's *Seasons of the Cranes* (Walker, 1989), which follows the whoopers as they migrate from Wood Buffalo National Park in northern Canada to the Aransas National Wildlife Sanctuary in Texas. Other books by Patent about threatened or endangered animals include *The Way of the Grizzly* (Clarion, 1987) and *Where the Bald Eagles Gather* (Clarion, 1984). The emphasis in these books is on natural history rather than efforts to protect species. Award: OSTB, 1988

■ Pringle, Laurence. LIVING TREASURE: SAVING EARTH'S THREATENED BIODIVERSITY. Illus. by Irene Brady. Morrow, 1991. 64pp. (LB 0-688-07710-2) Nonfiction. Interest Level: Ages 11 up
Any middle- or upper-level class studying endangered species should read this excellent book on biodiversity and the mass extinction of species. Pringle takes a look at the big picture in *Living Treasures* as he discusses evolution, distribution, and potential numbers of species. Theories of past mass extinctions are explored and lead into the factors contributing to the current extinction of species: population pressures, destruction of wildlife habitats, pollution, and invasion of nonnative species. Pringle calls this a quiet crisis. Although some popular endangered species garner much media attention, the extinction of what he calls living treasures, thousands of little-known, even undiscovered, animals and plants may be irreplaceable losses to humankind. Says Pringle, "the earth's biodiversity offers us *possibilities*. We cannot even imagine all of the usefulness and intangible values of its well-stocked genetic library, yet we continue to toss out thousands of unread volumes." But he offers other reasons to maintain this rich biodiversity, including species' aesthetic, intrinsic, and practical values, and he cites several examples of food and medical benefits of once unknown species to people. He also cites worldwide efforts to preserve biodiversity of species and suggests ways individuals can get involved. The larger format and open, inviting design of *Living Treasures* will appeal to readers. The book is illustrated with black-and-white drawings, and it has a colorful, attractive cover.

■ Pringle, Laurence. SAVING OUR WILDLIFE. Enslow, 1990. 64pp. (0-89490-204-0) Nonfiction. Interest Level: Ages 10 up
Beginning with a discussion of the value of wildlife and its basic requirements for survival, Laurence Pringle, a noted science writer, looks at the diverse efforts, both public and private, to protect the diminishing wildlife of North America. Noting that game animals were the first to be protected, Pringle states that overhunting was responsible for the establishment of the

first wildlife refuges in this country, which are part of the millions of acres set aside in public and private parks and refuges. He provides numerous examples of threats to wildlife (overhunting, poaching, loss of habitat, pollution) and examples of legislation and programs designed to protect existing populations or to increase numbers of threatened or endangered species. Captive breeding programs, reintroduction programs, and specific efforts in selected states are noted. Pringle includes current statistics on populations, making this a useful resource for student researchers. He acknowledges differences in opinion among scientists, business leaders, and political leaders on conservation. In a final section he encourages the involvement of young people in conservation efforts, listing several national organizations and their goals. A list of further reading follows, including both adult and juvenile books and periodical articles. Ilustrated with black-and-white photographs, the format is not eye-catching, but the up-to-date, well-organized information will be useful to young readers and researchers.

Award: OSTB, 1990

■ Rinard, Judith. WILDLIFE MAKING A COMEBACK: HOW HUMANS ARE HELPING. National Geographic, 1987. 104pp. (LB 0-87044-661-4) SERIES: Books for World Explorers. Nonfiction. Interest Level: Ages 11 up
For older readers than those of *Saving Our Animal Friends* (National Geographic, 1986), this is a thorough, visually appealing introduction to the problems facing wildlife around the world and efforts to protect and save threatened and endangered species. Overhunting, destruction of habitats, and pollution are cited as three major causes of the rapid extinction of species. Conservation efforts discussed include legislation to protect wildlife, preservation of habitat, research, education, and captive breeding programs. Rinard provides many examples for students researching endangered species and ends with suggestions for readers who want to help in the wildlife conservation movement. The narrative is broken up with spreads that expand on the text: keystone species, habitats, alien species, and a world map showing about 40 endangered species. Excellent full-color photographs include a multiethnic blend of men, women, and children involved in education, conservation, and research programs for wildlife. The book includes an index, a list of conservation organizations, and a brief bibliography.

■ Schlein, Miriam. THE YEAR OF THE PANDA. Illus. by Kam Mak. Harper, 1990. 83pp. (LB 0-690-04866-1) Fiction. Interest Level: Ages 8–10
A young, rural Chinese boy finds and rescues an orphaned panda cub and cares for it in this story for young readers. In an easy-to-read style with

full-page illustrations interspersed, this is an engaging and informative introduction to an endangered species. Schlein, author of the nonfiction book *Project Panda Watch* (Macmillan, 1984), writes a simple but convincing story about Lu Yi, whose small village is adjacent to panda habitat. Approximately every 60 years, the bamboo, which pandas depend on for food, dies off. Because of this and because farmland has taken over some of their former habitat, the pandas are in serious trouble. Lu Yi cares for the orphaned cub and travels with it to a rehabilitation center where he learns of the government's efforts to save the panda. Robert McClung's *Lili: A Giant Panda of Sichuan* (Morrow, 1988) also integrates factual information on the endangered panda into a story format for the same age group.

Award: OSTB, 1990

■ Steiner, Barbara. OLIVER DIBBS TO THE RESCUE! Illus. by Eileen Christelow. Macmillan, 1985. 122pp. (0-02-787890-2) Fiction. Interest Level: Ages 8–11
Ten-year-old Oliver Dibbs has his heart in the right place, but his schemes often seem to backfire. A born organizer, he puts much of his energy into creative projects to preserve wildlife. He paints orange tiger stripes on his dog and then takes him to the local mall to raise money for the World Wildlife Fund—but he gets hauled in to the police station for soliciting without a permit. He operates a semipermanent garage sale to raise money for future causes, but when he plays his wolf-call record to attract attention to the sale, he attracts most of the neighborhood dogs and gets into trouble. But eventually his good ideas and hard work culminate in a successful project when he organizes a protest to protect a nearby prairie-dog town from a shopping mall expansion. Steiner keeps the tone light, but she gives children a budding conservation activist for a hero.

■ Stone, Lynn M. ENDANGERED ANIMALS. Childrens, 1984. 48pp. (LB 0-516-01724-1) SERIES: New True. Nonfiction. Interest Level: Ages 6–9
Full-color photographs of dozens of rare and endangered species illustrate nearly every page of this New True book for primary grade readers. In simple language, Stone discusses some of the reasons animals have become extinct or are currently endangered. He reports on animals in trouble around the world and lists 200 endangered species worldwide. Various efforts to save animals are discussed—the Endangered Species Act of 1973, Project Tiger in India, and the establishment of protected parks and refuges, captive breeding programs, and zoos. In the last chapter he encourages readers to find out what animals are in trouble locally and to volunteer or find other ways to help. The book includes a short glossary and an index. *Endangered Animals* is good, basic, introductory material for young students.

Pollution

■ Aschenbrenner, Gerald. JACK, THE SEAL AND THE SEA. Trans. by Joanne Fink. Illus. by author. Silver Burdett, 1988. Unp. (LB 0-382-09985-0) Fiction. Interest Level: Ages 5–9

Jack is a commercial fisherman who can not imagine doing anything else for a living. Jack worries about his dwindling catch as the ocean becomes polluted and fish become scarce. One day, he finds a small seal in his net who is starving and covered with oil. Jack takes him aboard his boat and as the seal recovers, Jack looks vainly for other seals. Reluctantly he lets the seal go in a clear patch of ocean. The little seal quickly discovers a large school of mackerel. Relieved to have an excuse to take the seal back aboard, Jack throws out his nets and fills his boat with fish, his first good catch in a long time. That night, as Jack is sleeping on his boat, the sea roils up and speaks to him, pleading with Jack to help save the oceans. In the morning, Jack is unsure if the sea did speak to him or whether it was a dream. Jack, however, has been called to action. He becomes a crusader for clean oceans and sails up and down the coast talking about marine pollution and its effect on the environment.

This book is a cautionary tale, used by the author to warn against water pollution, particularly in the dramatic scene in which the sea speaks to Jack. The gray and brown pencil illustrations add to the book's realistic feeling. The drawings of the seal are especially appealing.

This unusual picture book, originally published in German, was a feature selection of the public television series *Reading Rainbow*. It could be used with both preschoolers or children in the lower grades of elementary school to begin discussions of the environment, the oceans, or pollution.

■ Baines, John. ACID RAIN. Steck-Vaughn, 1989. 48pp. (LB 0-8114-2385-9) SERIES: Conserving Our World. Nonfiction. Interest Level: Ages 10–14

Excellent color photos, charts, and diagrams combine with a smoothly written text that describes the formation of acid rain, how it affects the environment, and efforts to control it. With only 48 pages, Baines provides an overview for readers. They will want to read further for more information and explanation. But, the attractive format and balanced coverage of basic information and issues make *Acid Rain* a good choice. Some simple experiments to test soil acidity, seed growth, and acid rain require litmus paper and other easily obtainable supplies. Baines ends with a plea for individual responsibility to maintain a healthy environment—the less energy we use, the less pollution we produce. The book includes a glossary, list of books, and pamphlets for further reading as well as addresses of organizations such as the *Acid Rain Foundation* and other general conservation organizations. Other titles in the *Conserving Our World* series include *Conserving the Atmosphere* (Steck-Vaughn, 1990), and *Conserving the Oceans* (Steck-Vaughn, 1990).

■ **Bright, Michael. POLLUTION AND WILDLIFE. Watts, 1987. 32pp. (LB 0-531-17046-2)** SERIES: Survival. Nonfiction. **Interest Level: Ages 11–14**
Bright provides a quick, but sobering, look at the effect various pollutants have on wildlife around the world. Part of the *Survival* series, with its oversized and heavily illustrated format, *Pollution and Wildlife* will not suffice for in-depth research. It does, however, offer an overview of the effects on specific species of pesticides, runoff from fertilizers, sewage and wastes discharged into rivers and lakes, acid rain, oil spills, nuclear wastes, and ocean dumping. Bright looks at individuals and populations and an appendix notes specific causes of pollution and the consequences in several countries. The book includes an index and addresses of conservation organizations.

■ **Brown, Ruth. THE WORLD THAT JACK BUILT. Illus. by author. Dutton, 1991. Unp. (0-525-44635-4)** Fiction. **Interest Level: Ages 6–8**
Author-illustrator Ruth Brown's variation on the nursery rhyme *The House That Jack Built* may take unsuspecting readers by surprise. A black cat chases a blue butterfly through a landscape of sunny skies, flower-filled meadows, and sparkling streams in a lovely valley that surrounds the house that Jack built, leading readers to believe this is "just another" version of the rhyme. But when the cat (and reader) gets to the *next* valley, the idyllic scene changes. Images become cloudy, the vegetation is dying, a pipe carries pollutants to the stream, and in the final spread, the culprit–the factory that Jack built–appears in a brown smoky haze. It's a heavy message for young children, with no promise of a better world. *The World That Jack Built* may struggle to find the right audience and may be best suited to a post-preschool class. The story may serve as a springboard for discussions of pollution.

■ **Carr, Terry. SPILL! THE STORY OF THE *EXXON VALDEZ*. Watts, 1991. 64pp. (LB 0-531-10998-4)** Nonfiction. **Interest Level: Ages 9–13**
Terry Carr, an editorial writer for the *Anchorage Daily News*, presents a factual, shocking account of the 1989 collision of the oil tanker, *Exxon Valdez* that caused one of the worst environmental disasters of the century to the Prince William Sound region of Alaska.
Captioned color photographs have been carefully chosen to enhance the

well-written text. The overall design of *Spill!* is excellent and will captivate readers of all ages. A map of shipping lanes and another map that superimposes the oil spill area onto a map of the eastern seaboard of the United States will help children more easily understand the enormous extent of the spill's damage.

Carr has provided background on the history of oil development and the construction of the Alaskan pipeline. Although the oil has always posed a threat, it has also brought riches and, Carr says, complacency. The author blames inadequate disaster preparation for hampering early clean up efforts. Extremes of weather right after the spill also prevented chemicals from being quickly dispersed.

The effect of the spill on wildlife has been catastrophic. Tens of thousands of sea birds died, hundreds of vulnerable sea otters, and many other mammals were poisoned by eating contaminated food. It appears that the entire food chain may be adversely affected.

Despite the heroic efforts of more than 11,000 paid and volunteer rescue workers, the thick, black oil proved nearly impossible to clean up. Rocks, cleaned by hand, were fouled by more oil washed in by the tide. High pressure washing proved to be harmful to the ecologically sensitive beaches. A natural, slow-acting fertilizer that works by increasing the growth of oil-eating bacteria may be the best process.

This ruinous spill has caused much sadness and anger, almost all of which has been directed at Exxon. As a result new laws and new oil industry regulations have been passed. The detrimental effects of the Exxon Valdez oil spill on the land, water, and wildlife of Alaska will not be known for a decade or more, but every effort is now being made to guard the environment from future disasters.

A reading list and an index are appended.

■ **Collier, James Lincoln. WHEN THE STARS BEGIN TO FALL. Delacorte, 1986. 224pp. (paper 0-385-29516-2) Fiction. Interest Level: Ages 12 up**
The cards are stacked against Harry White. He comes from a poor and neglectful family; his father steals, his mother is disturbed, and his sister, who is his only friend, runs away from home. When his father mentions that the local carpet factory pollutes the river, Harry decides to investigate. His efforts to prove the factory is polluting and to expose the polluters become a path to self-respect. In trying to become a local hero he learns that most of the locals and officials already know about the pollution and are willing to go to great lengths to keep him silent because this one-industry town depends on the carpet factory for its livelihood. Collier writes a suspenseful, fast-paced story that will hold readers' attention. Teachers may find this useful in discussions of personal and civic responsibility in relation to environmental issues.

■ dePaola, Tomie. MICHAEL BIRD-BOY. Illus. by author. Prentice-Hall, 1987 (repr. of 1975 ed.). Unp. (LB 0-671-66468-9) Fiction. Interest Level: Ages 5–9

Talk about problem solving. It's not too hard when Michael Bird-Boy is at hand. When a black cloud pollutes the air around his rural home, he sets out to find the source. In the city he heads right to the culprit, Boss-Lady's Genuine Shoo-Fly Artificial Honey Syrup factory. The pollution comes from the sugar she melts in the furnace. Michael Bird-Boy tells her to use bees to make honey and sends her some. After some trial-and-error, it works; the air is clean, and Boss-Lady thanks Michael Bird-Boy. DePaola's familiar watercolors are not the least bit dated. His moral is obvious but handled with warmth and a light touch. The child solves the problem. This is a good introduction for the youngest children to pollution and what we can do to stop it.

■ Dolan, Edward F. OUR POISONED SKY. Dutton, 1991. 121pp. (0-525-65056-3) Nonfiction. Interest Level: Ages 11 up

This is a well-organized, up-to-date reference on air pollution. Dolan highlights several major instances of air pollution in history. He notes that problems began about the time of the Industrial Revolution when large quantities of fossil fuels began to be used. Subsequent chapters focus on identifying pollutants, on specific problems such as the ozone layer, acid rain, and the greenhouse effect. The author examines national and international efforts to control air pollution, which have been only partially successful, including the 1990 Clean Air Act. A final chapter suggests 10 things readers can do, for example, being aware of the issues "with further reading of books and magazines, joining environmental groups, discussing issues with friends, supporting efforts to curb pollution, and endorsing alternative energy sources. A lengthy bibliography includes both books and periodical articles. The book is indexed and includes black-and-white photographs.

■ Duggleby, John. PESTICIDES. Crestwood, 1990. 47pp. (0-89686-540-1) SERIES: Earth Alert. Nonfiction. Interest Level: Ages 9–11

This brief, attractive book will acquaint middle grade readers with the environmental concerns surrounding pesticide use in this country. Duggleby defines pesticides and discusses their known and suspected dangers. He recounts the impact of and controversy over Rachel Carson's 1962 book, *Silent Spring,* which alerted the American public to dangers of pesticides. He also notes the mixed success of the EPA and FDA in protecting the public from harmful substances. Alternative methods of ridding crops of pests such as companion planting, natural predators, and "safe" pesticides are mentioned. Duggleby also offers some tips for children: buy organic produce if it's available and families can afford it, otherwise wash all produce thoroughly with dishwashing liquid to remove wax and chemical residues. Suggestions of further reading, glossary, and index are appended.

■ **Freeman, Don. THE SEAL AND THE SLICK. Illus. by author. Viking, 1974. Unp. o.p. Fiction. Interest Level: Ages 4–7**
Deeply affected by a disastrous 1969 oil spill off the coast of Santa Barbara, California, resident author-illustrator Don Freeman wrote this picture book to draw public attention to the dangers of off-shore drilling. Freeman says, "I remember being especially impressed by the way the young people pitched in and tried to save the oil-soaked shore birds and seals."

"It wasn't until much later, when I happened to see a young sea lion swimming in a surfing area, that a story for children began forming in my mind. I couldn't keep from wondering if this seal might have been one of the lucky pups that managed to survive the oil slick—with the help of a boy and girl, of course."

The story begins with a family of sea lions basking in the sun. Sensing danger, the father sea lion barks out a warning, which is ignored by a heedless young pup who decides to go exploring. Suddenly, he is caught in an oil slick caused by a blowout on an offshore drilling rig. Near death, the little sea lion is carried to shore by the tide, where he lies helpless and immobile. Fortunately, a large-scale cleanup effort is underway and he is rescued by a boy and a girl who come to his aid. The heroic children pull the seal up onto their rubber raft and begin to wash the sticky oil from his fur. When they leave the pup to go for fresh water, the rising tide catches the raft and carries it out to sea. Much recovered and much wiser, the seal pup swims safely home while the waves return the raft to the children on shore.

Unfortunately, recurring oil spills continue to make *The Seal and the Slick* relevant. Freeman's watercolors deftly capture the drama and urgency of the rescue effort. The large pictures and exciting story make this book a good read-aloud choice. While Freeman has given *The Seal and the Slick* a happy ending, no child who hears this story will fail to grasp an understanding of the terrible consequences an oil spill has on the environment.

■ **Garden, Nancy. PEACE, O RIVER. Farrar, 1986. 245pp. (0-374-35763-3) Fiction. Interest Level: Ages 12 up**
Sixteen-year-old Kate returns with her family to a small Massachusetts town after four years. She resumes the close relationship she had with Jon, a childhood friend, but soon finds that hostilities have escalated between the middle class kids from her town and the less affluent kids from the town across the river. She also learns that both towns have been chosen as possible sites for an experimental nuclear waste disposal plant. The river,

which has always been a source of comfort and strength to Kate, now becomes a symbol of division—both between the fighting kids on either side of the river, and their parents who won't unite to fight the plant. Getting the kids to get along and the towns to unite to fight the plant become all-consuming issues for Kate in this coming-of-age story. While she succeeds in building some bridges between the two towns, the story has a tragic ending. There is an old-fashioned quality to *Peace, O River* although contemporary situations and events such as violence and drug use are present. Like Collier's *When the Stars Begin to Fall*, this book may be useful in initiating discussions on personal responsibility and civic duty.

■ Gay, Kathlyn. WATER POLLUTION. Watts, 1990. 144pp. (LB 0-531-10949-6) SERIES: An Impact Book. Nonfiction. Interest Level: Ages 14 up
Science writer Gay's well-organized book covers many aspects of water pollution and should be useful to upper level students studying the subject. She begins with some general information on the water cycle and pollution. In ensuing chapters she describes how groundwater, waste water, wetlands, lakes, rivers, and oceans become contaminated, noting some of the efforts to clean up, conserve, or manage water. She also devotes a chapter to problems of water supply and distribution in the United States. In a final chapter on protective measures she gives an overview of legislation, cooperative programs, demonstration projects, bioremediation, and educational programs in schools and communities. Gay urges readers to develop the habit of conservation and preservation. She offers several ways water can be protected and conserved at the local level. Source notes, glossary, list of books, and periodical articles for further reading, and index are appended. The text is illustrated with black-and-white photographs. See also Gay's *Air Pollution* (Watts, 1991) in the Impact series.

■ George, Jean. WHO REALLY KILLED COCK ROBIN? AN ECOLOGICAL MYSTERY. Harper, 1991. 176pp. (LB 0-06-021981-5) Fiction. Interest Level: Ages 9–12
Inspired by the mysterious death of a dying robin brought to her door, Jean George wrote this ecological mystery that uncovers the many forms pollution takes and the complexity of relationships in nature. First published in 1971, *Who Really Killed Cock Robin* wins as a mystery and for the enormous amount of information on ecology and pollutants that it imparts. Like many mystery books, characterization is a bit weak, but the plot moves and thickens at a good pace as Tony Isidoro and his friends try to solve the mystery of the death of the robin that has been nesting on the mayor's porch. By story's end, they have tracked several leads: aniline dyes, detergents, fertilizers, fungicides, mercury, DDT, and PCBs. George's knack for

weaving science into her narrative makes for an enjoyable mystery with a (still) timely message.

■ **Gold, Susan Dudley. TOXIC WASTE. Crestwood, 1990. 47pp. (0-89686-542-8)** SERIES: **Earth Alert. Nonfiction. Interest Level: Ages 9–12**
This quick review of toxic wastes for middle grade readers just introduces them to the subject. Gold discusses several major toxins—DDT, PCBs, herbicides, waste oil, nuclear wastes, radon, and household chemicals devoting a few paragraphs to each. She also highlights some of the major toxic accidents and spills such as the nuclear explosion at Chernobyl in the USSR, the chemical plant accident at Bhopal, India, and Love Canal in the United States. A list of Federal laws and regulations pertaining to toxic wastes, a brief list of suggestions for children, a glossary, and an index are included. Color photographs and accessible format make this small book attractive.

■ **Greene, Carol. CARING FOR OUR WATER. Enslow, 1991. 32pp. (0-89490-356-X)** SERIES: **Caring for Our Earth. Nonfiction. Interest Level: Ages 6–8**
Ideal for beginning readers, Greene's unpretentious text explains why water is so important and the many ways we use it. Sources and effects of water pollution are given and ways water can be conserved and cleaned suggested: "People can make laws to stop factories from dumping pollutant," and "Farmers can use safe ways to kill pests and make crops grow tall." Greene also suggests simple ways readers can conserve water. The black-and-white photographs may disappoint some, but the colorful cover and clean, open design is inviting. This is one of a series of series of books introducing environmental issues to beginning readers. The book includes a brief glossary and an index.

■ **Hare, Tony. POLLUTING THE SEA. Watts, 1991. 32pp. (LB 0-531-17290-2)** SERIES: **Save Our Earth. Nonfiction. Interest Level: Ages 10–14**
In his introduction, Hare stresses the richness of marine life and the important resources oceans offer people such as oil, gas and most important, food. In short two-page chapters current threats to oceans worldwide are examined: oil pollution, ocean litter, sewage, metal and chemical pollution, and radioactive wastes. A world map highlights areas that are particularly threatened by pollution. The oversize format with colorful, well-chosen photographs, charts and maps will interest readers. In an appendix, Hare offers a few suggestions for helping solve problems of ocean pollution. A glossary and an index are appended. This brief, but succinct, treatment will be useful to student researchers.

■ Hoff, Mary King, and Mary M. Rodgers. OUR ENDANGERED PLANET:
GROUNDWATER. Lerner, 1991. 64pp. (LB 0-8225-2500-3) SERIES: Our
Endangered Earth. Nonfiction. Interest Level: Ages 9–12
The inviting format, good organization, and writing of the *Our Endangered
Earth* series is evident in Hoff and Rodgers' *Groundwater*, which describes the
uses of groundwater and its vulnerability to pollution and depletion. The
authors begin with some of the same information on the water cycle found in
Rivers and Lakes but go on to explain the particular uses to which groundwater is put. Used for drinking water, growing and irrigating crops, carrying
away wastes, and in industry uses, this valuable resource is threatened by the
growing demand and by the many landfill pollutants, pesticides, fertilizers,
industrial wastes, salts, chemical spills, septic tanks, and the polluted surface
water of rivers and lakes. Hoff and Rodgers use examples from around the
world and suggest ways young people can help protect and conserve groundwater. They highlight a teenage winner of the Environmental Youth Award
who alerted her town to the dangers of household chemicals to groundwater.
Middle school researchers will find this useful. Full-color illustrations combine with the well-written text in a cleanly designed format. Words defined in
the glossary are bolded in the text. An index is included.

■ Hoff, Mary King, and Mary M. Rodgers. OUR ENDANGERED PLANET:
RIVERS AND LAKES. Lerner, 1991. 64pp. (LB 0-8225-2501-1) SERIES:
Our Endangered Earth. Nonfiction. Interest Level: Ages 9–12
Attractive design, good organization, and a happy balance of illustrations
and text combine to produce this introduction to water pollution in *Rivers
and Lakes*, part of Lerner's *Our Endangered Earth* series. Ideal for middle
school researchers, Hoff and Rodgers set the stage with an explanation of
the water cycle and the importance of water to all living things. The role of
water in the food chain and as a habitat are described as well as major uses
of water: agriculture, industry and personal use. They cite sources of pollution, many the result of our modern life: sediment from agriculture, fertilizers, pesticides, industrial wastes, thermal pollution, and their effect on life
in rivers and lakes. They use examples of pollution of rivers, lakes, and
wetlands around the world. A final chapter suggests ways young people can
help protect water in rivers, lakes, and wetlands. The authors highlight the
efforts of an organization "Kids Against Pollution" that was formed by
students. The books include a glossary and an index. Words defined in
glossary are bolded in the text.

■ Kronenwetter, Michael. MANAGING TOXIC WASTES. Messner, 1989.
118pp. (LB 0-671-69051-5) SERIES: Issues for the 90s. Nonfiction. Interest
Level: Ages 12 up

The EPA estimates that "as much as 90 percent of all the wastes produced in the United States each year are unsafely stored." For junior high students, Kronenwetter offers a thorough and fascinating look at types of toxic wastes produced in this country, environmental effects (pollution of air, water, and ground), major sources of toxic wastes, disposal methods, and issues and government efforts, some successful, some not, to control wastes and regulate disposal sites. He devotes a chapter to Love Canal and other serious events. Kronenwetter concludes, "The single most important thing that needs to be done to control toxic wastes is also the most obvious: We need to produce fewer of them." The book includes a bibliography and an index, but no glossary for the challenging vocabulary students will encounter. Good organization, writing, and an eye-catching cover are not supported by the inside format, which is illustrated with black-and-white photographs.

■ **Lee, Sally. PESTICIDES. Watts, 1991. 143pp. (LB 0-531-13017-7) SERIES: An Impact Book. Nonfiction. Interest Level: Ages 12 up**
The use of chemical pesticides for controlling a variety of animals, weeds, fungi, viruses and especially insects has mushroomed over the past 50 years. Author Lee examines the development and use of pesticides and looks at the mounting evidence of the environmental damage caused by these chemicals. Lee acknowledges the competing interests of industry, farmers, environmentalists, consumers, and the role of the government, especially the EPA in regulating the chemical industry. She also looks at alternatives to pesticides including biological control, different farming methods, and integrated pest management. Her presentation is balanced, her viewpoint moderate: "We cannot entirely escape the chemical world we have created. The best we can do is to use pesticides selectively, combined with nonchemical means of controlling pests. . . ." The book includes a glossary, sources, books for further reading, and an index. Illustrated with black-and-white photographs, this is a good resource for upper level students.

■ **Miller, Christina G., and Louise A. Berry. ACID RAIN: A SOURCEBOOK FOR YOUNG PEOPLE. Messner, 1986. 114pp. (LB 0-671-60177-6) Nonfiction. Interest Level: Ages 11–14**
Two features make Miller and Berry's well-organized book on acid rain stand out. The authors emphasize the importance of forming one's own opinions on controversial issues such as acid rain. They encourage readers to keep a journal of newspaper and magazine clippings to keep abreast of new information on the continuing debate. They also incorporate easy projects to engage reader interest and involvement. Projects include testing solutions for acids or bases, demonstrating how calcium carbonate reacts

with an acid, observing how acids dissolve metals, and observing the effect of acid, alkaline, and normal water on seedling growth.

After defining acid rain the authors discuss known or suspected effects on lakes, forests, wildlife, drinking water, air, buildings, and human health. Maintaining a concerned but objective tone, they examine some of the efforts to control acid rain and conclude with specific suggestions for readers to become involved. Further reading, a glossary, addresses of organizations such as the Acid Rain Foundation are appended. The book has an index. Black-and-white photographs and charts inform, but do not enhance the book's appeal.

■ Miller, Christina G., and Louise A. Berry. COASTAL RESCUE: PRESERVING OUR SEASHORES. Macmillan, 1989. 120pp. (0-689-31288-1) Nonfiction. Interest Level: Ages 11 up
"Seventy per cent of the population of the United States lives within fifty miles of the ocean." Authors and environmentalists Christina G. Miller and Louise A. Berry have written *Coastal Rescue* to educate students about the importance of beaches because this fragile ecosystem is increasingly threatened. The book presents an overview of coasts, their geologic history and development, and the problems of pollution, and erosion that have adversely affected seashore ecology. The authors advocate laws requiring communities to "preserve, protect, and restore coastal resources for the future."

Black-and-white illustrations of average quality and an occasional diagram, such as one of North American ocean currents, support the text. Simple instructions for making a small wave tank are also included.

Global warming, poor land management, and natural erosion have all contributed to the disappearance of the shoreline. Animal, fish, and bird populations along the coasts are also declining, as valuable wetlands are filled in to make way for the construction of buildings and roads. Miller and Berry urge individuals to explore new ways to preserve the beaches as the problem of erosion increases. They praise legislation that created national seashores and wildlife refuges.

The authors firmly believe that the coasts will be rescued and preserved if the public is educated about their importance and work together to monitor, protect, and clean up the environment. Special emphasis has been given to projects in which students participated.

Important words that are italicized in the text are defined in the glossary. There is also a list of information sources, a list of books chosen especially for young people, and an index.

■ Peet, Bill. THE WUMP WORLD. Illus. by author. Houghton, 1970. 44pp. (LB 0-395-19841-0) Fiction. Interest Level: Ages 6–10

When aliens from the planet Pollutus settle on the peaceful planet of the Wumps, the gentle, grass-eating Wumps become victims of a highly technological and polluting civilization. The Wumps are driven to forage in underground caves while the new settlers, called Pollutions, build cities, roads, and factories polluting water and air. When the pollution gets too bad, even for the Pollutions, they scout out a new planet to plunder and leave as suddenly as they came. The Wumps emerge to find only a small pasture of trees and grass left and the Wump world will never be the same. Peet takes on the issue of pollution with exagerrated humor and cartoon-like drawings. Pollution on Earth, teachers and parents will tell their students and children, is not caused by aliens from outer space, but by all of us.

■ Pringle, Laurence. RAIN OF TROUBLES: THE SCIENCE AND POLITICS OF ACID RAIN. Macmillan, 1988. 121pp. (LB 0-02-775370-0) Nonfiction.
Interest Level: Ages 13 up
Pringle's thorough, well-researched discussion of acid rain, although not the most recent book published, will provide student researchers with plenty of information for reports. In the first four chapters Pringle explains what acid rain is, tells how it was discovered, and what scientists have learned about how it forms, is transported, and the damage it does to lakes, rivers, forests, and people. In the final two chapters he looks at ways of controlling acid rain and the reasons behind the intense political controversies over acid rain. The book includes charts, diagrams, and black-and-white photographs. A list of periodical articles is appended. Pringle suggests readers examine the most recent issues of the periodicals cited for up-to-date information. As always, Pringle notes the political and economic controversies that surround environmental issues such as acid rain. An index is included.

Award: OSTB, 1988

■ Smith, Roland. SEA OTTER RESCUE: THE AFTERMATH OF AN OIL SPILL. Photos by author. Dutton, 1990. 64pp. (0-525-65041-5) Nonfiction.
Interest Level: Ages 9–12
Told simply as a story of wildlife rescue, this book, with its excellent photos and an appealing subject, has great appeal. But *Sea Otter Rescue* can also be used to discuss the larger issue of pollution, its effect on wildlife, and in the case of oil spills, the huge cost of cleaning up. When the *Exxon Valdez* tanker spilled 11 million gallons of crude oil into Prince William Sound off the coast of Alaska in 1989, sea otters were just one group of victims. The author, who led a team from the Point Defiance Zoo & Aquarium to help injured sea otters, gives readers background on the spill and on sea otters, to understand how deadly this catastrophe was to them. He chronicles the

efforts of rescue workers and volunteers to capture, clean, and release oil soaked otters. The book includes a glossary and an index.

Award: OSTB, 1990

■ **Stille, Darlene R. WATER POLLUTION. Childrens, 1990. 48pp. (LB 0-516-01190-1)** SERIES: **New True.** Nonfiction. **Interest Level: Ages 7–10**
Large print and a simple vocabulary aimed at students in grades 2–4 characterize the New True series, and this volume on water pollution is no exception. Captioned, color photographs illustrate a factual, well-researched text. Unfamiliar terms are explained in context to make them more understandable. These terms also appear in the glossary at the end of the book.

The importance of water to the existence of life is strongly emphasized. Author Darlene Stille points out that our need for water is often accompanied by its misuse, and that "water pollution has been a problem for thousands of years", since the Romans were poisoned by the lead pipes that they used to carry water.

Many causes of water pollution by both people and nature are described, including algae, sewage, and saltwater contamination of groundwater. Heat is also a source of pollution because changing the water temperature in a lake or a river can kill both plants and animals. However, Stille states that most water pollution, including acid rain, is caused by chemicals. The poisonous chemicals that pollute water also adversely affect the food chain. Dramatic, color photographs of dead fish and decaying plants show how pollution can destroy the natural balance of plants, animals, and oxygen. Oil spills and illegal dumping are sources of pollution in the oceans and along the coastlines.

Stille suggests several ways to prevent water pollution. First, clean-water legislation must be increased to prevent illegal dumping and protect the oceans. And, although it is expensive, it is essential to clean up already polluted water.

The author has packed a surprising amount of useful information into this slim volume that is a solid introduction to an important topic. An index is included.

Two other titles by Stille on pollution in the New True series include *Soil Erosion and Pollution* (Childrens, 1990) and *Air Pollution* (Childrens, 1990).

■ **Szumski, Bonnie, and JoAnne Buggey. TOXIC WASTES: EXAMINING CAUSE AND EFFECT RELATIONSHIPS. Greenhaven, 1989. 32pp. (paper 0-89908-496-6)** SERIES: **Opposing Viewpoints Juniors.** Nonfiction. **Interest Level: Ages 11–14**

Toxic Wastes, one of a series, Opposing Viewpoints Juniors, fills a specific curriculum need. The author, supported by an educational consultant, examines the cause and effect relationships that surround the subject of hazardous wastes. This analysis is intended to help middle or junior high school students acquire better skills in critical thinking and reading. Opposite viewpoints on toxic wastes from expert opinion-makers, such as consumer advocate Ralph Nader or DuPont Company vice president William G. Simeral, have been paraphrased from their original books or speeches to make them easier to understand.

The book is divided into three chapters, each presenting one of the following questions: Are Chemical Companies Poisoning America?; Are Toxic Wastes Causing Cancer?; and, Should Toxic Wastes Be Dumped in the Ocean? Following each question a positive and a negative response is explored. The chapters conclude with a page that examines causes and effects and includes activities to assess the discussion points. Chapter 3 concludes with questions to help analyze editorial cartoons that have been used throughout the book to support various statements with humor.

Speech and debate teachers and their students will find this book useful. Students preparing an oral or written report on hazardous wastes will also benefit.

■ **Van Allsburg, Chris. JUST A DREAM. Illus. by Chris Van Allsburg. Houghton, 1990. Unp. (0-395-53308-2) Fiction. Interest Level: Ages 4 up** Walter, a young boy, has a careless disregard for the world in which he lives. Symbolic of public apathy toward environmental issues, Walter is not intentionally malicious, but only self-centered and insensitive. Littering is easy; recycling is too much trouble. He derides the little girl next door when she expresses her excitement at receiving a live tree for her birthday. Walter likes television and his favorite program is set in the future. One night, he falls asleep wishing that he could live in the future only to wake up in a dump. Like *The Polar Express,* Caldecott medalist Van Allburg sets much of this book within a child's dream. The book's arrangement is original. Each dramatic two-page spread precedes a page of explaination. Another small block illustration follows. Van Allburg's use of color is masterful. An unusual pastel palette effectively conveys the smoke and murkiness of air pollution in contrast to the final pages of the book, which are filled with the crisp, vibrant colors of a clean world.

In Walter's dream, the seemingly small environmental concerns of the present have become alarming, overwhelming problems in the future. Almost no trees remain; the air and the oceans are polluted, automobiles clog the highways, and a hotel has been built atop Mount Everest. Walter's nightmare is not just a dream, but a cautionary tale that provides him with the impetus to change his ways.

Just a Dream is not a bedtime story, nor is it particularly entertaining. Much of the author's abstract imagery and symbolism will not be understood by young children. Nevertheless, the book, though didactic, is also provocative and can be used in discussions of environmental issues as well as in art classes. *Just a Dream* is reminiscent of both *A Christmas Carol* and *The Little Prince*. However, Walter's character has not been fully developed, therefore he does not engage the reader as do both Scrooge and the prince. The book is lucid and intelligent, but not a good choice for everyone.

Award: OSTB, 1990

■ Wildsmith, Brian. PROFESSOR NOAH'S SPACESHIP. Illus. by author. Oxford Univ. Pr., 1980. Unp. (0-19-279741-7) Interest Level: Ages 4–8
In Wildsmith's variation on the biblical story of the Ark, the forest animals find their world slowly being destroyed. Air pollution, pesticides, hunting, and eventually fire threaten their existence. They are rescued by Professor Noah who builds a spaceship to take them into the future to another unspoiled planet. Forty days and forty nights later the homesick crew lands. However, they discover that because of a malfunction they are back on earth many hundreds of years *earlier* in a clean, unspoiled environment. Professor Noah says, "It's a wonderful world, and we must keep it that way." Wildsmith's familiar style is as colorful as ever and his elephant astronaut worth the price of the book. This cautionary tale with its oversize format and festive air should hold the interest of young children. Teachers can use it to introduce the topic of pollution.

■ Zipko, Stephen J. TOXIC THREAT: HOW HAZARDOUS SUBSTANCES POISON OUR LIVES. Messner, 1990 (rev. ed.). 249pp. (LB 0-671-69330-1) Nonfiction. Interest Level: Ages 12 up
Zipko, a high school biology teacher, writes a fairly technical, curriculum-oriented book on hazardous wastes for upper level students. This revised edition begins by explaining food webs and water, nitrogen, carbon, phosphorous cycles. The author shows how toxins can disrupt their delicate balance. A chapter on how scientists define and test toxins is followed by chapters that identify various wastes that pollute our water supply, soil and air endangering our health. Zipko discusses industrial wastes, landfills, detergents, acid rain, pesticides, herbicides, nuclear wastes noting the damage that well-publicized catastrophes such as the accident at the Union Carbide pesticide plant in Bhopal, India, and the nuclear power plant explosions at Chernobyl in the U.S.S.R. caused.

He discusses the role of the EPA and legislative efforts to control pollution and concludes with a chapter on public involvement. Guidelines for writing effective letters to representatives, a summary of federal legislation on hazardous substances, and a list of environmental and science magazines, organizations, and agencies are appended. Projects and activities are interspersed throughout the text. Some choppy organization and an unfortunate error in the index pagination—the entire index seems to be off by a few pages—weaken an otherwise informative, up-to-date book. The book is illustrated with black-and-white photographs, charts, and diagrams.

Garbage and Recycling

■ Asimov, Isaac. SPACE GARBAGE. Stevens, 1989. 32pp. (1-55532-370-7) SERIES: Isaac Asimov's Library of the Universe. Nonfiction. Interest Level: Ages 7–12
Space Garbage, one volume in the Library of the Universe series by the prolific and respected writer Isaac Asimov, is an excellent introduction to this topic. Asimov anticipates questions that students may pose about space pollution and answers each one in two pages, briefly and clearly. This question-and-answer format is effective because it allows the reader to scan rapidly through the book without becoming mired in detail or missing any important facts. Color and black-and-white photographs and drawings help to provide an objective understanding of the problem. The causes of space garbage, its dangers, and new but insufficient efforts now being made to clean up space are explained. Asimov points out the need to track space debris in order to avoid collisions. Space junk includes broken spacecraft on Mars and Venus, scientific equipment left on the moon to perform experiments, and various memorials to accomplishments in space exploration. The author says that the solar system is filled with satellites that continue in orbit even after they have stopped working. He expresses concern that space debris is increasing. However, while most non-working space probes have no value, others contain messages about earth and its location. These will be left to drift deeper into space in the hopes of discovery by intelligent beings from other planets. Although some space shuttle missions have either repaired or removed malfunctioning satellites, little more than that is being done.

Though this book does not have the glossy, browsing appeal of Richard Maurer's *Junk in Space* (Simon & Schuster, 1989) Asimov's book is easier to understand and is suitable for elementary school use.

A simple chart of the types of space garbage with good and bad points explained, reference lists, sites to visit and sources to write for further information, a one-page glossary, and an index are included.

■ Condon, Judith. RECYCLING PAPER. Watts, 1990. 29pp. (LB 0-531-14078-4) SERIES: Waste Control. Nonfiction. Interest Level: Ages 10–12

We hear about recycling, but what happens to aluminum cans, paper, glass, and plastic once they leave our homes or are dropped at recycling centers is a mystery. Watts' *Waste Control* series of books that includes *Recycling Paper* provides an overview of the methods used to recycle materials and will be a useful supplement to recycling discussions. Condon does a good job in *Recycling Paper* of discussing the value of recycling, methods used, relative costs, and specific policies and projects. Suggestions for readers are appended along with a glossary, index, and addresses of useful organizations. Full-color photographs, charts, and diagrams enrich the text. Other titles in the series include: *Recycling Glass, Recycling Plastic, Recycling Metal.*

■ Gay, Kathlyn. GARBAGE AND RECYCLING. Enslow, 1991. 128pp. (0-89490-321-7) SERIES: Issues in Focus. Nonfiction. Interest Level: Ages 12 up

In this up-to-date and well-researched examination of garbage disposal, veteran author Kathlyn Gay gives special emphasis to recycling. Two introductory chapters outline the extent of the crisis and the importance of recycling; subsequent chapters look at how various materials are recycled: paper, glass, cans, scrap metal, and plastics. She also examines waste-to-energy programs, composting, and motor oil and car tire recovery. Further chapters examine hazardous waste disposal and clean-up, and nuclear waste disposal. Problems of disposal and recycling methods are discussed. Gay includes numerous examples of the efforts of individuals, corporations and communities to either produce less waste or recycle. Gay ends with suggestions for readers, an extensive list of recent books, booklets, and magazine articles that will be helpful to student researchers.

Addresses of about three dozen organizations, such as the National Recycling Coalition, Environmental Defense Fund, and the Alcoa Recycling Company are appended along with addresses of six magazines: *Garbage* and *E Magazine*. Good black-and-white photographs and pictures of various recycling symbols add to an otherwise undistinguished format and even less appealing cover. Chapter notes, glossary and index are included.

■ Hadingham, Evan, and Janet Hadingham. GARBAGE! WHERE IT COMES FROM, WHERE IT GOES. Simon & Schuster, 1990. 48pp. (LB 0-671-69424-3) SERIES: A NOVA Book. Nonfiction. Interest Level: Ages 11 up

Dramatic, full-color photographs provide a highly visual orientation for *Garbage!*, which is based on the PBS series *NOVA*. Pictures of both garbage problems and solutions, ranging from an actual mountain of discarded computers to a waterwheel made from recycled milk cartons and a polar bear foraging in a city dump, invite immediate discussion.

The Hadinghams give the garbage problem historical perspective by comparing Eskimo, or Inuit, villages in 1908, when native peoples, out of necessity, wasted very little, to today, as the increased use of plastic, paper and cans has resulted in ugly garbage mounds in every village. The huge problem of garbage disposal in New York City is also shown now and as it was at the turn of the century. The contrasts and similarities are striking and thought-provoking. The authors also analyze worldwide garbage problems, including the practice of shipping waste to poor countries and illegal dumping in the oceans, as well as auspicious developments in Europe and Japan where successful programs for waste disposal and recycling are established. A chapter on recycling stresses the economic advantages and offers plans for the implementation of new programs. Environmental activities are suggested for children who may want to become "garbage detectives" or dig a mini landfill. "Amazing Garbage Facts" appear in boxes next to maps and diagrams. *Garbage!* concludes with a description of a New Jersey social studies class that founded an activist organization, Kids Against Pollution.

Unfortunately, *Garbage!* does not contain a glossary of new or unfamiliar terms mentioned in the text such as "drift net" or "biodegradable." Although the word "recycling" is found in the index, a significant reference on page 31 has been omitted. Despite some flaws, this is a factual, well-organized book that urges children to think about the problem of garbage, who takes care of it, and where it goes.

■ **Johnson, Jean. SANITATION WORKERS A TO Z. Walker, 1988. 44pp. o.p. SERIES: Community Helpers. Nonfiction. Interest Level: Ages 4–8**
One of a series of non-fiction books for young children about community helpers, author-photographer Jean Johnson has chosen the alphabet as a framework to describe the many kinds of jobs performed by sanitation workers. Her purpose is to help children become aware of a valuable and necessary occupation that is often unappreciated.

Large, clear, black-and-white photographs illustrate each letter of the alphabet. Simple, descriptive sentences in large print are appropriate for reading aloud to preschoolers or to a kindergarten class. Alphabet books can often be contrived, but here the author, a former teacher and librarian, has adroitly matched terms to letters, such as I is for "illegal dump." The always difficult Q is used appropriately enough for "quitting time." While "recycling" is not found under R ("rear loader"), this term is explained under K for "kitchen garbage." Many kinds of garbage and garbage disposal methods are described. For children who are fascinated by trucks, various types are shown, including rear- and side-loading garbage trucks, earthmovers, vacuum sweepers, and even a washer truck.

A special seven-page section, which follows the alphabet is offered to promote classroom discussion with more detailed information about the role of sanitation workers and their importance in keeping cities and towns clean and healthy places to live, work, and play.

Types of landfills and the environmental regulations required to operate them are briefly discussed. Waste-to-energy facilities, which burn garbage cleanly and efficiently, are also described. Hazardous waste is mentioned in relation to The Resource Conservation and Recovery Act of 1973, which restricts the cleanup of hazardous substances to specialists.

The author, who helped to collect garbage in Charlotte, North Carolina while researching this topic, has provided teachers with a useful overview of an important community service.

Award: OSTB, 1988

■ **Kilbourne, Frances. THE RECYCLERS. Illus. by Ann Powell. Women's Pr., 1979. Unp. (paper 0-88961-060-6) Fiction. Interest Level: Ages 6–10**
This delightful, unpretentious picture book without words features two imaginative sisters (or friends) who are determined to renovate, recreate, and ultimately recycle the accumulated junk in and around their neighborhood. Over the course of several weeks the girls scavenge their neighborhood, keeping one step ahead of the garbage truck (and their parents who do not seem pleased to see the garage filling with junk). After collecting a sizable amount of discarded flower pots, broken appliances, bikes, buggies, lawn chairs, and other items, they close the garage doors, hang up a "do not enter" sign and go to work. Finally, curious neighbors are allowed to inspect an assortment of re-creations: fixed-up scooters and chairs, toys and handicrafts, and creations fashioned from discards. The final spread shows several happy children heading home with their recycled treasures. Two-color cartoon-like drawings in black and red are expressive and tell the story with humor and drama. This small press came up with a big winner in an area where little has been published.

■ **Lee, Sally. THE THROWAWAY SOCIETY. Watts, 1990. 128pp. (LB 0-531-10947-X) SERIES: An Impact Book. Nonfiction. Interest Level: Ages 12 up**
This book provides up-do-date information on solid waste disposal methods and problems in the United States. Lee begins with an overview of the problems, among them the growing amount of trash Americans generate, the rising cost of disposal, closed landfills, and the reluctance of residents to allow waste disposal sites near their homes. The author discusses waste collection, transportation of the waste, and disposal. Lee explains incineration and resource recovery methods, recycling, and ocean dumping. She

also notes the danger of toxic wastes. A confusing, contradictory summary muddles the issues. On one page Lee implies that recycling and conservation are not achievable goals. She says, "some idealists suggest that we go back to a simpler life with less packaging and fewer throwaway items . . . Americans are not about to give up their disposable diapers and TV dinners." However, on the following page she says, "The most obvious way to solve the garbage problem is to produce less garbage to begin with" and advocates reducing packaging waste. The book is illustrated with charts and mediocre black-and-white photographs, includes a glossary, and an index.

■ **Lefkowitz, R. J. SAVE IT! KEEP IT! USE IT AGAIN! A BOOK ABOUT CONSERVATION AND RECYCLING.** Illus. by John E. Johnson. Parents Magazine Pr., 1977. 64pp. o.p. SERIES: A Finding-Out Book. Nonfiction. Interest Level: Ages 8–11
With little available for children in the primary grades on recycling, it's unfortunate that this easy-to-read book on natural resources, conservation, and recycling is out-of-print. But, those who have copies should hold on to them. In simple, understandable terms, Lefkowitz explains the differences between renewable and non-renewable resources and the importance of conserving the resources we need. Filled with practical suggestions, this precursor to today's action-oriented handbooks offers down-to-earth advice, "Using less stuff such as fuel, having fewer things and keeping them longer, fixing up old things instead of getting new ones, recycling whatever you can—all are good ways to make our natural resources go further." Two-color line drawings effectively reinforce the text. One picture shows a broken chair and bookshelf tossed out with the garbage. In the next picture the salvaged and repaired furniture is being painted by two children. The book includes an index.

■ **Levin, Betty. THE TROUBLE WITH GRAMARY.** Greenwillow, 1988. 198pp. (LB 0-688-07372-7) Fiction. Interest Level: Ages 10–14
Set in a Maine fishing village, *The Trouble with Gramary* features a girl named Merkka whose family lives with their grandmother, Gramary. Gramary operates a scrap metal business on their waterfront property. Now that the fishing industry is declining, many townspeople are attempting to develop the tourist industry. The state of Gramary's "eyesore" oceanfront property becomes an issue among the townspeople and within the family. Merrka longs for conventionality—a new, tidy home inland would please her, but she also admires her grandmother. Merkka's actions unknowingly lead to Gramary's discovery as an artist, which changes everyone's attitude toward Gramary. Levin's good characterizations help create a believable story. Teachers may find this (like *Galimoto* (Lothrop, 1990) for younger readers) an unusual supplement to discussions of recycling.

■ Madden, Don. THE WARTVILLE WIZARD. Illus. by author. Macmillan, 1986. Unp. (0-02-762100-6) Fiction. Interest Level: Ages 4–8

Author-illustrator Madden pokes fun at litterbugs in this humorous story with a message. A tidy, old man gets tired of picking up trash that ends up in his yard and along the road. One particularly vexing day he stops in a clearing in the woods saying, "Mother Nature, I've tried to keep your hill and green places clean, but I can't go on. I'm tired." In the drop of a gum wrapper he acquires the "power over trash" and becomes the Wartville Wizard. To his delight he discovers that he has only to point to a piece of trash and it sticks to the person who dropped it. This creates several awkward and ridiculous situations among the townspeople but they are finally shamed into picking up after themselves. Madden makes the most of the "trashed-townspeople" in his cartoon-style watercolors.

■ Maurer, Richard. JUNK IN SPACE. Simon & Schuster, 1989. 48pp. (paper 0-671-67767-5) SERIES: A NOVA Book. Nonfiction. Interest Level: Ages 9–14

Adapted from the award-wining NOVA series on public television, *Junk in Space*, is a visually appealing book that will be a useful source of information for upper elementary and junior high school students writing research reports. Full-color, captioned photographs and graphics on every page enhance a sophisticated, well-written text.

Space junk is a broad term that includes any broken or discarded object in space. By the autumn of 1988, more than 7000 pieces of orbiting debris had been tracked. This debris includes old weather stations, navigation beacons, and broken satellites, as well as bolts, cylinders, and even, paint chips. In 1983, a small piece of white paint damaged a $50,000 window in a U.S. space shuttle. While the author says that it is unlikely that any of this debris could cause a catastrophe, small objects traveling at orbital speed are difficult to detect. Although many of these objects reenter the earth's atmosphere and burn, any increase in their number poses a risk to human space exploration.

The potential hazards of junk in space are further explained through a metaphorical comparison of lost space relics to shipwrecks in the ocean, a comparison that provides continuity throughout the book.

The author devotes one chapter to the scientific and mathematical explanation of orbits and gravitational fields. Understanding orbits is essential to comprehending space junk and how it travels through space.

Another chapter discusses the flight of the Apollo 11 to the moon. A "wreck chart" shows locations of both successful and crash landings on the surface of the moon as well as orbiting spacecraft. A list of items that astronauts left on the moon is particularly interesting.

The exploration of space is a scientific challenge. Much of the space debris described by the author consists of probes that have missed, malfunctioned, or crashed as part of the learning process.

While Maurer occasionally digresses from his discussion of space debris and does not offer any solutions to this problem, *Junk in Space* is both informative and fascinating. A too-brief glossary, an index, and a suggested reading list are included.

Award: OSTB, 1989

■ **Miller, Christina G., and Louise A. Berry. WASTES. Watts, 1986. 64pp. (LB 0-531-10130-4) SERIES: A First Book. Nonfiction. Interest Level: Ages 9– 14**
"What happens to the water flushed down the toilet, or trash and garbage emptied into the garbage truck?" ask authors Christina Miller and Louise Berry. They discuss household waste treatment, the harmful environmental effect of sewage and garbage disposal methods, and new methods of waste treatment that aim to recover and reuse as much as possible. The book is well-organized and easy to read. They begin by explaining the difference between sewage and solid wastes and trace the history of solid waste and sewage disposal from ancient Greece and Rome through the Middle Ages to the present. Interesting diagrams show how sewage treatment plants, septic tanks, and other waste treatment methods work. Conservation, recycling, composting, aquaculture, dry toilets, and sewage recycling projects are among new or alternative methods discussed. Black-and-white photographs, a glossary, and an index are included.

Award: OSTB, 1986

■ **O'Connor, Karen. GARBAGE. Lucent Books, 1989. 80pp. (LB 1-56006-100-6) SERIES: Overview. Nonfiction. Interest Level: Ages 9–13**
Humans are polluting the land, the water, the air, and even space. Tens of thousands of people and animals have become ill or died because of pollution. Since mankind is responsible for causing this problem, author Karen O'Connor says that it is vital that we educate ourselves and work together to clean up the environment. In *Garbage*, O'Connor takes a serious survey of the waste disposal dilemma, an expensive problem with no simple solutions.

Each chapter of *Garbage* discusses a specific issue surrounding pollution including ocean dumping, hazardous waste disposal, space junk, and recycling. Black-and-white photographs, editorial cartoons, and diagrams illustrate the text. Whenever possible, O'Connor has selected actual incidents in which citizens have united to take action, clean up a polluted area, and restore the environment. Specific laws and treaties that control pollution are also mentioned.

O'Connor sees recycling as a sign of hope and describes several successful programs in California and Georgia. She sees recycling as part of a total effort to take a new, "greener" look at product design, manufacture, packaging, and use. Practical suggestions for protecting the environment are provided, as are the addresses of concerned conservation and environmental organizations to contact and a reading list.

Garbage is a very persuasive and practical book that is highly recommended for students learning about the problem of pollution.

■ **Pringle, Laurence. THROWING THINGS AWAY: FROM MIDDENS TO RESOURCE RECOVERY. Harper, 1986. 90pp. (LB 0-690-04421-6) Nonfiction. Interest Level: Ages 12 up**
People have always produced garbage and our garbage tells a lot about us. Author Pringle begins *Throwing Things Away* with an interesting look at garbage and trash content and disposal from earliest times to the present. He discusses dumps and what they reveal about a culture, landfills and the environmental problems associated with them, various reclamation schemes for closed landfills, and some of the more current issues surrounding waste disposal: recycling programs, incineration of garbage and production of fuel from refuse. Because of its publication date, *Throwing Things Away* will not provide the most up-to-date information on landfill issues, but Pringle's broader, historical perspective will give readers some background on contemporary issues. Illustrated with black-and-white photographs. Includes bibliography and index.

■ **Tesar, Jenny E. THE WASTE CRISIS. Facts on File, 1991. 112pp. (0-8160-2491-X) SERIES: Our Fragile Planet. Nonfiction. Interest Level: Ages 12 up**
Tesar's well-organized examination of the waste crisis in the United States explores the sources of wastes (municipal, medical, industrial) and the methods we use to dispose of them. Other chapters discuss problems of hazardous and radioactive waste disposal, sewage and sewage treatment, and the importance of waste reduction and recycling. Numerous up-to-date examples, supporting information in insets, black-and-white photos, charts and diagrams combine in an attractive format. Two sets of full-color photographs on coated paper are inserted. Books for further reading, a glossary and an index appended. *The Waste Crisis* will be useful for students researching waste and waste disposal.

■ **Wilcox, Charlotte. TRASH! Illus. by Jerry Bushey. Carolrhoda, 1988. 40pp. (LB 0-87614-311-7) Nonfiction. Interest Level: Ages 9–11**

Large, color photographs of children taking out the trash introduce this factual, interesting book on the garbage disposal dilemma and its relationship to the environment.

Text and photographs are well-organized, with new and unfamiliar terms such as "solid waste" and "leachate" appearing in bold type. Pictures of different models of garbage trucks and dumpsters are followed by an extensive discussion of landfill uses and operations. The dangers of animals, insects, and fires from improper garbage disposal are described, as are the harmful consequences of chemical runoff from landfills to nearby lakes and streams. Simple, half-page diagrams compare an open dump to a sanitary landfill and show how each one affects groundwater.

Methane, the natural gas formed by decomposed garbage, is also explained, as is the use of methane as a power source for generating electricity.

Methods used to dispose of solid waste such as mass burn and the refuse-derived fuel (RDF) process, which results in a dry fuel, are outlined. Composting yard waste and recycling old tires, paper, glass, and metals are also discussed. As the book concludes, the author urges individuals to reduce the amount of unusable trash.

A glossary is appended, but unfortunately there is no index. Nevertheless, *Trash!* is a readable, well-executed book that may be considered a primary source of information for middle-grade students.

■ **Williams, Karen Lynn. GALIMOTO. Illus. by Catherine Stock. Lothrop, 1990. Unp. (LB 0-688-08790-6) Fiction. Interest Level: Ages 4–8**
The author and the illustrator of this multicultural story were inspired by their experiences with the children of Malawi in creating this appealing picture book. A "galimoto," they explain, is an intricately crafted push toy popular among African children. Old wires or other simple materials are shaped into cars, trucks, planes, trains, and helicopters.

Kondi, a creative and resourceful seven-year-old boy, lives in a village in Malawi. He keeps his treasures in an old shoe box, in the universal manner of children around the world. For some time he has been saving wire to make a "galimoto," but he needs more. Ignoring his brother's discouraging advice, Kondi begins his quest for wire, first trading his knife to a friend for a handful of precious pieces. More wires are salvaged from his slightly perplexed uncle and the miller. His tenacity brings him to the attention of a local police officer who catches Kondi climbing the fence behind the bicycle repair shop to search their trash heap. At last, wires safely in hand, Kondi settles under a shady red flame tree and begins to make a pickup truck. After working diligently all afternoon, he joins his admiring friends to play with his new toy and falls asleep dreaming of the "galimoto" he will make tomorrow.

The illustrations by Catherine Stock are bright, full-page watercolors that capture the activity of the African village and its residents.

It is hard to resist the urge to recycle some wire to make your own "galimoto" and most children would be delighted with the opportunity for a hands-on art experience after listening to this story read aloud. Teachers who use *Galimoto* with young children will find it to be an unexpected and original addition to recycling discussions.

Energy

■ **Cross, Mike. WIND POWER. Watts, 1985. 32pp. (LB 0-531-17007-1)** SERIES: Energy Today. Nonfiction. Interest Level: Ages 10–14
Cross examines various techniques and technologies used in creating wind power. He notes that as world supplies of fossil fuels dwindle, energy sources such as wind power may provide a ready source of electricity, especially in developing countries. The book is arranged by chapter, each two pages, with excellent color photographs, charts or diagrams, and a few paragraphs of text. Wind pumps, wind turbines, the "Savonius rotor," sail power, and wind rafts are among the applications discussed. More descriptive than issue oriented, *Wind Power* will serve classes seeking information on alternative energy sources. This brief and attractive book is not an automatic purchase. It includes a glossary and an index.

■ **Cross, Wilbur. SOLAR ENERGY. Childrens, 1984. 100pp. (LB 0-516-00511-1)** SERIES: Science and Technology. Nonfiction. Interest Level: Ages 10–14
Cross's thorough exploration of the history, problems, applications, and future promise of solar energy offers good background information for report writers and readers. Although this book does not provide current statistical information, Cross gives many examples of solar technology and research projects in the United States and abroad, discusses the importance of NASA in the development of solar energy, and concludes with some predictions for the role of solar energy in the future. Colored photographs, diagrams, a glossary, a bibliography and an index are included.

■ **Fradin, Dennis B. NUCLEAR ENERGY. Childrens, 1987. 48pp. (LB 0-516-01237-1)** SERIES: New True. Nonfiction. Interest Level: Ages 7–10
The author provides a well-written introduction to nuclear energy for younger readers. Fradin explains how nuclear energy is produced, the history of its development, use in the atomic bomb, and as nuclear power. Nuclear power now supplies about one–sixth of the world's electric power. He discusses the pros and cons of nuclear energy—in weapons and in the

production of electricity—with mention of Three Mile Island and Chernobyl. The large print and abundant photographs are characteristic of the New True series. A glossary and index are included.

■ Gardiner, Brian. ENERGY DEMANDS. Watts, 1990. 36pp. (LB 0-531-17197-3) SERIES: Green Issues. Nonfiction. Interest Level: Ages 10–14
Gardiner's overview of world energy needs and problems strikes an urgent tone. One of the Green Issues series, this book is characterized by good, full-color photographs and charts in a busy but uncluttered design. Gardiner looks at present world energy consumption, our dwindling source of fossil fuels, and the pros and cons of nuclear energy. He urges research on alternative, renewable energy sources and briefly looks at hydro power, solar energy, thermal energy, wind power, and biofuels. Along with development of these sustainable fuels, Gardiner urges energy conservation and international cooperation to help solve energy problems and supply energy needs, although he avoids analysis or discussion of the political and economic factors that play such a significant role in energy issues. A glossary and an index are included.

■ Goldin, Augusta. SMALL ENERGY SOURCES: CHOICES THAT WORK. Harcourt, 1988. 178pp. (0-15-276215-9) Nonfiction. Interest Level: Ages 13 up
The strength of Goldin's discussion of alternative energy sources is the text's focus on successful, small-scale projects around the world. She has researched and reported on dozens of projects—a New York dairy farmer who uses his cows' manure to produce methane, which in turn produces electricity; a wind farm in California; a micro hydroelectric plant in China; a geothermal well in Indonesia—that demonstrate the axiom "Think globally, Act Locally." The practicality and success of small-scale projects, especially those in developing countries, is apparent and often overlooked in discussions of energy. Goldin's enthusiasm for her subject is apparent. Her intent is to open readers' eyes to the creative possibilities in supplying our energy needs. The book is illustrated with black-and-white photographs and diagrams. Bibliography, further sources of information, a glossary and an index are appended.
Award: OSTB, 1988

■ Hawkes, Nigel. NUCLEAR POWER. Rourke, 1990. 48pp. (0-86592-098-2) SERIES: World Issues. Nonfiction. Interest Level: Ages 10–14
Following initial chapters on the history of nuclear energy and the development of the nuclear power industry, Hawkes does a credible job of explain-

ing the debate on nuclear power from a global perspective. He cites the accidents at Three Mile Island, Chernobyl, and the lesser known Windscale accident in England. The possible health risks associated with living near nuclear power plants and the dilemma of waste disposal are also discussed. He traces the history of public opinion about nuclear power and the opposition, exploring how environmental, political, and economic factors all have an influence on the present and future success of the industry. Illustrated with color photographs, the book includes a glossary, an index, a short bibliography, and the names and addresses of several organizations to write for more information on nuclear issues. All of the organizations listed except one are against nuclear power.

■ Helgerson, Joel. NUCLEAR ACCIDENTS. Watts, 1988. 128pp. (0-531-10330-7) SERIES: An Impact Book. Nonfiction. Interest Level: Ages 12 up
Helgerson writes about nuclear power and the major nuclear accidents that have occurred. After explaining nuclear fission and the history and development of the nuclear power industry, he describes how nuclear reactors work. In separate chapters on two major accidents, Three Mile Island in the United States and Chernobyl in the Soviet Union, Helgerson describes why the accidents occured, how the plants were cleaned up, medical casualties, and world reaction. He writes in an objective style that contrasts with the catastrophes he describes. Other accidents are mentioned as well as some of the pros and cons of alternative sources of energy. Some of the issues surrounding the safety and use of nuclear energy are summarized at the conclusion along with the need for continued development of safety features in the nuclear power plant design, more careful training of operators, and planning for emergencies. No mention is made of energy conservation as a factor in the nuclear power issue. Pringle covers the issues more thoroughly, albeit with an anti-nuclear position in *Nuclear Energy* (Macmillan, 1989). The book includes notes, sources, further readings, an index and is illustrated with black-and-white photographs.

■ Hoban, Russell. ARTHUR'S NEW POWER. Illus. by Byron Barton. Harper, 1978. 40pp. (LB 0-690-01371-X) Fiction. Interest Level: Ages 6–9
What do crocodiles have to do with energy conservation? Crocodiles have everything to do with energy conservation in Russell Hoban's funny story. After blowing three fuses in one week from plugging in his "Dracula Hi-Vamp" Arthur, a young but hip crocodile, and his family realize they must do something. They decide to try living a bit less electrically. They unplug a lot of extra gadgets. By week's end Arthur has rigged up a generator at the stream behind the house. They all plug in again. Soon they blow the

generator too and come to the conclusion they can live without so much power. Hoban never gets "preachy" in this easy-to-read story that pokes fun at our passion for electrical gadgets.

■ **Keeler, Barbara. ENERGY ALTERNATIVES. Lucent Books, 1990. 112pp. (LB 1-56006-118-9)** SERIES: Our Endangered Planet. **Nonfiction. Interest Level: Ages 10–14**
Beginning with a brief history of our use and depletion of fossil fuels, Keeler discusses advantages and disadvantages of these and other energy sources, including nuclear energy, hydropower, solar energy, wind power, geothermal energy, and alternative biofuels. A final chapter on energy conservation recommends energy conservation measures for individuals. Keeler writes in a textbook style. She does not offer an analysis of political or economic factors influencing energy research and policy, but students reporting on current energy issues will find *Alternative Energy Sources* covers the major energy sources used or under consideration. Illustrated with black-and-white photographs, the book includes a glossary, an index, suggestions for further reading, and a list of energy related organizations.

■ **Kerrod, Robin. FUTURE ENERGY AND RESOURCES. Watts, 1990. 32pp. (LB 0-531-17221-X)** SERIES: Today's World. **Nonfiction. Interest Level: Ages 10–14**
Kerrod offers capsule summaries of current and potential energy and mineral resources in this 32-page addition to the Today's World series. Oversize, with colorful pictures and diagrams in a busy design, the series' purpose is to present, rather than analyze the pros and cons of various resources. Fossil fuels, nuclear energy, fusion, solar, wind, geothermal, and ocean energy resources are mentioned along with a brief look at mineral, ocean, and water resources. This overview is presented within the context of our dwindling resources and emphasizes the need to conserve and recycle. It includes a chart showing energy resources and consumption by continent in the late 1980s. A glossary and an index are included.

■ **Moeri, Louise. DOWNWIND. Dutton, 1984. 121pp. (0-525-44096-8) Fiction. Interest Level: Ages 11–14**
Not for the faint hearted, *Downwind* is an engrossing, frightening novel about a family's attempt to flee after an accident at a nuclear power plant. Set in southern California, the story's main character is 12-year-old Ephraim Dearborn, a clear-headed kid, who with his family, sets off on a frightening journey in their trailer away from the dangerous nuclear power plant. The story of their escape becomes a survival story as Ephraim's mother can't cope, his younger brother and sister are injured, and the

highways are jammed. People are panicked and become violent. As happened in the real accident in 1986 at Chernobyl, information is scarce. Conflicting reports from the media confuse and frighten people. Moeri's characterization and fast-moving plot will appeal to readers who like survival stories. The book will be useful in enriching a study of nuclear energy issues.

■ New Mexico People and Energy Collective. RED RIBBONS FOR EMMA. New Seed Pr., 1981. 48pp. (0-038678-07-8) Nonfiction. Interest Level: Ages 8–12
This is the story of Emma Yazzie, a Navajo woman in New Mexico, and her fight against the destruction of Navajo land by energy companies, power plants, and coal mines now operating. Emma, who herds sheep, and her Navajo neighbors live simply, without electricity on land near the coal mines. They resent the power lines, polluted air, and destruction of the land they live on. Emma has used both legal and subversive methods to fight the companies. The companies' presence is sanctioned by tribal leaders, who according to Emma, live in the cities, not on the land. The red ribbons of the title refer to red-flagged survey stakes Emma has defiantly pulled. The authors present her side of the story only, but this story reveals the striking clash of cultures, white and Navajo, as well as lack of agreement among the Navajos on the use of their land in a changing society. The text is illustrated with black-and-white photographs.

■ Petersen, David. SOLAR ENERGY AT WORK. Childrens, 1985. 48pp. (LB 0-516-01942-2) SERIES: New True. Nonfiction. Interest Level: Ages 6–9
Although this introduction to solar energy does not shine, it fills a need for energy information in the primary grades. Stressing that solar energy is not new, Petersen notes the renewed interest in this form of energy is stimulated by dwindling sources of gas, coal, and oil and the uncertain future of the nuclear power industry. Although he is correct in stating that solar energy is abundant, it is misleading to say that it is free. Current methods of collecting and using solar energy are relatively expensive. Petersen explains the difference between passive and active solar systems. He discusses aspects of solar energy—how it works in a greenhouse, how electricity is produced, and water heated. Several pages are devoted to the role of solar energy in the space program. The book includes a few simple experiments, large type, many colored photographs, a glossary, and an index.

■ Pringle, Laurence. NUCLEAR ENERGY: TROUBLED PAST, UNCERTAIN FUTURE. Macmillan, 1989 (rev. ed.). 124pp. (0-02-775391-3) Nonfiction. Interest Level: Ages 12 up

In this revision of his 1979 book on nuclear energy, Pringle presents a history of nuclear energy production and applications in the United States. He brings readers up-to-date on recent developments in the industry. Well-researched and written, Pringle's update approaches the topic from the anti-nuclear stand (the theme is the poor record of the industry), although he presents arguments on both sides. The role and failures of the Nuclear Regulatory Agency, safety issues, including chapters on Three Mile Island and Chernobyl, nuclear waste disposal, and prospects for the future are addressed. Illustrated with black-and-white photos, maps and charts the book includes a glossary, an index and a bibliography with books, pamphlets, and articles.

Award: OSTB, 1989

■ Rickard, Graham. THE CHERNOBYL CATASTROPHE. Bookwright, 1989. 32pp. (LB 0-531-18236-3) SERIES: Great Disasters. Nonfiction. Interest Level: Ages 9–12
When engineers carried out an experiment improperly at the nuclear power station in 1986 at Chernobyl, they caused the world's worst nuclear power plant accident. The accident killed 29 people. More than 135,000 people were evacuated from their homes within 19 miles of the plant; many will never return. Rickard recounts the events that led up to the explosion, the efforts to stop the fire, and worldwide reaction as tons of radioactive material were released into the atmosphere and drifted to Europe and Scandinavia. Some of the long-term effects of the disaster are mentioned, although the aftermath is greater than first realized. Illustrated with colored photographs, charts and a few garish drawings, this book will provide easy-to-read information on a high-interest topic. A glossary, an index and a list of names and addresses of anti-nuclear organizations are included.

Climate

■ Duden, Jane. THE OZONE LAYER. Crestwood, 1990. 48pp. (0-89686-546-0) SERIES: Earth Alert. Nonfiction. Interest Level: Ages 9–12
Duden clearly explains the role the ozone layer in blocking the sun's ultraviolet rays, and the effects of too much exposure to those rays: an increase in skin cancer, damage to human immune systems, loss of vision, disruption of the ocean food chain, and decreased food supply. She discusses the use of CFCs, developed in the 1920s, and how scientists learned of their role in the destruction of the ozone layer, and their contribution to the greenhouse effect. She covers international efforts to reduce production of CFCs and individual and organizational efforts to pressure companies producing CFCs.

Duden provides suggestions for children including a list of CFCs to avoid. Other suggestions include avoiding the use of polystyrene foam and writing to companies and legislators. She includes a brief list of organizations to contact and a list of specific pamphlets to request. The recommended reading is current and includes articles in children's magazines. An index is appended.

■ Facklam, Margery, and Howard Facklam. CHANGES IN THE WIND: EARTH'S SHIFTING CLIMATE. Diagrams by Paul Facklam. Harcourt, 1986. 128pp. (0-15-216115-5) Nonfiction. Interest Level: Ages 12 up
Good writing and a broad perspective make this older title on climate change worth keeping on the shelves. Veteran science writers Margery and Howard Facklam discuss natural forces that cause changes in climate such as the El Nino ocean current, ice ages, and volcanic activity, as well as the effect human activity has on both weather and climate. The greenhouse effect is discussed as well as a section covering the effects on climate of deforestation and desertification due to population pressures, and poor farming practices. The impact of nuclear power on climate is also included. Illustrated with black-and-white photographs and diagrams, the book includes a glossary and an index.

■ Gay, Kathlyn. THE GREENHOUSE EFFECT. Watts, 1986. 88pp. (LB 0-531-10154-1) SERIES: A Science Impact Book. Nonfiction. Interest Level: Ages 12 up
Despite its 1986 publication date and lack of colored photographs, Gay's balanced, well-researched, and thorough examination of the greenhouse effect should serve student researchers for a few more years. Gay explains the greenhouse effect and examines the continuing debate among scientists on global warming. She discusses the methods scientists use to study climate and the various computer-based systems used to predict the effects of increased greenhouse gases on climate, agriculture, water supplies, and human activity. Gay also discusses ice age theories, which introduces another factor in scientific speculation on climate change. Two final chapters are devoted to methods of reducing consumption of fossil fuels and both international and local efforts to conserve energy. Gay refers to research studies throughout the text. A list of books and articles (adult) is appended along with an index. Another of Gay's book to consult is *Ozone* (Watts, 1989).

■ Hare, Tony. THE OZONE LAYER. Watts, 1990. 32pp. (LB 0-531-17218-X) SERIES: Save Our Earth. Nonfiction. Interest Level: Ages 9–12
This oversize, colorful, encyclopedic overview of the ozone layer and chemicals that are destroying it is a part of a British series. The book is visually

appealing and has a high picture-text ratio, two-page spreads, each with charts, diagrams, and photographs. Hare offers suggestions for readers and includes addresses of organizations, such as the Acid Rain Foundation and Environmental Defense Fund. The appended "fact files" offer information that could have been integrated into the text. A glossary and an index are included. Other titles in the series include *The Greenhouse Effect, Acid Rain,* and *Rainforest Destruction.*

■ Harris, Jack C. THE GREENHOUSE EFFECT. Crestwood, 1990. 48pp. (LB 0-89686-543-6) SERIES: Earth Alert. Nonfiction. Interest Level: Ages 9-12
Harris' non-technical overview for younger readers on the greenhouse effect is well-organized and well-written. He stresses, more than other writers, that the greenhouse effect, or global warming, is a scientific theory. There is no consensus on global warming and it's possible effects. He details scientists' first awareness of the possibility of a greenhouse effect, the causes, predictions of the effect on climate, plants, animals, and people.

Actions to slow the effects of global warming are suggested, including reducing our dependence on fossil fuels (using cars less, saving energy, recycling, and the development of other technologies such as solar power), and tree planting. He also discusses the importance of environmental legislation and international cooperation. A final chapter suggests individual action plans that may help stop global warming. Illustrated with fine colored photos, the text includes a brief list of environmental organizations, a glossary, and an index.

■ Johnson, Rebecca L. THE GREENHOUSE EFFECT: LIFE ON A WARMER PLANET. Lerner, 1990. 112pp. (LB 0-8225-1591-1) Nonfiction. Interest Level: Ages 11 up
Johnson offers a detailed look at the greenhouse effect, a natural phenomenon that keeps Earth's atmosphere warm, and global warming, caused by relatively recent human interference in the environment. She discusses the increasing levels of carbon dioxide and other gases that are building up in the atmosphere. She explains how scientists have developed computer models to predict the effects of rising global temperatures, to describe predicted effects of climate change on precipitation, plant zones, and seasons. The author also discusses the potential impact of global warming on human society and the natural world.

A final chapter offers suggestions by scientists to reduce the amount of carbon dioxide released into the atmosphere through energy conservation, reforestation, and reducing our reliance on fossil fuels by finding alternative forms of renewable energy resources. Johnson stresses the global aspect of warming and the importance of nations working together to solve the problems. Excellent color photographs and diagrams illustrate this thorough, well-balanced account. The book includes a glossary and an index.

■ **Koral, April. OUR GLOBAL GREENHOUSE. Watts, 1989. 64pp. (LB 0-531-10745-0)** SERIES: A First Book. Nonfiction. Interest Level: Ages 10–14
Koral clearly explains the greenhouse effect and the predicted changes in climate and environment due to global warming. She emphasizes, for the younger reader, the reasons for the increase in greenhouse gases, caused by burning of fossil fuels, stem from changes in society, particularly since the Industrial Revolution. She acknowledges the differences in opinion among scientists regarding the kinds of changes that may occur and the solutions to the problem. Emphasis is given to international cooperation. Excellent colored photos illustrate the text, although the captions, bolded and in caps, are difficult to read and not always informative. Four rather simple projects, intended to add to readers' knowledge of the greenhouse effect, make up the final chapter. They do not add to the book's value. An index and a glossary are included.

■ **Peckham, Alexander. GLOBAL WARMING. Watts, 1991. 32pp. (LB 0-531-17274-0)** SERIES: Issues. Nonfiction. Interest Level: Ages 11–14
In this addition to Gloucester's "Issues" series, Peckham emphasizes the predicted consequences of global warming, providing specific examples—flooded coastlines, violent weather, droughts, disease, and extinction of species—and the impact of those changes on people and society—food and water shortages and political instability as nations compete for scarce resources. He points out the huge differences in energy use by industrialized countries and developing countries and the impact population growth has on land and energy use. These factors also increase the amount of carbon dioxide added to the air. Peckham stresses international cooperation in tackling the problem of global warming; he cites the findings and recommendations of the IPCC, an international committee of climate experts as well as some of the specific policies and actions that individuals, organizations, and nations have taken or are planning to take. Coverage is superficial but current. Peckham mentions the Chipco movement in India, the murder of Brazilian rubber tapper Chico Mendes, and the Center for Alternative Technology in Wales. Color photographs and diagrams illustrate this book, which is organized in two-page sections. An index is included.

■ **Pringle, Laurence. GLOBAL WARMING: ASSESSING THE GREENHOUSE THREAT. Little, 1990. 46pp. (1-55970-012-2)** Nonfiction. Interest Level: Ages 10–14

In his usual clear, readable style Pringle explains the greenhouse effect, the predicted effects of global warming, and actions that should be taken both to prepare for climate changes and to limit warming. Although he acknowledges the differences in opinion among scientists on the types of changes we may anticipate and the actions to take, he doesn't mince words: "The earth is getting warmer." Less detailed than Rebecca Johnson's or Kathlyn Gay's books on global warming, Pringle nevertheless covers the subject well. Design, choice, and quality of color photographs, diagrams, and organization make this book, which includes a glossary and an index stand out.

Award: OSTB, 1990

■ Stille, Darlene R. THE GREENHOUSE EFFECT. Childrens, 1990. 48pp. (LB 0-516-01106-5) SERIES: New True. Nonfiction. Interest Level: Ages 6–9

The large print and colorful photographs on coated paper make this book an attractive addition to the *New True* series for young readers. Stille explains how the earth's atmosphere helps trap heat that keeps the temperature warm, just as the glass in a greenhouse helps to retain warmth. She discusses human activities thought to add to the greenhouse effect, those changes global warming may cause, and how scientists think global warming can be slowed. The author acknowledges the differences of opinion among scientists. The book provides basic information for those seeking material for young readers.

■ Tesar, Jenny E. GLOBAL WARMING. Facts on File, 1991. 112pp. (0-8160-2490-1) SERIES: Our Fragile Planet. Nonfiction. Interest Level: Ages 12 up

Author Tesar examines several aspects of global warming in a well-organized and well-written book for upper level students. Beginning with the role of carbon dioxide in the atmosphere, Tesar looks at the many human activities that contribute to the greenhouse effect and the methods scientists use to make predictions. Further, the author discusses predicted effects of climate change and the adaptations that may be necessary with global warming. Tesar devotes chapters to the hole in the ozone layer, energy conservation, and the kinds of actions that must be taken to slow a warming trend. *Global Warming* includes an up-to-date bibliography that includes a list of magazines and other publications that regularly cover issues associated with global warming. A directory of several government and private organizations concerned with environmental issues is also included. Black-and-white photographs, (two sections of full-color photos have been inserted also), a glossary and an index enhance the book.

Population and Food Supply

■ Aaseng, Nathan. ENDING WORLD HUNGER. Watts, 1991. 143pp. (LB 0-531-11007-9) SERIES: Science, Technology & Society. Nonfiction. Interest Level: Ages 14 up
This well-researched and timely examination of world hunger is a good source of information for upper level students. Aaseng examines the numerous interrelated causes of world hunger. He shows how such things as loss of arable land, water shortages, overpopulation, natural disasters, modern farming methods, war, national and international policies all affect the production and distribution of food. Readers will learn how science, technology, values, and policies all play a part in treatment of the environment. The impact on the food supply and the ultimate effect on people's lives is explored. A case study of the Ethiopian famine, the pros and cons of improved food technology, and prospects for the future are discussed. Aaseng argues for sustainable production and concludes that we can end world hunger. The author asserts that we need only to decide to end it. Readers may also find Aaseng's related *Overpopulation* (Watts, 1991) in the Science, Technology & Society series useful. The book includes source notes, a bibliography, and an index. Black-and-white photographs are used.

■ Becklake, John, and Sue Becklake. THE POPULATION EXPLOSION. Watts, 1990. 36pp. (LB 0-531-17198-1) SERIES: Green Issues. Nonfiction. Interest Level: Ages 10 up
This brief but well-organized overview of population growth and the associated problems has an urgent tone. The Becklakes trace the history of population growth and explain the differing rates of growth in industrialized and developing countries. Pressures on our natural resources because of increased need for energy and food, pollution, and problems of the green revolution are discussed. Family planning, other population control measures, the importance of health care and health education, particularly in the developing countries, are also discussed. The Becklakes suggest several possible consequences of uncontrolled population growth: famine, pollution, plagues, or wars over remaining resources. An up-to-date resource for student researchers, this book is illustrated with attractive color photographs and charts. The captions do not relate specifically enough to the text. A glossary and an index are included. *Food and Farming* (Gloucester, 1990), another title in the *Green Issues* series, examines the issues of food production in relationship to the world's growing population.

■ Dolan, Edward F. DROUGHT: THE PAST, PRESENT, AND FUTURE ENEMY. Watts, 1990. 144pp. (LB 0-531-10900-3) Nonfiction. Interest Level: Ages 11 up
Dolan looks at the forces, especially natural forces, that trigger droughts throughout the world. Several chapters are devoted to the effect of wind, lack of rain, atmospheric pressure, and ocean currents on drought. The cyclical nature of droughts are discussed with both current and historical examples. In the chapter discussing the Dust Bowl, Dolan blames both natural and human events, drought years, and increased farming on the Great Plains that led to loss of soil. These conditions created a major economic disaster for the nation. Strategies to prevent drought in the United States are discussed including soil conservation, irrigation projects, planting of windbreaks, development of new strains of wheat and corn, and weather modification. In the final chapters the author discusses future threats including pollution, global cooling and warming. He says the need to reduce pollution worldwide, prevent global warming, slow deforestation, and conserve water is critical. Source notes, bibliography and an index are included. Black-and-white photographs illustrate the text.

■ Fine, John Christopher. THE HUNGER ROAD. Macmillan, 1988. 148pp. (0-689-31361-6) Nonfiction. Interest Level: Ages 12 up
In *The Hunger Road,* Fine discusses many elements that contribute to hunger and starvation: population, pollution, destruction of habitats, depletion of the food supply by overfarming and other poor land use decisions, war, greed, corruption, and abuse of natural resources. But, the heart of this book is Fine's observations on the grim, horrifying conditions of hunger and starvation in countries where he has traveled as a relief volunteer and has investigated famine relief programs. Fine establishes a strong link between starvation and war, revolution, corrupt governments, and corrupt people. He chronicles many examples of inadequate food relief programs that do not reach the people in need. He emphasizes the importance of long range projects to ensure education, health, and a reliable food supply. Separate chapters on Cambodia, Ethiopia, the Congo, The Sahel, Asia, Egypt, the Middle East, Latin America, and the United States include historical background. A helpful bibliography for students researching world hunger is included. The book is illustrated with black-and-white photographs.

■ Fradin, Dennis B. FAMINES. Childrens, 1986. 64pp. (LB 0-516-00859-5) SERIES: Disaster! Nonfiction. Interest Level: Ages 10 up
In a world so rich with resources, it is difficult to comprehend the fact that "hunger is an ordinary part of life for a half a billion people" and that "15

million children die annually as a result of malnutrition and diseases."
When a serious shortage of food results from drought, floods, plant disease,
or war; famine occurs and millions of people's lives are threatened. Concen-
trating on famine in Africa in the 1980s, Fradin presents sober, heartrend-
ing stories told by relief workers in Africa in the 1980s. He discusses the
causes and effects of famine, highlights several major famines, and signals
that predict and may prevent famines. Among the recommendations discussed are reducing population growth (famine-prone countries are among
the poorest and most populous), developing more irrigation projects, im-
proving farming methods, and soil conservation. A glossary and an index are
included. Both color and black-and-white photographs illustrate the text.

■ Gallant, Roy A. THE PEOPLING OF PLANET EARTH: HUMAN POPU-
LATION GROWTH THROUGH THE AGES. Macmillan, 1990. 163pp.
(0-02-735772-4) Nonfiction. Interest Level: Ages 12 up
While most books on population have a contemporary focus, author Roy
Gallant's multi-faceted look at human population growth throughout history will help readers better understand and evaluate current population
issues. He begins with the origin of life on earth and traces both human
evolution and population demographics. He includes both creation theories
and scientific theories on the origin of human life. He examines the historical impact on population of the move from hunter-gatherer to farmer, the
rise of cities, industrialization, disease, famine, and medicine. This discussion sets the stage for chapters on population growth rates and the question
of the earth's "carrying capacity." A final chapter on population and quality
of life addresses the environmental impact of the increasing population and
population control. Well-researched and written, this broad look at population growth will serve upper level students well. The book includes a glossary, an index and a bibliography. The text is illustrated with black-and-
white photographs, charts, and maps.

Award: OSTB, 1990

■ Knapp, Brian. DROUGHT. Steck-Vaughn, 1990. 48pp. (LB 0-8114-
2376-X) SERIES: World Disasters! Nonfiction. Interest Level: Ages 10–14
Knapp's overview of the causes and effects of drought begins with descriptions of droughts in America and Europe, but much of the focus of this book
is on the drought-prone developing countries (India, Ethiopia, Kenya)
where poverty and over-populations increase the problems. Knapp discusses economic, political, and environmental influences on droughts, and
relief efforts. He surveys the methods that can be used to prevent droughts.
Modern farming methods, irrigation projects, resevoirs, conservation, and

changing lifestyles are discussed. Good photographs and an appealing layout is marred by the lack of specific country identifications in the captions. A glossary and an index are included.

■ **Lee, Jeanne M.**, retold by. **TOAD IS THE UNCLE OF HEAVEN: A VIETNAMESE FOLK TALE.** Illus. by reteller. Holt, 1985. Unp. (0-8050-1146-3) Fiction. Interest Level: Ages 4–10
The devastating effect of a drought drives Toad to journey to the King of Heaven to ask for rain. He is joined by a swarm of bees, a rooster, and a tiger, who are also suffering greatly. The King does not take kindly to Toad and sets his guards, the Thunder God, and the Hound of Heaven upon him. Toad is rescued by his friends and earns the respect of the King who tells him that when he needs rain, not to come all the way to heaven, but to signal with a croak. That way, the King of Heaven will know to send rain. This pourquois story from Vietnam, like *The Name of the Tree* (Macmillan, 1989) reminds us of the close connection to the natural world people had long ago. Classes studying ecology or drought will find this a useful supplement. Lee uses intense colors and a flat, stylized design.

■ **Lottridge, Celia Barker**, retold by. **THE NAME OF THE TREE: A BANTU FOLKTALE.** Illus. by Ian Wallace. Macmillan, 1989. Unp. (LB 0-689-50490-X) Fiction. Interest Level: Ages 5–10
Set on the drought-stricken African savanna, this Bantu folktale tells the story of hungry animals trying to survive on the parched landscape. Searching far and wide for food, they find nothing until they come upon a strange fruit laden tree rising like a mirage in the middle of the plain. But, the branches are high and the animals are despondent because they are so hungry and cannot reach the fruit. At last the old tortoise tells them that only when they go to the king of the jungle and learn the name of the tree will they be able to reach the fruit. First the quick gazelle goes to the lion king who tells her its name. But, by the time the gazelle returns, she has forgotten it. Next the elephant trudges off to the lion, but he too forgets. Finally the young tortoise, slow but determined, learns the name from the lion and returns to share his knowledge with the others. Full-page illustrations in muted colors suggest the parched landscape and unrelenting sun. Drought is not new to Africa; *The Name of the Tree* will enrich the knowledge of classes studying about drought and the hardships it causes.

■ **McGraw, Eric. POPULATION GROWTH.** Rourke, 1987. 46pp. (0-86592-276-4) SERIES: World Issues. Nonfiction. Interest Level: Ages 10–14
McGraw's discussion of worldwide population growth, although now slightly dated, is a good resource for middle and upper level students

studying population issues. He briefly discusses the history of population growth since the eighteenth century, noting that achievements in agriculture, industry, transportation, and medicine have enabled us to sustain ever larger numbers of people on earth. He surveys growth trends around the world using China, India, Kenya, Mexico City, and Europe as examples. In McGraw's view a major problem is that "numbers are increasing most rapidly in the developing counties, often those nations least equipped in terms of social and economic resources to absorb vast numbers of additional people." Problems associated with increased demand for food—loss of agricultural land because of overgrazing, urbanization, and other pressures on the land—are addressed as is the role of education in maintaining health, family planning, and the difficulty of earning a means of living in overcrowded, developing countries. In a final chapter McGraw refers to the 1984 United Nations World Population Conference, which included proposals to coordinate population development, environment programs, and increase financial support for population control activities. Charts, color, and black-and-white photographs add to the appeal, but unattributed quotations inset throughout the text are less helpful. A glossary and an index are included.

■ **Timberlake, Lloyd. FAMINE IN AFRICA. Watts, 1986. 32pp. (LB 0-531-17017-9)** SERIES: **Issues. Nonfiction. Interest Level: Ages 10 up**
Timberlake makes the point that "while nature triggers famine, it does not create it. People do that." He maintains that in countries where the balance between population and the country's ability to feed itself is already precarious, famines are likely to occur. Focusing on several African countries, he examines the causes of famine—overgrazing, deforestation, desertification, over-dependence on cash crops, and development of industry and cities at the expense of agriculture. In looking at relief efforts, which are often sabotaged or mismanaged, and development aid, he is critical of some of the development aid projects, but maintains that "if development aid was spent wisely, emergency relief aid might not be needed." This is a brief but thought-provoking look at a multifaceted issue; it will be useful for research and reports. Excellent photographs include faces of hunger, land under drought conditions, and a few hopeful projects.

■ **Versfield, Ruth. WHY ARE PEOPLE HUNGRY? Watts, 1988 (LB 0-531-17082-9)** SERIES: **Let's Talk About. Nonfiction. Interest Level: Ages 6–10**
This book provides a good introduction to the problem of world hunger for the primary grades. *Why Are People Hungry?* answers nine questions about hunger and the food supply. Versfield, a teacher employed by the relief agency Oxfam, covers the subject well using simple language and an objective approach to a devastating issue. Poverty, growing populations, poor

land conditions, and war are cited as reasons for hunger. Versfield also discusses the politics and economics of hunger. While world food production is sufficient to feed everyone, she says, "the main reason why all the world's food can't get around to everyone is always the same. Food is only sold to those who can pay for it." The text includes a map indicating areas where the highest numbers of people suffer from malnutrition. A glossary, an index and a list of three hunger relief organizations are appended. The book is illustrated with color photographs.

■ **Winckler, Suzanne, and Mary M. Rodgers. OUR ENDANGERED PLANET: POPULATION GROWTH. Lerner, 1991. 64pp. (LB 0-8225-2502-X) Nonfiction. Interest Level: Ages 10–14**
With clear writing, good examples, and an appealing layout, the authors do a fine job of condensing a lot of information on population growth and the environmental problems caused by "more people using more resources." They show how famine, dwindling non-renewable resources, depletion of the ozone layer, deforestation, desertification, and extinction of species are all related to population pressures and affluent lifestyles. They also point out that populations of Third World countries are increasing at a faster rate that those of developed nations, resulting in severe strains on the people and resources in those countries. They discuss various methods used to control population growth around the world, including contraception, abortion, China's one-child program, and family planning in India. The text stresses the importance of family planning education and respect for cultural differences regarding family size. They remind readers of a shared responsibility for keeping our planet liveable: "People who live in the developed nations of the world use a huge share of the earth's resources. Their impact on the earth is at least 10 times greater than the effect of people living in the Third World." This is a condensed but informative look at interrelated environmental issues. The book includes a glossary, a list of organizations concerned with population, and an index.

■ **Xiong, Blia. NINE-IN-ONE GRR! GRR! Adapted by Cathy Spagnoli. Illus. by Nancy Hom. Children's, 1989. 32pp. (LB 0-89239-048-4) Fiction. Interest Level: Ages 4–10**
In this folktale from Laos, Tiger is promised by the great god, Shao, that she will have nine cubs a year, but only if she remembers that number. When the black Eu bird learns of this, she is upset. "That's terrible! If Tiger has nine cubs each year, they will eat all of us. Soon there will be nothing but tigers in the land." So she tricks Tiger into thinking she will have not nine cubs in one year but one cub in nine years, thus saving the world from an overabundance of tigers. The tale shows that people have long had an

understanding of the importance of the balance of nature. Classes studying ecology as well as population issues will find this an enriching supplement. Colorful silkscreen illustrations executed in the style of Hmong embroidery story cloths add to the appeal of the book.

Animal Rights

■ Ames, Mildred. WHO WILL SPEAK FOR THE LAMB? Harper, 1989. 216pp. (LB 0-06-020112-6) Fiction. Interest Level: Ages 12 up
In Mildred Ames' out-of-print *Philo Potts* (Scribner, 1982), she writes about mistreated and stray dogs and two schoolmates who rescue them. In *Who Will Speak for the Lamb?* Ames writes more pointedly about the subject of animal exploitation. This story, for slightly older readers, concerns the use of animals for school lab experiments and the use of animals for research. It begins with a graphic description of a lamb being slaughtered during a high school science class and the demonstration at the high school against this incident. The plot revolves around former 17-year-old model Julie, who may have been exploited as well, and her growing friendship with Jeff. Jeff's family is active in an animal rights organization. Julie's father conducts abusive experiments using animals in his psychology laboratory. Readers may enjoy the glamour of Julie's career and the budding romance. They may find the animal rights theme enlightening—or too controversial.

■ Bloyd, Sunni. ANIMAL RIGHTS. Lucent Books, 1990. 128pp. (LB 1-56006-114-6) SERIES: Overview. Nonfiction. Interest Level: Ages 12 up
This is an up-to-date, well-balanced overview of animal rights. *Animal Rights* is organized in much the same way as Pringle's and Dolan's books on the same subject. Bloyd discusses the history of attitudes toward and treatment of animals, the development of humane societies, and the development of animal rights organizations. Like Pringle, she begins with a philosophical discussion of the question of animal rights before devoting separate chapters to animals used in research, classrooms, agribusiness, the fur and pet industry, hunting, and trapping. She suggests ways readers can be involved, noting that animal rights begins at home with the humane treatment of pets. Black-and-white photographs tone down the gruesomeness of some of the examples. Bloyd includes a glossary and an index, a list of organizations, sources, and suggested fiction and non-fiction books for further information.

■ Curtis, Patricia. ANIMAL RIGHTS: STORIES OF PEOPLE WHO DEFEND THE RIGHTS OF ANIMALS. Macmillan, 1980. 148pp. (0-590-07650-7) Nonfiction. Interest Level: Ages 11 up

Seven people talk about their involvement in animal rights issues. Curtis chose to use fictional characters who represent various concerns: a student who protested dissecting frogs in biology class; a veterinarian who discusses factory farming; two young men who call attention to the plight of whales; a lawyer who helps enforce animal welfare laws for a humane organization and others. The technique is effective and these first person accounts will hold reader interest while they raise awareness of issues concerning treatment of animals. They also offer students ideas for career paths. Cutis ends with a brief history of treatment of animals. A reading list and addresses of humane organizations are appended.

■ Curtis, Patricia. ANIMALS AND THE NEW ZOOS. Dutton, 1991. 60pp. (0-525-67457-4) Nonfiction. Interest Level: Ages 10 up
Animal rights defender Patricia Curtis looks at the changing role of zoos from little more than "freak shows" to institutions that educate the public on wildlife and that more and more often take excellent care of their animals. The improved zoos work to protect and preserve endangered species. Curtis aims to "make zoo goers more critical and appreciative of the role of zoos." Rather than focus on any one zoo, Curtis looks at animals from five basic habitats: grasslands, deserts, tropical rain forests, woodlands, and tundras. The author describes how "new" zoos try to recreate conditions close to each animal's natural habitat. She concludes with a list of things to look for when visiting a zoo and a list of exemplary zoos to visit throughout the United States. The book is illustrated with both color and black-and-white photographs in a pleasing format. An index is included.

■ Dickinson, Peter. EVA. Delacorte, 1989. 219pp. (LB 0-385-29702-5) Fiction. Interest Level: Ages 12 up
Thirteen-year-old Eva wakes up from a coma after a serious car accident only to discover that her brain has been transplanted into the body of a chimpanzee. So begins this futuristic novel that considers not only the ethics of the transplant but also what it is to be human (and chimpanzee), humanity's relationship with animals, and the rights of animals. Dickinson writes compellingly of Eva's thoughts and feelings as she slowly discovers what has happened to her and her transformation from Eva the girl to Eva, part human, part chimp. Dickinson also explores the theme of exploitation, for Eva lives on an overpopulated and exploited Earth. Natural resources have been depleted; many species are extinct and there is little wilderness remaining. Chimpanzees, however, are bred and used for experiments. Once Eva's transformation is made public, she is exploited in new ways until she eventually finds her way to a remote island with other chimps where she lives out her life as a chimp. *Eva* is an unsettling book and best used with

mature, good readers. For a much simpler look at animal rights in a novel, choose *Castaways on Chimp Island* by Landsman (Macmillan, 1986).

Award: ALA Notable Children's Book, 1989

■ **Dolan, Edward F., Jr. ANIMAL RIGHTS. Watts, 1986. 144pp. (LB 0-531-10247-5) Nonfiction. Interest Level: Ages 12 up**
Dolan briefly traces the history of animal treatment and the development of the animal rights movement. He covers the same issues Laurence Pringle explores in *The Animal Rights Controversy* (Harcourt, 1989) including animals used in research, factory farming, commercial hunting and trapping, sport hunting, and animals in zoos and rodeos. But Dolan is less interested in presenting the philosophical issues of the treatment of animals; clearly he's interested in exploring more humane ways of treating animals in all areas discussed. He encourages readers to become active in organizations that work to protect animals and their rights. A list of 25 national organizations and their goals is appended. An index is included. The book is illustrated with black-and-white photos, some showing suffering animals.

■ **Keller, Beverly. FOWL PLAY DESDEMONA. Lothrop, 1989. 183pp. (LB 0-688-06920-7) Fiction. Interest Level: Ages 9–12**
Light-hearted treatment of animal rights? In Beverly Keller's hands, it works. Without moralizing, Keller lets her characters act out their beliefs in what turns into a series of comic mishaps. Desdemona, at a new school, gets roped into helping design posters for the junior high production of *The King and I.* She doesn't question her friend Sherman when he volunteers to help, but soon discovers that Sherman, who is a vegetarian, has painted animal rights messages on the backs of all the posters, such as "Thanksgiving's No Treat / For the Bird That You Eat" and plans to get double use out of them when they are distributed around town just before Thanksgiving. Soon Desdemona is caught up in the issue. After reading literature from the animal rights organization *People for the Ethical Treatment of Animals,* she decides to become a vegetarian. She and Sherman liberate two ducks slated for a family dinner and get involved in other escapades. While this is not strong enough fare to convert readers to vegetarianism, it informs them of another point of view, and offers a good read.

■ **Landsman, Sandy. CASTAWAYS ON CHIMP ISLAND. Macmillan, 1986. 203pp. (0-689-31214-8) Fiction. Interest Level: Ages 10 up**
An intelligent laboratory chimp outsmarts himself when he inadvertently convinces scientists that chimps can't communicate with humans through

sign language. This results in an end to research funding and his banishment to an island where he and other lab chimps are to be trained to live in the wild. Told from the point of view of the chimp, Danny, Landsman writes a humorous but poignant tale of their desperate attempts to get themselves off the island and back to the comforts of civilization they depend on. Landsman's chimps have distinct personalities and they don't all get along together on the island. They even ostracize one chimp who can't sign very well, only to discover later that he learned to communicate using a typewriter. In spite of the zany plot antics, readers will sympathize with Danny, his companions, and their predicament. *Castaways on Chimp Island* could be used in a discussion of animal rights and our responsibility toward the animals we use in research.

■ **Pringle, Laurence. THE ANIMAL RIGHTS CONTROVERSY. Harcourt, 1989. 103pp. (0-15-203559-1) Nonfiction. Interest Level: Ages 12 up**
Pringle tackles the controversial subject of animal rights with balance, while aiming to get readers to think about the ethical issues surrounding our treatment of animals. He first asks: "Do animals have rights?; Are we morally obliged to respect their lives and to ensure their well-being?; To what extent can we use animals for scientific research or for food?." He outlines the history of attitudes toward animals and the development of the animal rights movement. Separate chapters on the treatment of animals in the livestock industry and animals used for research spell out the issues and conflicts between animal rights activists and scientists. Black-and-white photographs include some graphic pictures of suffering animals. A final chapter deals with other animal rights issues—zoos, circuses, rodeos, racetracks, hunting, and trapping. An extensive list of books and articles and a list of 13 organizations involved in animal rights issues is appended. An index is included.

Awards: NSSB, 1989; OSTB, 1989

■ **Taylor, Theodore. THE HOSTAGE. Dell, 1991 (repr. of 1988 ed.). 176pp. (paper 0-440-20923-4) Fiction. Interest Level: Ages 10 up**
Fourteen-year-old Jamie Tidd and his family live in a remote fishing village near Vancouver, British Columbia. It is not easy to make a living, so when they learn that a marine park in the United States is willing to pay $100,000 for a killer whale captured live, they start dreaming of a better life. Jamie and his dad eventually capture one of the huge whales that frequents their fishing waters by luring it into a small cove. They soon find themselves embroiled in an environmental controversy, however. Greenpeace, other environmental groups, and even Jamie's friend, Angie, protest the keeping

of whales in captivity for exhibition. In the end their hopes for fortune slip away when the marine park backs down from the negative publicity and the "hostage" whale is freed. Abundant information about the killer whale and representation of the fishermen's point of view give this story balance.

■ **Thomas, Jane Resh. FOX IN A TRAP. Illus. by Troy Howell. Clarion, 1987. 78pp. (0-89919-473-7) Fiction. Interest Level: Ages 9–12**
In this sequel to *The Come-back Dog* (Houghton, 1981), Daniel, a farm boy, idolizes his dashing uncle who escaped the life of the farm and now travels and writes for a sporting magazine. Uncle Pete is a knowledgeable hunter and trapper. He has promised to show Daniel how to trap foxes on the farm. Thomas captures the inner turmoil young Daniel experiences as he sorts out his conflicting feelings toward farming, his father who doesn't trap, and trapping itself, which to him represents some of the excitement of his uncle's lifestyle. Astute readers will predict the outcome of the plot in which Daniel realizes trapping isn't for him and all conflicts are neatly tied up at the end. Thomas doesn't moralize, although she graphically describes what happens when a fox's foot gets caught in a trap. There is no anti-hunting message; in the final chapter Daniel and his father talk about hunting deer. *Fox in a Trap* will certainly stimulate discussion on the treatment of animals and may be a good supplementary source for classes studying animal rights issues.

People and Nature

Sometimes we need to step back and contemplate the big picture. Who are we and what is our place in this world? Books in Chapter Four focus on people's relationships with and attitudes toward the environment. In *Natural History*, M.B. Goffstein conveys a sense of beauty and purpose in the natural world while reminding readers of their responsibility to care for and protect all living things. Patricia Lauber's stunning photographs in *Seeing Earth from Space* remind readers of both the magnificence and fragility of our planet.

Our attitude toward the land affects how we use it. Current interest in Native American views of their relationship to the earth suggested the *People and the Land* section. The chapter includes some books by Native Americans, such as Edward Benton-Benai's *The Mishomis Book*, an important work that explains Ojibway history and beliefs; and Gary McLain's *The Indian Way*, which, through recollected stories, illustrates Native American respect for the earth. Other views round out this section. Barbara Cooney's *Island Boy* demonstrates the deep love of family and land by an early American settler. Contemporary farmers in Betsy Imershiem's *Farmer* along with George Ancona's and Joan Anderson's *The American Family Farm* demonstrate a relationship and respect for the land.

One theme that appears again and again in environmental literature is the alarming rate at which humanity is changing and harming the earth. Change is natural and inevitable; it is the unprecedented rate of change that worries environmentalists. Can the earth recover? In *The Changing Landscape* authors explore change from a variety of perspectives. Virginia Lee Burton's classic, *The Little House*, and Jeannie Baker's *Window* chronicle urbanization, while John Chiasson's moving *African Journey* documents changes to people and land in six regions of Africa. In Nadia Wheatley's *My Place*, readers travel from present to past to understand the changes in Australia over 200 years.

Reading about people who have helped protect or preserve habitat or have added to our knowledge about the environment helps children see the many ways people can positively affect the environment. Biographies offer a taste of hope. Johnny Appleseed sits with Rachel Carson, John Muir, Henry David Thoreau, and John Cronin, riverkeeper of New York's Hudson River, at this environmental dinner table.

Our Earth, Our Home

■ Allen, Thomas B. WHERE CHILDREN LIVE. Illus. by author. Prentice, 1980. Unp. (0-13-957126-4) Nonfiction. Interest Level: Ages 8 up
One aim of environmental education is to encourage the development of a global view of the world. If children grow up understanding that they live in a world community, they may begin to see the interdependence of life on Earth. In *Where Children Live*, Thomas B. Allen tries to encourage that concept. He says his aim was to "dramatize the notion that, no matter how dissimilar the conditions, which govern the lifestyles of people, there is a unifying force . . . which is always so evident in children."

Where Children Live is a series of portraits in colored pencil and oils of 13 children from different countries. The children are shown in or outside their homes and an adjacent illustration reveals another view of their home or environment. The very brief text tells the reader a little about each child. Despite the differences in environments-climate, land, means of making a living, and customs, the children have alot in common. They share the need for home, family, food, and play. Allen's portraits also reveal the children's relationship to their environments. Each child appears wonderfully part of his or her place on Earth.

Award: NSSB, 1980

■ Ekker, Ernst A. WHAT IS BEYOND THE HILL? Illus. by Hilde Heyduck-Huck. Harper, 1986. Unp. (LB 0-397-32167-8) Fiction. Interest Level: Ages 2–8
Ekker and Heyduck-Huth take young readers on a journey through the vastness of the universe in this simply executed picture book on a complex subject. As a young boy and girl look over a fence, they seem to ask, "What is beyond the hill? Does the world stop there?" As each succeeding page is turned, the reader sees farther and farther into the distance, beyond hills and mountains and finally, to the stars, "and another star and another star . . . and another star and still another star. And the stars go on forever." The large two-page spreads are done in soft, muted watercolors showing vistas of hills and mountains that move further away from civilization until they reach the stars.

■ Frasier, Debra. ON THE DAY YOU WERE BORN. Illus. by author. Harcourt, 1991. Unp. (LB 0-15-257995-8) Fiction. Interest Level: Ages 4–9
Celebration of life and reverence for the natural world combine in this unique picture book that describes all the things that happen on the eve and day of a child's birth. Although this child seems to exist at the center of the universe, Frasier conveys the interrelatedness of all things as well. Animals migrate, gravity pulls, the sun shines, the moon glows, the North Star glitters, and air rushes in and blows about protecting "you and all living things on Earth." Frasier's warm prose welcomes the child to the Earth and gives children a mini-science lesson too. A five-page epilogue with small-sized pictures from the book describes in more detail concepts and phenomena mentioned in the text: migration, gravity, sun, moon, rain, tides and stars. Frasier's paper collage illustrations are banner-like with warm colors. A cut-out child appears in most spreads in various hues of buff, brown, black, or red. This is a fine book to celebrate a birthday or even Earth Day!

■ Goffstein, M.B. NATURAL HISTORY. Illus. by author. Farrar, 1979. Unp. (0-374-35498-7) Fiction. Interest Level: All ages
Goffstein's strength lies in simplicity and her ability to condense big ideas into small, child-size formats. In *Natural History* she paints a picture of earth where "tiny grains of sand keep the powerful waters from flooding lands where trees grow skyward." With just a few words and telling images she conveys the richness, interdependence, and problems of life on our planet. She gently tells the reader that we have a responsibility to care for and protect all life. "Every living creature is our brother and our sister . . .", she says. "So let us be like tiny grains of sand, and protect all life from fear and suffering!" This is gentle encouragement to small children and adults who may often feel powerless. The illustrations are executed in her familiar small size. Each page of *Natural History* features a small rectangular picture framed with ample white space. The line drawings are washed with soft colors. Bijou Le Tord's creation story, *The Deep Blue Sea* (Orchard, 1990), is kindred in spirit to this book, without any specific call to care for the earth.

■ Goffstein, M.B. THE SCHOOL OF NAMES. Illus. by author. Harper, 1986. Unp. (0-06-021984-X) Nonfiction. Interest Level: Ages 4 up
Respect for the earth and all that's in it is subtly expressed in *The School of Names*. It provides a unique starting point from which to view our world and think about our place in it. The jacket notes refer to the age-old belief that if you possess an object's true name, you hold its spirit. Like a young child full of enthusiasm and curiosity, the narrator wants to go to "the School of Names" to learn about everything on earth and in the universe. "I want to know / what's in the ocean, / every school of fish, / every watery

motion by name." Softly colored and defined pastel drawings of rocks, trees, islands, rivers, and horses illustrate each page in this small book about a person who earnestly wishes to be at one with the world.

■ **Hirst, Robin, and Sally Hirst. MY PLACE IN SPACE. Illus. by Roland Harvey and Joe Levine. Orchard, 1988. Unp. (LB 0-531-08459-0) Nonfiction. Interest Level: Ages 8 up**
As they board a bus to go home, Henry and his sister are asked by a mean-spirited bus driver if they're sure they know where they live. "Yes, I do," replies Henry and so begins a clever astronomy lesson about "my place in space." The rest of the book is Henry's long-winded answer placing him and his sister outside a small Australian town, in the Southern Hemisphere, on Earth, in the solar system, and the universe. The illustrations combine detailed pictures of the Earth, the planets, stars, and the solar system on the upper half of each page with cartoonish pictures of the very odd little town (with a "Five Star Hotel" a "Galaxy Restaurant," and "Black Hole Disco") and its inhabitants (some comical, some murderous, others alien). The book creates a lesson on our niche in the universe that will appeal to older children and their parents, especially those who appreciate the bizarre. This book presents a cosmic, and perhaps far-fetched, way of teaching children to think about their place, not only in the big picture of space, but also in the smaller niches or communities they are part of.

■ **Jaspersohn, William. HOW THE UNIVERSE BEGAN. Illus. by Anthony Accardo. Watts, 1985. 48pp. (LB 0-531-10032-4) Nonfiction. Interest Level: Ages 8–10**
Environmentalists alert us to the quickness with which people alter the face and health of our planet. Children reading *How the Universe Began*, or its companion book, *How Life on Earth Began* (Watts, 1985), may see the very different pace creation of the universe took and the comparatively slow process of evolution. In this 48 page picture book Jaspersohn presents the "big bang" theory covering twenty billion years of history that culminated in the formation of the universe and our solar system where "only one planet, Earth, has the air and water and warmth for things to live." Jaspersohn's simple prose and black-and-white illustrations capture this broadest of subjects in a readable style for children in the early elementary grades.

■ **Lauber, Patricia. SEEING EARTH FROM SPACE. Illus. with photos. Orchard, 1990. 80pp. (LB 0-531-08502-3) Nonfiction. Interest Level: Ages 9 up**
Lauber's stunning book allows readers to step back and see the Earth from a new perspective. Remarkable color photographs taken by astronauts, photos from satellites using infrared sensors, and radar images all provide

new and valuable information that help scientists to better understand our home in space. *Seeing Earth from Space* demonstrates the interdisciplinary study of our environment. Biologists use satellites to track wildlife to understand how human activities affect it; climatologists interested in global climate change use satellite images to record temperature changes in polar lands and ice; scientists also use satellite images to study the upper atmosphere and learn about the hole in the ozone layer. And, Lauber says, many astronauts who have seen earth from space return with a sense of earth's beauty and fragility.

Many photographs require interpretation, which Lauber provides in her essay. However, captions would have been helpful, especially in the section that includes infrared and radar images. The book includes a glossary, a list of books for further reading, and an index.

Award: ALA Notable Children's Book, 1990

■ **Le Tord, Bijou. THE DEEP BLUE SEA. Illus. by author. Orchard, 1990. Unp. (LB 0-531-08453-1) Nonfiction. Interest Level: Ages 4-9**
Bijou LeTord's beautifully conceived story is a poetic and moving interpretation of creation that celebrates the interdependence of all living things. There is a sense of peace and harmony in this world. Everything has its place and purpose. "He let the streams and rivers flow for birds to nest in cattails, for ducks to swim in ponds, and for little frogs to hop on lily pads." He made "coyotes for the desert, snakes for dust and sand." Le Tord's masculine, but unseen, God made man and woman "to love each other and their children and their families." With simple text and lovely watercolor illustrations, Le Tord's optimistic view of the world is a welcome gift that allows readers a moment to reflect, dream, and appreciate the beauty of Earth.

■ **Livingston, Myra Cohn. EARTH SONGS. Illus. by Leonard Everett Fisher. Holiday, 1986. Unp. (LB 0-8324-0615-6) Nonfiction. Interest Level: Ages 8-12**
Earth sings of itself in Livingston's *Earth Songs*. She launches the poem with a reference from Shakespeare, "The little O, the earth," and returns to it at the end where little "O" is transformed to "Big O, great planet, spinning in space . . ." On the way Earth describes itself, its continents, mountains, forests, deserts, and core with energy, inviting readers to follow, roam, and explore.

Fisher's intense, abstract paintings on two-page spreads bleed off the page suggesting the energy and magnificence of the earth. Livingston and Fisher also collaborated on *Sea Songs* (Holiday, 1986) and *Sky Songs*

(Holiday, 1984). The trilogy is an effective tool with which to introduce the wonders of earth.

■ **Scarry, Huck. OUR EARTH. Illus. by author. Simon & Schuster, 1984. 106pp. (0-671-49846-0) Nonfiction. Interest Level: Ages 10 up**
Best suited for browsing, Scarry's oversize *Our Earth* encompasses the creation of the universe and the evolution of people and culture. The topical arrangement covers a bit of everything related to science and the development of civilization. Scarry writes in a conversational style; each two-page topic, e.g., *Earth's Neighborhood, the Solar System, Earth's Changing Face, Keeping Time with the Sky, From Hunter to Herder, Resources and Conservation,* is illustrated with captioned, colorful drawings, and diagrams. Two scales run across the top and bottom of each page. One is a time scale marked in millions of years showing the evolution of life on earth. The other scale shows distance in millions of miles demonstrating the distance from the sun to the planets in the solar system. The book is successful in stimulating curiosity and giving readers a broad perspective of their place in the universe. The book is not useful as a source for reports, although it does include an index.

■ **Scholes, Katherine. PEACE BEGINS WITH YOU. Illus. by Robert Ingpen. Sierra Club, 1989. Unp. (0-316-77436-7) Nonfiction. Interest Level: Ages 6–10**
With simple and direct prose author Scholes explores the concept of peace and how peace allows us to survive and fulfill our needs and wants. The author explores how conflicts arise and the choices we make in resolving them. Scholes defines peace broadly, incorporating an environmental perspective into the narrative when she talks about how our needs and wants sometimes conflict with those of the natural world. She stresses the interdependence of all living things and the importance of "living in peace with the land." Teachers introducing environmental concepts may find this picture book will add a new dimension to environmental education. Realistic illustrations in soft colors illustrate the text.

Award: NSSB, 1989

■ **Simon, Seymour. EARTH: OUR PLANET IN SPACE. Macmillan, 1984. Unp. (0-02-782830-1) Nonfiction. Interest Level: All ages**
This is a simple, scientific explanation of Earth's place in the solar system. *Earth, Our Planet in Space* offers dramatic views of Earth that will appeal to all ages. The impressive design with high contrast black-and-white photographs, many taken from space, illustrates the effectiveness of black-and-

white photography in information books. The photos and diagrams are balanced by a clearly written text set in fairly large type with alot of white space. Simon explains Earth's position in the solar system, its orbit around the sun, the seasons, atmosphere, and the Earth's surface. No issues or philosophy are discussed, but there is straightforward science writing. Pair this book with Hirst's *My Place in Space* (Orchard, 1988) for an entirely different (and humorous) approach. Another good addition would be Lauber's *Seeing Earth from Space* (Orchard, 1990), which uses color photographs effectively.

People and the Land

■ Ancona, George, and Joan Anderson. THE AMERICAN FAMILY FARM. Harcourt, 1989. 94pp. (0-15-203025-5) Nonfiction. Interest Level: Ages 9–12

Ancona and Anderson's tribute to the farming tradition in America will open readers' eyes to a way of life that was and continues to be closely connected to the land. Three families are profiled in this photo essay—the MacMillans, Massachusetts dairy farmers; the Adamses, Georgia chicken farmers; and the Rosmanns, Iowa hog and grain farmers. Hard work, close families, independent spirits, dependence on weather, and their interdependence with each other and the land characterize these people. Ancona's excellent black-and-white photographs show the farms and farm families at work and occasionally at rest. Of particular note is the Rosmann family that successfully farms without artificial fertilizers or pesticides. Says Ron Rosmann, "I was lucky to inherit well-cared for land when my father died, and that's why I'm able to have a successful farm. I hope to pass on healthy land to my sons someday." His wife Maria concurs, "We believe we're caretakers of the land and we must treat it with reverence."

Awards: ALA Notable Children's Book, 1989; NSSB, 1989

■ Ashabranner, Brent K. MORNING STAR, BLACK SUN: THE NORTHERN CHEYENNE AND AMERICA'S ENERGY CRISIS. Illus. by Paul Conklin. Dodd, 1982. 154pp. (0-396-08045-6) Nonfiction. Interest Level: Ages 12 up

Upper level social and environmental studies programs will be enriched by this excellent social studies book that chronicles the clash of two forces, America's growing energy needs and Cheyenne culture. Ashabranner's lengthy summary of Northern Cheyenne history provides an illuminating background for the bulk of the book, which follows the Cheyenne's more recent struggles to preserve their land and culture as energy companies have sought reservation land for strip coal mining. The Montana reservation, home to the Northern Cheyenne since 1884, lies on huge quantities of coal. If mined, the damage to the land, pollution, and influx of outsiders to support the mining development would change the Cheyenne's way of life forever. Ashabranner is clearly sympathetic to the tribe's struggles among themselves, with the Bureau of Indian Affairs (BIA), and with Congress. Interviews with tribal members and Ashabranner's historical perspective demonstrate the importance the land has for the Cheyenne and their respect for it. Their reluctance to lease mining rights despite their poverty supports this respect. Seldom do we think about the results of our individual, let alone collective, consumption of energy. *Morning Star, Black Sun* gives readers a chance to think about environmental issues within their social and economic contexts. The book is illustrated with black-and-white photos. Books for further reading and an index are appended.

Award: NSSB, 1982

■ Baylor, Byrd. THE DESERT IS THEIRS. Illus. by Peter Parnall. Macmillan, 1975. Unp. (LB 0-684-14266-X) Nonfiction. Interest Level: Ages 6–10
Byrd Baylor understands the close connection between the Papago Indians and their desert home. In this lyrical free-verse poem she explains how everything in the desert has its place and how it is right for the people living there. "Ask how they live in a place so harsh and dry. / They'll say they *like* the land they live on so they treat it well—the way you'd treat an old friend. They sing it songs. They never hurt it / And the land knows." She incorporates Papago Indian legends about the creation of Earth into the poem. She also gives a lesson in desert ecology. The result is a tribute to the desert and desert people that celebrates the harmony these people have with their environment. Parnall's graceful and fluid line drawings are washed with intense desert colors where yellows and golds predominate and where people and animals blend harmoniously into the landscape.

Awards: Caldecott Honor Book, 1976; NSSB, 1975; OSTB, 1975

■ Bellville, Cheryl Walsh. FARMING TODAY YESTERDAY'S WAY. Carolrhoda, 1984. 40pp. (LB 0-87614-220-X) Nonfiction. Interest Level: Ages 7–10
A family-run dairy farm in western Wisconsin is featured in book discussing alternative farming. Author Bellville follows the Saunders family throughout a year as they operate their small dairy farm. With one exception, their lives are not much different than other farm families in the United States. On most farms, tractors are used for all the field work; on the Saunders' farm draft horses do all the work a tractor might. The Saunders enjoy working with draft horses, but their use of horse rather than machine power

offers them both economic and environmental benefits. The Saunders can grow food for their horses instead of buying gasoline, breed horses rather than buy new tractors, and use the horses' waste products for fertilizer instead of buying it. The draft horses are a non-polluting, renewable resource. Excellent color and black-and-white photos illustrate the text. A glossary is included.

■ Benton-Banai, Edward. THE MISHOMIS BOOK: THE VOICE OF THE OJIBWAY. Illus. by Joe Liles. Red School House (643 Virginia Street, Saint Paul, MN 55103), 1988. 114pp. Nonfiction. Interest Level: Ages 12 up
Based on the oral traditions of the Ojibway people, *The Mishomis Book* is an impressive introduction to Ojibway culture. Presented as a series of teaching stories, *The Mishomis book* explains Ojibway history, culture, and spiritual beliefs. It was written by Edward Benton-Banai, an Ojibway educator and former director of the Red School House, an alternative school serving Native American children in St. Paul, Minnesota. Mishomis is the Ojibway word for grandfather and the stories are written in the voice of an Ojibway named Mishomis who calls this a "journey to rediscover a way of life that is centered on the respect for all living things. It will be a journey to find the center of ourselves so that we can know the peace that comes from living in harmony with powers of the universe." The stories trace the history of the Ojibway from creation through to the coming of the "light-skinned race" prophesied in Ojibway stories. Many of the stories end with suggestions of how the stories have meaning today. The Native American respect for the land and their connection to the Earth is a theme throughout the book. The stories are told with honesty and simplicity. The author's respect for the body of teachings is also evident. The book is illustrated with line drawings.

■ Bingham, Sam, and Janet Bingham, eds. BETWEEN SACRED MOUN-TAINS: NAVAJO STORIES AND LESSONS FROM THE LAND. Univ. of Ariz. Pr., 1984 (repr. of 1982 ed.). 288pp. (0-8165-0855-0) SERIES: Sun Tracks. Nonfiction. Interest Level: Ages 12 up
This is a handsome collaboration that offers readers insights into the Navajo people and their connection to the land. It was produced for the young people of Rock Point Community School on the Navajo Reservation to make them "aware of their own unique history and to understand its relevance to the problems and challenges of today." It joins other recent works by Native Americans that explain their history, culture, and philosophy. Chapters with interviews, stories, poems, commentary, and questions for discussion cover broad subjects as land, plant watchers, hunters,

Anasazi, ancestors, Spaniards, war, the reservation, the Navajos and the Hopis, modern times, and the future. Contemporary issues such as the Navajo-Hopi land dispute and mining are discussed.

It ends with profiles of several Navajo men and women working in different ways for the Navajo people. The authors make interesting connections between Navajo beliefs and ecological concepts. Readers will have a much deeper understanding of the Navajo people, changes to their land, and changes to their culture over time. The book is illustrated with black-and-white photographs, line drawings, maps, and diagrams. The book also includes a bibliography, help in reading Navajo words, which are used frequently in the text, and an index. The book is best used in a classroom setting.

■ Connolly, James E., ed. WHY THE POSSUM'S TAIL IS BARE: AND OTHER NORTH AMERICAN INDIAN NATURE TALES. Illus. by Andrea Adams. Stemmer, 1985. 64pp. (LB 0-88045-069-X) Fiction. Interest Level: Ages 8 up
Thirteen stories form this attractive collection of nature tales and myths from eight Native American tribes. Connolly, who edited the tales, writes a thoughtful introduction that describes the diversity of Native American traditions. He acknowledges the shared "keen obesrvation of nature, desire to teach virtues, and respect for all living things" found in the folklore. Connolly introduces each tale often providing background on the animals featured or Native American beliefs about the animal. Sources for each story are given. Full page black line drawings illustrate each story.

Award: NSSB, 1985

■ Cooney, Barbara. ISLAND BOY. Illus. by author. Viking, 1988. Unp. (0-670-81749-X) Fiction. Interest Level: Ages 4–8
Like Tony Johnston's *Yonder*, this is a story of our sense of place and our connection to the land and each other over time. While *Yonder* is written in broad strokes, *Island Boy* tells a moving story of a boy whose family settles an island off the coast of Maine in the early part of the nineteenth century. Cooney depicts the hard work, self-reliance, and deep love for his family and island that characterize Matthais' life. He goes to sea for several years, but eventually marries and returns to the island to raise a family. A daughter and grandson feel the same connection to the land and join him after his wife dies. Cooney's paintings reflect the simplicity of life then and the much closer connection to the natural world that people of Matthais' time had than most of us have today. A "red astrakhan apple tree" planted

by Matthais' mother appears throughout the book; beneath the tree becomes a place to sit and reflect. The tree becomes Matthais' final resting place.

Award: NSSB, 1988

■ **George, Jean. MY SIDE OF THE MOUNTAIN. Dutton, 1988 (repr. of 1959 ed.). 166pp. (0-525-87-27556) Fiction. Interest Level: Ages 9 up**
Wilderness survival stories are a genre in children's literature. They reflect our need of yearning to connect with nature, and to prove to ourselves that we are capable and courageous enough to survive without the comforts of modern life. In Jean George's classic book, the experience is self-imposed, and like Thoreau's experiment at Walden Pond. This book is about the details of day-to-day life in the wilderness, rather than brushes with danger or death that young Sam Gribley recounts and readers will relish. After leaving his home in New York City, Sam Gribley spends a year on his family; land in the Catskill Mountains. Through his first person narrative, and excerpts from his diary, readers learn how Sam forages, fishes, hunts, creates his treehouse home, tames a falcon, and becomes attuned to the rhythms of life in nature. George's sequel, *On the Far Side of the Mountain* (Dutton, 1990), published 30 years later, picks up where the first book ends and adds another character, Sam's sister Alice, who comes to live with him on the mountain.

Award: Newbery Award, 1960

■ **Gerson, Mary-Joan. WHY THE SKY IS FAR AWAY. Illus. by Hope Meryman. Harcourt, 1974. Unp. o.p. Fiction. Interest Level: Ages 6–10**
The consequences of wastefulness and our abuse of natural resources is the theme of a Nigerian folktale retold by Mary-Joan Gerson that explains why we must grow our own food. In the beginning the sky was close to the Earth and was also a source of food. When people got hungry, they simply sliced off a piece of sky and ate it. But food was so plentiful and easy to obtain, people became wasteful, took more than they needed, and threw out the rest. The sky grew angry: "I am tired of seeing myself on heaps of garbage everywhere. I warn you. Do not waste my gift any longer, or it will no longer be yours." When the people once again abuse their privilege, the sky moves out of reach and from that day forward people have had to grow their own food. Brown and blue woodcuts illustrate this tale set in the time of the Benin kingdom. This is an excellent choice for storytelling that would also enrich a social studies curriculum.

■ **Goble, Paul. BUFFALO WOMAN. Illus. by author. Bradbury, 1984. Unp. (0-02-737720-2) Fiction. Interest Level: Ages 6–9**

For the Plains Indians, buffalo provided food, clothing, shelter, and tools. The Indians felt a deep connection to and respect for the buffalo. Many legends that reflect this kinship were first told by Indians of the Plains. Author-illustrator Paul Goble says that "it was felt that retelling the story had power to bring about a change within each of us; that in listening we might all be a little more worthy of our buffalo relatives." In *Buffalo Woman* he retells the story of a young hunter who marries a buffalo in the form of a beautiful woman. When his people reject her she returns to her buffalo family with their son. The hunter follows her and after several challenges, he is transformed into a buffalo. The buffalo remember that this hunter "became a buffalo because he loved his wife and little child." In return the Buffalo People "have given their flesh so that little children, and babies still unborn, will always have meat to eat." Goble's dramatic and stylized illustrations are richly colored and will invite close inspection. The message of love, sacrifice, and kinship with the buffalo, on which the Indians were so dependent, is conveyed with beauty.

Awards: ALA Notable Children's Book, 1984; NSSB, 1984

■ Hall, Donald. OX-CART MAN. Illus. by Barbara Cooney. Viking, 1979. Unp. (0-670-53328-9) Fiction. Interest Level: Ages 4–9
While there is no turning back the clock to a simpler time, this glimpse of a year in the life of an early nineteenth century New England family offers a message for our time. Both Hall and Cooney give dignity and grace to an era when hard work, frugality, and simple pleasures were the norm in this 1980 Caldecott Medal book. Set in a time when a family's well-being depended upon nothing being wasted, the oxcart man's life stands in sharp contrast with today's excessive consumption and wastefulness. It was a time too, when an agrarian economy dictated a way of life far more in tune with the cycles of nature and the seasons than most of us experience today. The spare text has a rhythm and movement that is enhanced by Cooney's flat folk-style paintings that evoke the period. Teachers can incorporate environmental themes such as interdependence, living in harmony with nature, and even recycling when sharing this book with students.

Awards: Caldecott Medal, 1980; NSSB, 1979

■ Imershein, Betsy. FARMER. Photos by author. Messner, 1991. 32pp. (LB 0-671-68185-0) SERIES: The Work People Do. Nonfiction. Interest Level: Ages 7–10
Children will get a glimpse into the work and life on an organic farm in this profile of owners Guy and Peggy Jones and their young son, Travis. Blooming Hill Organic Farm produces flowers, fruits, vegetables, and herbs, which are sold at a nearby farmer's market. Hay, a cash crop, is sold for animal

feed. Imershein shows the many tasks involved in running a farm. She explains some of the things that are unique to organic farming, for example, no pesticides are used. Since two people cannot do all the work at Blooming Hill, the Jones' hire workers at some times during the year. Many of them are young people who are attracted to this alternative kind of farming. The black-and-white photos that amply illustrate the text do not quite live up to the exceptionally appealing full-color photo of the Jones' family on the cover. But, this is a valuable addition to collections on farm life for its matter-of-fact look at chemical-free use of the land.

■ **Johnston, Tony. YONDER. Illus. by Lloyd Bloom. Dial, 1988. Unp. (LB 0-8037-0278-7) Fiction. Interest Level: Ages 5–8**
This is a story about our connection to the land and each other and the cycles of seasons and of life in an earlier time in this country. A young farmer brings his bride to land that they clear, then farm. Over the years they raise a family. Trees are a symbol of renewal and are featured in Lloyd Bloom's richly colored oil paintings. Each important event is celebrated by the planting of a tree. A plum tree is pictured throughout the seasons and over the years in the center of many two-page spreads. The tree provides shade and a spot to work or rest; children swing from it; deer feed under it in the winter; and when the farmer dies, he is buried under it. Johnston's text rolls along like the hills "that roll forever." The refrain "There, just over there" sets up the often panoramic views of the countryside from the family's house on the hill. *Yonder* suggests a romantic view of our past, but Johnston and Bloom's sense of family, of place, and of continuity are solid and refreshing.

Award: NSSB, 1988

■ **McLain, Gary. THE INDIAN WAY: LEARNING TO COMMUNICATE WITH MOTHER EARTH. Illus. by Gary McLain and Michael Taylor. John Muir, 1990. 114pp. (paper 0-945465-73-4) Nonfiction. Interest Level: Ages 8–12**
This is a fresh collection of thirteen stories that explain and illustrate Native American beliefs and respect for the Earth. McLain has recorded stories he remembers being told as a boy during full moon at his grandparent's house on the Wind River Range. As McLain introduces each story, he recalls arriving at his grandparents' house with his brothers and sisters and their activities before Grandpa Iron, an Arapaho Medicine Man, tells the story. In *The Food*, Grandpa Iron tells how a grandson, after killing his first deer, continued to hunt every day until the family had far more than they needed. The grandson became very ill and learned that his greed was the source of

his illness. "It is not good to take more than you can use." The blend of contemporary setting and traditional tale will give readers a sense of how beliefs and customs are passed on in some families. The stories are followed by a section called "Experiences," a collection of twenty activities related to the stories. The book is printed on recycled paper and illustrated with halftone drawings and paintings.

■ Mayo, Gretchen Will. EARTHMAKER'S TALES: NORTH AMERICAN INDIAN STORIES ABOUT EARTH HAPPENINGS. Illus. by author. Walker, 1989. 89pp. (LB 0-8027-6840-7) Fiction. Interest Level: Ages 9–13

The forces of nature can profoundly affect people, particularly those who live close to the land. Native Americans have passed down a rich tradition of stories that explain these forces. Mayo has collected 16 "earth happenings," legends about the origins of floods, tornados, thunder, earthquakes, and other natural events from across North America. Teachers may derive environmental themes from some stories; all reveal the big part nature and the environment has played in the lives of Native Americans. For example, in *The Mountain Roars*, a hunter who is greedy for haiqua (shells used for money) doesn't take time to appreciate his people or the natural world. He is punished by a mountain that erupts into a volcano. Each short tale is briefly introduced and provides some background to the story or refers to variations from other tribes. Sources for each story are provided at the end. A glossary is included. The book is illustrated with shaded black-and-white drawings.

Award: NSSB, 1989

■ Ortiz, Simon J. THE PEOPLE SHALL CONTINUE. Illus. by Sharol Graves. Children's Book Press (1461 Ninth Ave., San Francisco, CA 94122), 1988 (rev. ed.). 24pp. (0-89239-041-7) Nonfiction. Interest Level: Ages 8–11

Native American author Simon Ortiz offers a new perspective on Native American history for children in this picture book story of epic proportions. His story is the history of the "People," a word that encompasses *all* Native Americans, and ultimately all minorities. This history begins with creation and continues to the present. In Ortiz's vision, the "People," who come from many different tribes, share much in common. They all have leaders, healers, hunters, warriors, and teachers. The teachers all taught that, "The Earth is the source of all life. / She gives birth. / Her children continue the life of the Earth. / The People must be responsible to her. / This is the way that all life continues." Ortiz describes the coming of the Europeans and the destruction of Native American life and culture, and of the land as the country is settled by immigrants. In Ortiz's vision, the "People" must unite and part of his message is that "We must make sure that the balance of the Earth be kept. / There is no other way." While other Native American legends and books like *Between Sacred Mountains* (University of Arizona Press, 1982) and *The Mishomis Book* (Red Schoolhouse Press, 1988) also by Native Americans, provide an in-depth look at Native American respect for and connection to the Earth, Ortiz's perspective is not mainstream, but is one many teachers and parents will want to make available.

■ Seattle, Chief. **BROTHER EAGLE, SISTER SKY.** Illus. by Susan Jeffers. Dial, 1991. Unp. (LB 0-8037-0969-3) Nonfiction. Interest Level: Ages 6 up
The words of Suquamish Chief Seattle in the mid-1850s have been quoted often in recent years. His speech, translated into English and published some 30 years after he spoke, has been adapted several times. It has inspired people around the world. This contemporary version, however, differs somewhat in language and theme from the first version.

Artist Susan Jeffers has further adapted the speech in a beautifully designed and illustrated picture book. The book carries a strong message of environmental protection. Seattle says, "What will happen when the buffalo are all slaughtered?" and "Preserve the land and the air and the rivers for your children's children. . . ." Familiar phrases such as "All things are connected," and "What befalls the earth befalls all the sons and daughters of the earth," are also included. Readers may not realize these are contemporary additions to the speech and that Seattle, a Puget Sound Indian, may have known little of buffalo being slaughtered on the Plains.

Jeffers's characteristic illustrations, pen-and-ink and dyes, reveal her close affinity with the natural world. A bald eagle flying toward the reader across a two-page spread is particularly striking. The Native Americans depicted represent various tribes and Plains Indians predominate. The cover illustration portrays Seattle, apparently as a Plains Indian. While it is clear that Jeffers intended this, it is puzzling. She missed an opportunity to portray Seattle, if not in his own words, at least in his own dress. This could lead to misunderstandings regarding Seattle's background and the differences among Native Americans.

Teachers may find this book useful when introducing the themes of respect for nature and protection of the environment, but should be careful not to introduce *Brother Eagle, Sister Sky* as history.

■ Sewell, Marcia. **PEOPLE OF THE BREAKING DAY.** Illus. by author. Macmillan, 1990. 48pp. (0-689-31407-8) Nonfiction. Interest Level: Ages 7–12
The Wampanoag people, who lived in what is now southeastern Massachusetts at the time of the arrival of the Pilgrims, tell their story in this

companion to *The Pilgrims of Plimoth* (Atheneum, 1989) by author-illustrator Marcia Sewell. In *People of the Breaking Day,* Sewell doesn't mention encounters with the European settlers who changed forever their way of life and the land they lived on. Rather she concentrates on a time prior to their arrival and describes their way of life and beliefs. Readers will get a feel for their respect for and close connection to the natural world and the pattern of their lives throughout the year. The author discusses the food they grew, gathered, and hunted for, the division of labor, dwellings, spiritual beliefs, and games. Over a dozen Wampanoag/Narragansett words used in the text are defined in a section following the glossary. Earth-tone paintings, somewhat impressionistic in style, illustrate every page. Although the text is brief in this picture-book history, an index would have helped young researchers.

Award: NSSB, 1990

■ **Walker, Kath. STRADBROKE DREAMTIME. Illus. by Lorraine Hannay. Angus & Robertson, 1982. 64pp. o.p. Fiction. Interest Level: Ages 8 up**
Aboriginal writer Kath Walker grew up on Stradbroke Island off the coast of Queensland, Australia. This collection of stories, first published in 1972, includes reminiscences about the author's childhood on the island and Aboriginal legends, some traditional, others new. The legends are those the author recalls hearing as a child. Her stories capture a land and way of life now drastically changed. In her introduction she speaks of the once beautiful Stradbroke Island, much of which has been damaged or destroyed by development. "Greedy, thoughtless, stupid, ignorant man continues the assault on nature. But he too will suffer. His ruthless bulldozers are digging his own grave." Following these strong words, Walker's stories offer anecdotal accounts of family life with insights on Aboriginal attitudes, beliefs, and fate under white rule. Readers will see respect for life, economy of lifestyle, and a closeness to the natural world are all part of the Aboriginal culture. Hannay's pen-and-ink and pencil drawings, some in color, in earthy tones are a fine accompaniment to the stories.

■ **Wheeler, Bernelda. I CAN'T HAVE BANNOCK BUT THE BEAVER HAS A DAM. Illus. by Herman Bekkering. Pemmican Publications (412 McGregor St. Winnipeg, Manitoba, Canada), 1984. 32pp. (paper 0-919143-11-3) Fiction. Interest Level: Ages 4–7**
This simple, cumulative story delightfully shows the interconnections between us and the natural world. A boy asks his mother to bake him some bannock (a kind of griddle cake). She says she can't. He asks why. She says the electricity is off. He asks why. And so on until we learn that a beaver chopped down a tree that hit the power line, and until the line is fixed, Mom

can't bake bannock. His father, who works for the power company, helps fix the line. The story is told through the dialogue between mother and son. Children who are at the age of endless questioning should enjoy the story and the story offers possibilities for discussion such as our dependence on electricity, interconnections between people, and events in the natural world. Black charcoal sketches illustrate the text.

The Changing Landscape

■ Baker, Jeannie. WINDOW. Greenwillow, 1991. Unp. (LB 0-688-08918-6) Fiction. Interest Level: Ages 6 up
Baker's collage constructions, rich with detail, tell from the perspective of a mother, then her son, the change over a 24-year period to the land seen from his bedroom window. In the tradition of Jorg Müller's *The Changing Countryside* (Macmillan, 1977), *Window* chronicles the change brought and wrought by people as they "develop" the land and a once-rural area is urbanized. This is a wordless picture book but Baker's collages tell the story as well as any words could. The passage of time is noted by changes to the landscape. Roads are built, houses appear, a McDonald's is built, and the countryside slowly but surely disappears. Small details in the room also note the boy's growth: birthday cards, toys, and hairstyles all change with the years. In the final scene, the boy who has grown up, married, and fathered a son now looks out from a new window in a new house that is again in the country. A sign not too far away says "House Blocks for Sale." Change is inevitable, the cycle continues. *Window* is not only a wonderful aesthetic experience for children, but it will spark discussions of change in their environment. The book could be used in art, language arts, and social studies classes in many different ways. Companion books include *Acacia Terrace, The Little House,* and other titles in this section. Baker's *Where the Forest Meets the Sea* (Greenwillow, 1987) concerns threats of human encroachment in the Australian tropical rain forest.

■ Burton, Virginia Lee. THE LITTLE HOUSE. Illus. by author. Houghton, 1978 (repr. of 1942 ed.). Unp. (0-395-18156-9) Fiction. Interest Level: Ages 3–8
Author of the beloved picture book *Mike Mulligan and His Steam Shovel (Houghton, 1939),* Virginia Lee Burton published *The Little House* in 1942. Fifty years later, the book's theme of the effects of change on the landscape remains pertinent.
   Originally built to provide a home for generations of families, a little house sits solidly on a hill overlooking acres of farmland, a city barely visible

on the horizon. As the seasons change and years pass, the children who live in the house grow up and move away "and now at night the lights of the city seemed brighter and closer." More changes come to the countryside: paved roads, automobiles and new houses. An ugly, polluted city crowds around the little house, which becomes badly run down and neglected. And then, one spring, a descendent of the first owner recognizes the house, still a good house under layers of city grime, buys it, and moves it back to the country onto another little hill to be lived in and cared for once again.

The worthy recipient of the 1943 Caldecott Medal, this is a charming allegory for young children. The colorful illustrations are now quaint but retain their appeal. *The Little House* is a remarkably honest portrayal of the enormous changes brought on by technology and population growth that have taken place in this century.

Award: Caldecott Medal, 1943

■ Chiasson, John. AFRICAN JOURNEY. Photos by author. Bradbury, 1987. 55pp. (0-02-718530-3) Nonfiction. Interest Level: Ages 10 up
In this thought-provoking book, photojournalist Chiasson explores the ways environment shapes and changes the lives of people in six different regions of Africa. This work is full of opportunities for discussion of environmental issues. Nature's influence on people and people's impact on the land, deforestation, over-population, desertification, politics, and war are all discussed. Chiasson examines the nomadic Twareg and WoDaaBe of the Sahel, the Yoruba who farm on the coastal plains of Benin, the city people of Dakar on the coast of Senegal, a Senegalese coastal fishing village, a river port in Mali, and drought-stricken, war-ravaged Ethiopia. Chiasson discusses family life, how people make their living in different regions, and the challenges they face because of natural and man-made forces. The lack of an index is a weakness in this otherwise well-written and stunningly photographed book. A map at the beginning helps readers locate the six African regions discussed.

Awards: ALA Notable Children's Book, 1987; NSSB, 1987

■ Fiday, Beverly, and David Fiday. TIME TO GO. Illus. by Thomas B. Allen. Harcourt, 1990. Unp. (0-15-200608-7) Fiction. Interest Level: Ages 5-8
Forced by drought to leave the farm that his family has owned for generations, a young boy must say good-bye to the land and the only life he has known. Dedicated by the authors "to the farm children whose time to go has come already," this is a poignant and painful story.

As the boy and his dog walk around the farm for the last time, his happy memories when "I was the luckiest boy in the world," contrast sharply with the melancholy pictures, and charcoal and colored pencil drawings done in earth tones. The boy has lost a great deal more than his pony, his innocence is gone as well. The silos, once "protecting our hard work, measuring our success," stand empty as does the barn. The silos are sad reminders of the past. The pump handle becomes a symbol of the family's broken dreams.

The authors, Beverly and David Fiday, and the award-winning illustrator, Thomas B. Allen, see this book as a tribute to the farm children "who must seek a new future away from the land that they love." The book ends on a note of hope as the boy, mature beyond his years, voices his determination to overcome adversity and reclaim his legacy.

Award: NSSB, 1990

■ Goodall, John S. THE STORY OF A MAIN STREET. Illus. by author. Macmillan, 1987. 58pp. (0-689-50436-5) Fiction. Interest Level: Ages 5 up
The changes brought to an English town over time are given rich, historical perspective by illustrator John S. Goodall. Wordless, except for an introductory paragraph, and a table of contents, Goodall's soft watercolor paintings bring historic periods vividly to life, depicting the main street of a typical country community from Medieval times through the Restoration and Regency periods, from the Victorian era up to the present day. Goodall's characteristic half-page flips allow clever changes of scene, moving the reader from room-to-room through the centuries. The warmth and activity of the community are conveyed in charming, detailed drawings of shop interiors, cobbled streets, and a festive Christmas bazaar, anchored by the reappearance of a stone market cross in many of the spreads. Changes in architecture, transportation, and dress are evident as the reader travels along the street, observing adults and children at work and at play. Enjoyable for any age, Goodall's other works are in a similar style; among them *The Story of a Seashore* (Macmillan, 1990).

■ Hurmence, Belinda. THE NIGHTWALKER. Clarion, 1988. 140pp. (0-89919-732-9) Fiction. Interest Level: Ages 10 up
The descendents of the original settlers (some of them are part Coree Indian) on Breach Island off the North Carolina coast are fishermen who resent the changes that are coming to the island. Outsiders, known as "dit dots," are buying land moving in with more money, and different values. They also support the National Park Service's plans to make nearby Shackleford Banks, where the fisherman have their fishing shacks, part of the National Seashore. When that happens, the fisherman will lose their shacks. Hurmence's novel is about twelve-year-old Savannah, daughter of a fisherman. She is worried that her younger brother Poco, who sleepwalks, is

somehow involved in the mysterious fires that are burning down the fishing shacks. She becomes friends with Mary Jean, a "dit dot" whose family has a vacation home on the island, and she begins to see that while the locals love the land, they have also strewn the banks around their fishing shacks with garbage. Hurmence has too many subplots going in this novel that includes arson, sleepwalking, and a minor mystery. But the themes of both development (of Breach Island) and conservation (of Shackleford Banks) and their effects on the local people are worth exploring. She presents a credible portrait of two preteen girls who become friends in spite of different backgrounds. Another good book to consider is Betty Levin's *The Trouble with Gramary* (Greenwillow, 1988)

■ **Jenness, Aylette, and Alice Rivers. IN TWO WORLDS: A YUP'IK ESKIMO FAMILY. Photos by author. Houghton, 1989. 84pp. (0-395-42797-5) Non-fiction. Interest Level: Ages 10 up**
This book, *In Two Worlds* is about changes that have taken place in Scammon Bay, Alaska, a Yup'ik Eskimo village, and to the Rivers family, who has lived in the area for generations. Fifty years ago the Yup'ik people lived a simple, close-to-the-land life. They hunted, fished, and moved with the seasons. Today Scammon Bay is a modern village of 350 people, still remote, but connected to the rest of the world through TV, telephones, and airplanes. This balanced account, drawn from interviews with the Rivers, shows both dramatic change to family and land, but also the many customs that remain. Many uncaptioned, black-and-white photos illustrate the book. Although specific environmental issues are not emphasized, this documentary-style look at a changing landscape and people will be useful in social studies classes.

Award: NSSB, 1989

■ **Locker, Thomas. THE LAND OF GRAY WOLF. Illus. by author. Dial, 1991. Unp. (LB 0-8037-0937-4) Fiction. Interest Level: Ages 6–10**
With his now familiar oil landscapes, Thomas Locker tells of the change over several hundred years to the northeastern landscape that he has often portrayed and to the Native Americans who were uprooted from their land by European settlers. This is the story of a group Native Americans living in New York's Hudson River Valley at the time of the arrival of white settlers. The story is told from the point of view of a young boy, Running Deer, who tells of his tribe's fate as settlers take over their hunting gounds and clear land for farming. Both wildlife and Indians suffer from loss of their home. The settlers eventually displace the Indians through land purchases and wars. The Indians are moved to a reservation. Locker contrasts the

native "earth friendly" use of land with that of the settlers whose farming methods depleted the soil. Eventually, the settlers abandoned their farms and moved west. At the end of the story the land is slowly returning to its former state. "Some of Running Deer's people still live nearby on the mountainside. Perhaps one day they will hear the howl of a wolf echoing in the forest light." Locker's majestic landscapes contribute to the romantic and somewhat idealized view of Native Americans.

■ Müller, Jorg. THE CHANGING COUNTRYSIDE. Illus. by author. Macmillan, 1977. Unp. (0-689-50085-8) Nonfiction. Interest Level: All ages
This award-winning book is a landmark sociological commentary on the change wrought on the land by an increasing population. First published in Switzerland in 1973 and still timely, the book has a unique format: a portfolio containing seven full-color prints on heavy paper, each of which folds out to one by almost three feet. The paintings have an enormous visual impact on the reader, especially when they are seen together.

Painted in the naif style, the pictures depict the same landscape at approximately three-year intervals from 1953 to 1972, spanning the seasons. The bucolic countryside of 1953 shows farms with grazing cows, blooming wildflowers, and children playing and daydreaming. Only a small white cat walks along the country road. The cat, a symbol of innocence, appears in each of the series. Gradually, but inevitably, change comes to the land. Roads are paved by 1956, the town has moved closer by 1959, ugly oil storage tanks appear by 1963, new buildings and more under construction are evident in 1966, and by 1972, an expressway dominates the landscape. In the final painting, children have only a small sandbox in which to play, and the white cat is in peril as it flees across the busy highway. Without a word, Jorg Müller has made a profound statement about urban and industrial growth. The portfolio of drawings is an excellent choice for classroom display, discussion and will serve as an inspiration for writing projects. Müller also produced a companion portfolio, *The Changing City* (Atheneum, 1977).

■ Peet, Bill. FAREWELL TO SHADY GLADE. Illus. by author. Houghton, 1966. 38pp. (0-395-18975-6) Fiction. Interest Level: Ages 4–8
Sixteen frightened, but plucky, forest animals band together after they are forced by development to abandon their peaceful home in Shady Glade. As they view the encroaching cranes and bulldozers, one raccoon says bluntly, "The brutes are indestructible, all powerful, and there's no stopping them. Shady Glade is doomed." The next day, the animals climb a sycamore tree and leap from it to the roof of a passing train, determined to seek a new home hundreds of miles away. As the train moves through a city, the

animals are shocked by the sight of a creek which has been polluted by factory waste. Continuing their journey, the weary animals face a new dilemma—how to get off the speeding locomotive. A fortuitous rockslide halts the train and the animals quickly disembark. To their dismay, they again hear an ominous rumbling. This time, however, they are relieved to discover that the noise is not a bulldozer, but only a thunderstorm.

Popular author-illustrator Bill Peet first published this picture book in 1966, dedicating it to environmentalist Rachel Carson "with the hope that the new generation will carry on her all-important work toward preserving what is left of the natural world." Peet, who began his career working for Walt Disney, skillfully uses colored pencils to draw scenes that are alive with color, humor, and action. Told from the animals' perspective, this appealing picture book can be compared to *Tucker's Countryside* by George Selden (Farrar, 1969), a novel for slightly older children that also deals with the theme of loss of wildlife habitat. Peet successfully manages to avoid didacticism, while reminding readers that animals have rights and that people must be responsible for preserving these rights.

Happily, in this book, the animals find a new Shady Glade, but with every Shady Glade that is lost, the natural world grows smaller.

■ **Provensen, Alice, and Martin Provensen. SHAKER LANE. Illus. by authors. Viking, 1987. Unp. (LB 0-670-81568-3) Fiction. Interest Level: Ages 5–10**
A Shaker Meeting House once marked the crossing of two rural roads in an area similar to the upstate New York home of Alice and Martin Provensen. As the genteel Herkimer sisters sell off their once prosperous family farm "in order to live," a motley row of tar paper and clapboard houses appears. An independent group of extended families lives on Shaker Lane, including more than a dozen children, dogs, cats "and a duck named Lucy." People seem casual, but a genuine sense of neighborhood exists. There is always someone to help weed a garden, chop firewood, or to move a chicken coop. Through the candid observations of the narrator, the reader senses that there are many stories behind the one that is being told. This slow but satisfactory way of life is interrupted by the county land agent's announcement that a reservoir is planned and that the county is going to buy their property. "One by one" the families pack up and leave without a fight, following a trail of giant power lines down the road. The Herkimer sisters stand forlornly at the back of one page, watching the water rise "slowly but surely," watching their land and their lifestyle disappear forever. This happens so quickly that the reader is shocked by the sudden appearance on the next two-page spread of a new neighborhood of relentlessly middle-class split level houses, their raw, bright colors in harsh contrast to the muted,

autumnal shades used in the preceding illustrations. "You wouldn't know the place," says the narrator. Implicit is the thought, "you wouldn't want to."

Caldecott medalists Alice and Martin Provensen state that they "have watched the vast changes that are taking place, profoundly altering the look and feel of our rural landscape." In *Shaker Lane*, the Provensens's have made an important statement about this loss that can be easily understood by children.

Award: NSSB, 1987

■ Pryor, Bonnie. THE HOUSE ON MAPLE STREET. Illus. by Beth Peck. Morrow, 1987. unp. (LB 0-688-06381-0) Fiction. Interest Level: Ages 5– 10

When one of Bonnie Pryor's daughters discovered an arrowhead near their home in Ohio, the author and her two young children began to daydream about its origins. From this experience evolved *The House on Maple Street*, a simple, circular story with the intent of giving young children a realistic sense of the past that they can comprehend.

Two young girls, Chrissy and Jenny, live with their mother and father and a cat and dog at 107 Maple Street. The scene shifts abruptly back in time three hundred years, when Maple Street was the site of a forest and a bubbling spring. A herd of buffalo arrives, followed by a tribe of Indians, including a small boy who makes and quickly loses an arrowhead. The tribe moves on and then wagon trains begin to pass through the area. Eventually, the land is claimed by a family of settlers who have a daughter, Ruby. Ruby unearths the long buried arrowhead, but in the manner of children everywhere, loses it again along with her own china doll teacup. Generations of Ruby's relatives inhabit the family farm and the passage of time is symbolized by the growth of a row of maple trees planted near the farmhouse. A town expands to the edge of the farm and then engulfs it. The original farmhouse is torn down and replaced by the home where Chrissy and Jenny live and where they find, while planting a garden, a tiny china teacup and an arrowhead. They wonder and dream about life long ago.

The changes in the ecology and landscape are illustrated with large pastel drawings, which vary in clarity and intensity from page to page. Scenes verge on the stereotypical—a buffalo herd, an Indian teepee, a covered wagon, a herd of cows, but are adequate as an introduction to the theme of westward expansion and its impact on the countryside.

An understanding of history is a difficult concept for young children to grasp. Pryor's attempt at making this semiautobiographical story more personal by choosing children as characters is, for the most part, successful.

This book will be useful to early elementary teachers when used in conjunction with other curriculum materials.

Awards: NSSB, 1987; OSTB, 1987

■ **Selden, George. TUCKER'S COUNTRYSIDE. Illus. by Garth Williams. Farrar, 1969. 167pp. (0-374-3-7854-1) Fiction. Interest Level: Ages 9–12**
Tucker's Countryside continues the adventures of Chester Cricket, Harry Cat, and Tucker Mouse, introduced in *The Cricket in Times Square* (Farrar, 1960). This time Chester's country home in Connecticut, known as the "Old Meadow," is threatened by land developers who plan to build apartment houses. Chester and the meadow animals try to figure out a way to save the meadow and protect their homes. They are aided by Harry Cat and Tucker Mouse who travel up from the City to help. Selden pokes gentle fun at city slickers Harry and Tucker who are a bit out of their element in the meadow. But, Tucker comes up with a clever plan and the animals help carry it out, successfully preserving the meadow from future development. This fanciful story presents the animal's view of urbanization.

■ **Sharpe, Susan. WATERMAN'S BOY. Macmillan, 1990. 170pp. (0-02-782351-2) Fiction. Interest Level: Ages 8–12**
Ten-year-old Ben Warren longs to be a waterman like his father, but his parents don't want him to follow in his footsteps. Times are changing in Marsh Hollow on Chesapeake Bay. There aren't as many fish (or oysters or crabs) as there once were. The small fishing town now attracts tourists, bringing new people and businesses, to the area. Ben and his friend Matt meet a young scientist, who is studying the pollution problems in the bay, and learn something about the causes of the declining marine life. Ben's father and the other local fishermen do not trust outsiders and experts. They are frustrated with their meager catches and restrictions on their fishing. When Ben and Matt stumble on an illegal oil dumping site on the bay, the whole town of Marsh Hollow has to confront the problems that pollution and development are bringing their town. Sharpe's environmental message comes through loud and clear in this easy-to-read-story about an environmental issue. But, Ben is a believable ten-year-old, the plot moves quickly, and Sharpe's Chesapeake Bay setting is nicely drawn.

■ **Tchudi, Stephen. THE GREEN MACHINE AND THE FROG CRUSADE. Delacorte, 1987. 221pp. o.p. Fiction. Interest Level: Ages 11–14**
Sixteen-year-old David Morgan is shocked to learn that a shopping mall is slated to be built on a local swamp where for years he has poked about enjoying its natural beauty and studying the frogs. He quickly enlists the aid

of his best friend, Mike, and a local lawyer; they literally take on city hall, lobbying for the swamp's preservation. Construction of the planned mall is eventually blocked—temporarily. As a lesson in local activism, Tchudi is right on target. Tchudi's character development is subordinate to the conservation issues he addresses. But, there are some funny moments when his spunky younger sister organizes her freshmen friends into the "Green Machine," (their chant is "Froggie, Froggie") canvassing neighborhoods dressed in green, and city council president Larry Jensen speaks for all the unconverted when he says: "But we're just talking frogs and turtles. It's not like we'd be damaging animal life . . . say, like deer." This book presents a good social studies and conservation lesson in a palatable story.

■ Thiele, Colin. FARMER SCHULZ'S DUCKS. Illus. by Mary Milton. Harper, 1988. 32pp. (LB 0-06-026183-8) Fiction. Interest Level: Ages 5 – 10
Farmer Schulz raises ducks in South Australia. These are not just ordinary ducks, but "the most beautiful in the world." Looking at Mary Milton's watercolors of ducks drawn from life, the reader agrees unequivocally. These ducks have "necks of opal and wings of amethyst." These are "ducks like burnished gold." Farmer Schulz is fiercely proud of his ducks and much of the premise of the story is dependent on how much the reader cares about them as well, especially as they are threatened.

Each morning, after their feeding, the ducks must cross the road that runs through the farm to get to the Onkaparinga River to swim. To avoid predators, the ducks return to the safety of the farm at dusk. As the years pass, the population of the surrounding area increases and traffic on the road becomes busier. Inevitably, an accident occurs. Farmer Schulz and his children hold a family meeting to discuss possible solutions. A "ducks crossing" sign is posted but ducks continue to be run over. Next, Farmer Schulz constructs a duck overpass. The "Bridge of Ducks" quickly becomes a tourist attraction creating more havoc until, one day, a speeding semi truck hits the bridge and destroys it, killing many of the ducks. This time the government intervenes and, after much frustration and delay, a compromise is reached and the problem is happily resolved.

This mini-drama begs to be read aloud in a classroom or library and is sure to spark a lively discussion about the issues of population growth and wildlife protection. Colin Thiele, a prize-winning Australian author, writes with emotion and sensitivity; each phrase is full of sounds and images. It is a worthy companion to Robert McCloskey's *Make Way for Ducklings* (Viking, 1941). The book is highly recommended.

Award: ALA Notable Children's Book, 1988

■ Turner, Ann Warner. HERON STREET. Illus. by Lisa Desimini. Harper, 1989. Unp. (LB 0-06-026185-4) Fiction. Interest Level: Ages 5–9

Ann Turner chronicles the changes in the American landscape, specifically that of a marsh on the Eastern seaboard, from the time of the Pilgrims through the Revolutionary War to the twentieth century and the emergence of the automobile and airplane.

Progress is appreciated, but the author makes it clear that it does not come without cost to both settlers who must fight to keep their land and to animals, like the wolves, who "loped away to a land where there were no churches, or schools, or bells." Turner's language is moving and lyrical, mimicking the diverse sounds of seagrass, of cannons and victory bells, of music from a doorway, and "roller skates on tar."

In her first picture book, illustrator Lisa Desimini masterfully evokes the historical imagery of the text. Her sense of design is strong, as is her choice of bright, primary colors, softened by shadows. The heron represents nature and is a fragile yet enduring symbol of change. It flies away in the book's final pages, a gentle warning. "On the land where herons rested, automobiles chugged down the streets," and a street named Heron is the only reminder of what once was.

Award: NSSB, 1989

■ Von Tscharner, Renata, and Ronald Lee Fleming. NEW PROVIDENCE: A CHANGING CITYSCAPE. Illus. by Denis Orloff. Harcourt, 1987. Unp. (0-15-200540-4) Nonfiction. Interest Level: Ages 9 up

Six full-color, two-page spreads by first-time illustrator Denis Orloff dramatically depict change in an imaginary but typical small American city during this century. Highlighting the years 1910, 1935, 1955, 1970, 1980, and 1987, the detailed paintings authentically illustrate changes in architecture, transportation, business, the environment, the arts, and the people of a cross-section of the United States.

The authors, an urban design consultant, and a city planner, credit Jorg Muller, author of The Changing Countryside (Atheneum, 1970), with the inspiration for this book. A team of architectural historians and designers created the city from an assemblage of old photographs of American buildings. Social studies teachers will find this book an invaluable introduction to topics such as urban renewal and historic preservation. This book effectively presents a portrait of socio-economic change in this century in a familiar and accessible way. It will also be useful to spark discussions of twentieth century history. Gradual urbanization is pictured as both a positive and a negative force.

Each scene is described in a short, factual narrative that precedes the series. Small black-and-white drawings are used to pull out important details. As the city changes, so do the seasons. In the book's final pages, sunlight streams onto the landscape, instilling the reader with a sense of optimism that after more than 70 years of mistakes, we may finally be learning from our errors.

Award: NSSB, 1987

■ **Wheatley, Nadia. MY PLACE. Illus. by Donna Rawlins. Australia in Print (110 W. Ocean Blvd., Long Beach, CA), 1989. Unp. (0-7328-0010-2) Fiction. Interest Level: Ages 8 up**
Two hundred years of Australian social, economic, and cultural history are chronicled in this intriguing picture book that shows the changes to people and land at a fictitious, but representative, place along the coast. Beginning in the present, Wheatley goes back in time pausing every ten years to introduce a child from that period. An unusual but effective device, it works because it begins with what kids understand: their own time and place. Of course, *My Place* can as easily be read from past to present, and children may want to do that once they've read it front to back. The children introduce themselves to readers, for example "My name's Sarah and this is my place," then describe something about their family and origins, present circumstances, and sometimes, national or world events of the day. A crude map shows each child's home and the surrounding landmarks with a stream and a big tree providing a bridge from present to past. The children come from a variety of ethnic and economic groups that settled in Australia. Readers will find numerous examples of changes to the environment throughout *My Place*. One telling difference in attitude about the land is revealed at the very end, or beginning, in 1788, when the Aboriginal boy, Barangaroo introduces himself. "I *belong* to this place," he says.

■ **Wilson, Barbara Ker. ACACIA TERRACE. Illus. by David Fielding. Scholastic, 1990. Unp. (paper 0-590-42885-3) Fiction. Interest Level: Ages 8–11**
This ambitious picture book traces the history of Australia through the lives of the Flynn family, who built three houses on a street they named Acacia Terrace in Sydney, Australia. The narrative begins in the 1860s and follows the Flynn descendents and other owners through the 1960s when the whole street is in decline and eventually renovated. Fielding's richly color stylized paintings, one on each right-facing page, reveal close-up views of the street, its houses, and inhabitants over the decades. *Acacia Terrace* helps young readers visualize change to their homes, streets, and towns

over time. The book also shows that change, urbanization, and urban decay aren't only the hallmarks of American cities. Small print mars this otherwise recommended picture book that should be useful in social studies or art education classes. This book is a good companion to Von Tscharner's *New Providence: a Changing Cityscape* (Harcourt, 1986), and Müller's *The Changing City* (Atheneum, 1977), and Wheatley's *My Place* (Australia in Print, 1989).

■ **Wiseman, David. BLODWEN AND THE GUARDIANS. Houghton, 1983. 163pp. (paper 0-395-33892-1) Fiction. Interest Level: Ages 11–14**
The Guardians are fairies whose duty is to protect an ancient site just outside a small English village. The Mow, as it is known by the villagers, has always been a "queer old place," and one which they avoid. Ten-year-old Blodwen and her family move from the city to an old cottage near the Mow and begin to enjoy the beauty of the countryside. Blodwen is attracted to the mow, but she and her brother feel something that warns them away. Soon the village learns that a highway will be built nearby, destroying the open country and the Mow. While the villagers are unhappy about the coming road, they do little to prevent it. The subversive fairies do what they can to deter the builders, causing minor setbacks to the construction. Only when the fairies allow Blodwen and her brother to enter the grove where the burial chamber is hidden, is a solution to the dilemma found. The ancient site is preserved and the highway is built elsewhere. Says Peridot, one of the fairies: "I do not know why they sweep so ruthlessly aside lands their forefathers tilled so lovingly. Their reasons seem insane to me and I cannot hope to make them clear to you. They have a need to create and destroy, destroy and create. Change is their god." Although Blodwen and the other human characters are not as well developed as they could be, the fairies are engaging and their pranks not unlike those of some contemporary environmental activists. This is a readable fantasy with a preservation theme.

■ **Wrightson, Patricia. MOON DARK. Illus. by Noela Young. Macmillan, 1988 (repr. of 1987 ed.). 169pp. (0-689-50451-9) Fiction. Interest Level: Ages 9–14**
Set in Australia, this fantasy features Blue, a fisherman's dog, who bridges the human and wild animal world. When houses begin dotting the riverbank in a heretofore remote area, Blue begins to notice changes in the behavior of the wildlife, a wonderfully portrayed collection of Australian wallabies, kangaroos, koalas, flying foxes, bandicoots, bush rats, and others. The encroachment of people has stressed the animals, who are now in competition for food. When a war breaks out between the bush rats and bandicoots,

Blue, and the other animals call on Keeting, an ancient moon spirit, to help them. Keeting may be confusing to readers, but the supernatural element adds a nice touch to this nocturnal novel that gives a dogs-eye view of the impact of development on wildlife.

People Make a Difference

■ Ancona, George. RIVERKEEPER. Photos by author. Macmillan, 1990. unp. (LB 0-02-700911-4) Nonfiction. Interest Level: Ages 9–12
With his clear prose and well-composed, black-and-white photographs, George Ancona introduces young readers to a new kind of environmentalist, John Cronin—river keeper of New York's busy Hudson River. Cronin's job is to help keep the river safe from polluters and other hazards that would endanger the lives of people and wildlife who depend on it. He monitors the fish and other wildlife in the river, looks for and catches polluters, pressures the local and federal governments to enforce the laws, promotes new legislation to protect the river, and educates the public on the importance of the river ecosystem and the dangers of pollution. Ancona explains the river's ecosystem and shows how it has been polluted. Cronin emerges as a good role model and a crusader against pollution. He says "pollution is a universal problem. But only if we take care of our own backyard can we go to our neighbors and ask them to take care of the tropical rain forest. So I believe we can change the world right here on the Hudson River." The uncaptioned photographs flow naturally from the text. There is no index.

■ Brenner, Barbara. ON THE FRONTIER WITH MR. AUDUBON. Putnam, 1977. 96pp. (LB 0-698-30637-6) Nonfiction. Interest Level: Ages 8–12
In this fictionalized journal, Brenner gives an account of 13-year-old Joseph Mason, who in 1820, accompanied artist and ornithologist John James Audubon on a trip down the Ohio and Mississippi Rivers to New Orleans. In exchange for chores and assistance in finding bird specimens to paint, Joseph was given drawing lessons and room and board on the 18-month trip. Many of the paintings Audubon made on this trip became part of his *The Birds of America Folio.* The trip was rough, for Audubon had little money, and in exchange for passage, they supplied game for the captain and crew of the boat. Mason describes the rich wildlife along the rivers and the passion Audubon had for birds and painting. The book is illustrated with some black-and-white reproductions of Audubon's drawings and historical photographs. Read this book along with some full-color reproductions of

Audubon's work. Social studies and language arts classes will find this book useful.

Awards: NSSB, 1977; OSTB, 1977

■ **Burleigh, Robert. A MAN NAMED THOREAU. Illus. by Lloyd Bloom. Macmillan, 1985. 31pp. (LB 0-689-31122-2) Nonfiction. Interest Level: Ages 9–12**
Author Burleigh has written a short biography of a man whose ideas over one hundred years ago have influenced today's conservation movement and continue to have relevance as our society's consumption of resources grows at an alarming rate. Thoreau is probably best known for his experiment in living simply at Walden Pond near Concord, Massachusetts. Burleigh portrays Thoreau as an oddity in his day, a thinker, and writer who sought a closeness with nature. "To Thoreau, nature was like a living being. He wanted to do more than just enjoy its beauty. He wanted to get so close to nature that he became one with it." Burleigh successfully weaves many quotations from Thoreau into the text as he recounts several events in Thoreau's short life. The biography is illustrated with soft black and white drawings, and includes a short chronology of events and a bibliography. The book is good introduction to a complex man for young readers.

Award: ALA Notable Children's Book, 1985

■ **Calabro, Marian. OPERATION GRIZZLY BEAR. Macmillan, 1989. 118pp. (LB 0-02-716241-9) Nonfiction. Interest Level: Ages 10–14**
In 1959, wildlife biologists Frank and John Craighead began a landmark twelve-year study of grizzly bears in Yellowstone National Park. Calabro does a fine job of writing about their innovative research methods, which included ear-tags and radio collars, the excitement and drama of work with these magnificent endangered animals, and the political battles fought over bear management policy in the parks, during which the Craigheads were forced to end their study. Readers develop an awareness of the plight of the grizzly, a taste of the work of a wildlife biologist, and an understanding of the political issues involved in preserving wildlife. A similar book of interest is Pringle's *Bearman* (Macmillan, 1989) about the work of another wildlife biologist with black bears. The book includes black-and-white photographs, a map of Yellowstone National Park, and an excellent list of books for further reading.

■ **Collins, David R. THE COUNTRY ARTIST: A STORY ABOUT BEATRIX POTTER. Carolrhoda, 1989. 56pp. (LB 0-87614-344-3) SERIES: Creative Minds. Nonfiction. Interest Level: Ages 8–12**

While Beatrix Potter is best known as the writer and illustrator of some of the best-loved children's books published, young readers of this biography will learn that she was also an early environmentalist. She had always loved her stays in the country and in her middle years she bought and moved to a farm in the Lake District of England. Over the years she acquired more land and began to raise and breed sheep. She loved what she called the "pure and simple life" of the country. When she died the 4,000 plus acres of land she owned around the Lake District were turned over to the National Trust to be preserved for everyone to enjoy. Readers who appreciate Potter's great talent in drawing from nature will be pleased to know that she also preserved land for the wildlife that was the source of her inspiration.

■ Faber, Doris, and Harold Faber. NATURE AND THE ENVIRONMENT. Macmillan, 1991. 288pp. (0-684-19047-8) SERIES: Great Lives. Nonfiction. Interest Level: Ages 10–14
With current high interest in the environment, this biographical profile of 26 naturalists, conservationists and environmentalists from around the world is timely and welcome. The Fabers span three centuries as they look at a diverse group of people who contributed in various ways to the study or protection of the environment. Some names are well-known, although their contributions may not be: Thoreau, Muir, Audubon, Darwin, Carson, Cousteau, Linnaeus, and Theodore Roosevelt; other names may be less familiar to young readers: Luther Burbank, Louis Agassiz, Frederick Law Olmsted, J.I. Rodale, Aldo Leopold, and Liberty Hyde Bailey. Information on many of those profiled is not readily available elsewhere and the Fabers bring an engaging writing style to their work. This book serves as a useful addition to collectons serving middle and upper grades. The text is illustrated with photographs, includes list of further reading, and an index.

■ Force, Eden. JOHN MUIR. Silver Burdett, 1990. 146pp. (LB 0-382-09965-6) SERIES: Pioneers in Change. Nonfiction. Interest Level: Ages 11–14
This thorough, fascinating, but lengthy biography of one of the most influential conservationists in America's history will reward the reader who stays with it. In addition to his many accomplishments—he was instrumental in the establishment of a national park system and was one of the founders of the Sierra Club—Muir can serve as a role model for young people. A youth spent in hard labor on a Wisconsin pioneer farm with a strict, demanding, and often hard-hearted father must have been very difficult. That he should have grown into such a likable, talented, and productive person is amazing. Of course, author Force offers insights into those people and places that influenced Muir. Fictionalized conversations in his early years between

John and his friends may jar readers—they're written in a Scottish dialect, then "translated." A chronology of important dates in Muir's life, an ample bibliography, and index are appended. The text is illustrated with occasional photographs.

■ Foster, Leila M. THE STORY OF RACHEL CARSON AND THE ENVIRONMENTAL MOVEMENT. Childrens, 1990. 32pp. (LB 0-516-04753-1) SERIES: Cornerstones of Freedom. Nonfiction. Interest Level: Ages 10–12
This slim biography of Rachel Carson for middle and upper level students offers a basic profile of the woman scientist and writer, best known for her book *Silent Spring*. While Foster doesn't go into much depth on Carson's childhood or personal life, she does discuss her books, the impact of *Silent Spring* in alerting the public to the dangers of pesticides, and her role in the environmental movement. Illustrated with both colored and black-and-white photographs, the book provides a quick look at an important figure in America's environmental movement who can serve as a role model for young people. The book includes an index.

■ Goodall, Jane. MY LIFE WITH THE CHIMPANZEES. Pocket, 1988. 124pp. (paper 0-671-66095-0) Nonfiction. Interest Level: Ages 10–14
Goodall writes an engaging autobiography for children that tends to ramble when she talks about her childhood in England, but turns into a fascinating account of how, in 1960 at the age of 26, she came to study chimpanzees at Gombe National Park in Tanzania, where she has since studied several generations of chimps. In the final chapter she encourages readers in nature watching and careers with animals. She also makes a plea for conservation and animal rights.

■ Graham, Ada. SIX LITTLE CHICKADEES: A SCIENTIST AND HER WORK WITH BIRDS. Macmillan, 1982. 56pp. (LB 0-590-07508-X) Nonfiction. Interest Level: Ages 9–12
This is an easy-to-read biography of Cordelia Stanwood, a teacher who, at the age of forty, became one of the first women to study bird behavior and contribute to the emerging science of ornithology. After a pet crow was shot, Stanwood began her study of birds in earnest and for the next 35 years observed, photographed, and wrote about the birds in and around her home in Ellsworth, Maine. She felt that if people knew more about birds, they would "understand how important they are in our own lives." Graham introduces Stanwood as she begins her bird observations in middle age, so the reader doesn't learn much of her life until that time. She focuses on Stanwood's fieldwork, particularly her study of chickadees and hawks. Black-and-white photographs taken by Stanwood illustrate the text.

■ Harlan, Judith. SOUNDING THE ALARM: A BIOGRAPHY OF RACHEL CARSON. Dillon, 1989. 128pp. (LB 0-87518-407-3) SERIES: People in Focus. Nonfiction. Interest Level: Ages 10–13
Harlan writes about the life and achievements of biologist and writer Rachel Carson, probably best known for her final book, *Silent Spring*, which in 1962 warned the world of the dangers of pesticides to both humans and wildlife. Harlan describes Carson's solitary childhood in a close-knit family in rural Pennsylvania and shows how her love of nature and her family's feel for the land shaped her future. "Rachel Carson saw the world on an ecological level. All things were connected, all things related." Harlan also shows how Carson's combination of intelligence, hard work, and concern for the environment (in an era when women scientists were almost unheard of) led her to write eloquently about ocean life and eventually about toxic chemicals. The book is illustrated with black-and-white photographs and includes a bibliography and an index. This is written for children older than those reading Kathleen Kudlinski's *Rachel Carson: Pioneer of Ecology* (Viking Kestrel, 1988) and younger than Marty Jezer's *Rachel Carson* (Chelsea House, 1988).

■ Jezer, Marty. RACHEL CARSON. Chelsea House, 1988. 110pp. (LB 1-55546-646-X) SERIES: American Women of Achievement. Nonfiction. Interest Level: Ages 10–14
Jezer's biography of the woman scientist who alerted the American public to the dangers of pesticide use focuses on the controversy her book, *Silent Spring*, created and on her social, political, and scientific environment. This book is for older readers than Harlan's *Sounding the Alarm* (Dillon, 1989) and Kudlinski's *Rachel Carson: Pioneer of Ecology* (Viking Kestrel, 1988). The biography is illustrated with black-and-white photographs, not only of Carson, but of people, places, and events that had bearing on her life and work. It includes a list of books for further reading, a chronology of events in Carson's life, and an index. The book has an introductory essay about the series "American Women of Achievement." The book's cover is colorful but not especially attractive. This is an excellent resource for middle and upper level students.
Award: OSTB, 1988

■ Kellogg, Steven. JOHNNY APPLESEED: A TALL TALE. Illus. by author. Morrow, 1988. unp. (LB 0-688-06418-3) Nonfiction. Interest Level: Ages 5–9
Young children will enjoy getting to know Kellogg's easily read introduction to American folk hero Johnny Appleseed. With fun-loving, exaggerated

illustrations and narration, Kellogg highlights several events attributed to real-life frontiersman John Chapman, who travelled west from his birth place in Massachusetts, clearing land, and planting apple orchards to welcome westward moving settlers. While "environmentalist" would be too strong a term to honor him with, Johnny's love of nature, respect for wildlife, and preoccupation with planting apple trees make him an appealing character to introduce on Arbor Day. Kellogg includes a note about known facts of Johnny's life; the back endpapers show a stylized map of his travels.

■ **Kudlinski, Kathleen V. RACHEL CARSON: PIONEER OF ECOLOGY. Illus. by Ted Lewin. Viking, 1988. 56pp. (LB 0-670-81488-1)** SERIES: **Women of Our Time. Nonfiction. Interest Level: Ages 7–11**
Kudlinski, a scientist and former teacher, has written a biography of ecologist Rachel Carson for young children. In short chapters, illustrated with black and white watercolors, she captures Rachel's early years on a 65-acre farm in Pennsylvania in the early 1900s and follows her through college where Rachel changes her major from English to biology, much to the consternation of friends and teachers, because "there was no place for a woman scientist in the 1920s." Rachel eventually combined her love of writing with her love of nature, especially the sea, both through her job at the U.S. Fisheries Bureau, and her books, *Under the Sea Wind, The Sea Around Us* and *The Edge of the Sea.* The biography ends with Rachel's growing awareness of the dangers of pesticides and after much research, publication of *Silent Spring* about the toxic effects of pesticides. The book's cover has a watercolor picture of Carson. There is no index.
Award: OSTB, 1988

■ **Lindbergh, Reeve. JOHNNY APPLESEED. Illus. by Kathy Jakobsen. Little, 1990. Unp. (LB 0-316-52618-5) Nonfiction. Interest Level: Ages 5–10**
Folk hero John Chapman, also known as Johnny Appleseed, is portrayed in this poem by Reeve Lindbergh. The poem is illustrated with paintings by Kathy Jakobsen. Her paintings capture the spirit of the early nineteenth century and help to create a dignified and respectful tribute to this Bible-carrying missionary whose other mission of planting and distributing apple seeds from Massachusetts to Indiana make him a memorable character.
   In the poem Lindbergh speaks of him through a family he visited. Through the years the family hears tales of him. Years later he returns and one daughter, Hannah, continues the tradition of storytelling and legend making. Jakobsen, a folk artist, was a good choice for illustrating a book about this folk hero. Full page paintings depict the rural landscape of the time. Jakobsen has a rich palette and uses deep blues and greens. The text

is framed by a checkered quilt pattern with small scenes of landscapes, of Chapman and, of course, apples throughout the seasons. An epilogue provides some additional facts about Chapman's life. The endpapers show a map of the states he traveled through. This book is an attractive choice.

Award: NSSB, 1990

■ **Pringle, Laurence. BATMAN: EXPLORING THE WORLD OF BATS. Photos by Merlin D. Tuttle. Macmillan, 1991. 48pp. (0-684-19232-2) Nonfiction. Interest Level: Ages 10–14**
Pringle's most recent profile of a scientist and the animal he studies is attractive and well-written. This book should do much to dispel the negative images people have about bats. Merlin Tuttle is the founder of Bat Conservation International, an organization that tries to counter the worldwide decline in bat populations. Pringle shows how Tuttle's childhood interest in nature was nurtured by his parents and led to his early fascination with bats and a professional career involving the study of bats. Pringle combines biographical information with information on bats, emphasizing their ecological role and their endangered status. Pringle discusses efforts by Tuttle and others to learn more about bats and to educate people about their value. The color photographs, taken by Tuttle, are outstanding, and like Pringle's text, may soften some readers attitudes about "nasty" bats. This is eye-catching and high-interest reading. The book includes an index and a list of further reading.

■ **Pringle, Laurence. BEARMAN: EXPLORING THE WORLD OF BLACK BEARS. Illus. by Lynn Rogers. Macmillan, 1989. 42pp. (LB 0-684-19094-X) Nonfiction. Interest Level: Ages 10–13**
Pringle, trained as a wildlife biologist, profiles Lynn Rogers who has been studying black bears in Minnesota for more than 20 years. Rogers' early love of nature led to his biology major in college and eventual career as a wildlife biologist. Pringle captures the inherent drama of Rogers' work as he tracks and studies bears. As in the Craighead's study of grizzly bears in Yellowstone National Park (see Calabro's *Operation Grizzly Bear*), Rogers traps bears and fits them with radio transmitter collars before releasing them. Using this technique he has been able to follow the bears for years and learn about their habits. Rogers downplays black bears' danger to humans; during one study the bears became accustomed to him and he was able to travel and rest with certain bears for a day or two at a time. Some of the photographs show him and his family in close proximity to bears, perhaps not the wisest choice of photographs. While there is alot of information on black bears woven into the story, Pringle has focused more on

Rogers' work as a researcher. The color photographs taken by Rogers are ample and excellent. The cover photo of the biologist with two bear cubs in hand is intriguing. Pringle's list of books and articles for further reading are adult titles. An index is included.

Award: OSTB, 1989

■ **Pringle, Laurence. WOLFMAN: EXPLORING THE WORLD OF WOLVES. Macmillan, 1983. 71pp. o.p. Nonfiction. Interest Level: Ages 10–14**
Pringle writes about wildlife biologist David Mech, who studies wolves and their behavior. Like Lynn Rogers, who Pringle wrote about in *Bearman* (Macmillan, 1989), Mech's early interest in nature and outdoor adventure led to a career as a wildlife biologist. Pringle covers his youth, graduate study of wolves on Isle Royale in Lake Superior, and further research in northern Minnesota, which included aerial and radio tracking. In order to learn more about wolves, nearly annihilated in the United States and still hunted and reviled by some, Mech even tried raising two wolf pups. While he learned more about wolves that way, he regrets what damage is done to wild animals in captivity. Pringle's *Wolfman* is longer than *Bearman* and not as visually exciting. *Wolfman* includes a list of adult books and articles for further reading and an index. It is illustrated with black-and-white photographs. This is a good choice for readers interested in this threatened species and for budding biologists.

■ **Ricciuti, Edward R. THEY WORK WITH WILDLIFE: JOBS FOR PEOPLE WHO WANT TO WORK WITH ANIMALS. Harper, 1983. 148pp. (0-06-025003-8) Nonfiction. Interest Level: Ages 12 up**
Ricciuti, a nature writer and former curator at the New York Zoological Society, writes about careers in several wildlife related fields, outlining responsibilities and educational requirements. By introducing men and women in various fields, readers will get a more vivid picture of what each job is like. For example, Ricciuti traveled to Amboseli National Park in Kenya where he visited field biologist Cynthia Moss, who studies elephants. Not all examples are so exotic, however. Other careers include wildlife management, wildlife law enforcement, animal keeping at an aquarium, nature writing, marine biology, education, and administration. *They Work with Wildlife* offers choices to ecologically or conservation minded students who may wish to pursue their interests in careers. An updated edition with photographs and a colorful, appealing cover would be welcome. Laurence Pringle's books profiling scientists who study bear, bats, and wolves offer a more colorful look at wildlife biologists. Libraries that own *Careers in Conservation* (Sierra Club, 1980) by Ada and Frank Graham, now out of

print, may find additional conservation career information for older readers there.

Award: OSTB, 1983

■ **Rose, Deborah Lee. THE PEOPLE WHO HUGGED THE TREES: AN ENVIRONMENTAL FOLKTALE. Illus. by Birgitta Saflund. Roberts Rinehart, 1990. Unp. (0-911797-80-7) Fiction.** Interest Level: Ages 6–10
Based on a folktale from Rajasthan, India, the story of *The People Who Hugged the Trees* tells of the first Chipko, or "Hug-the-Tree" people. It reminds us of several things—that people have long known of the value of the natural world and the importance of protecting it, the power of folklore, and the power of the individual to make a difference. Amrita was a young girl in India of long ago who loved the trees next to her village on the edge of a desert. The trees provided shade, protected the village from desert sandstorms, and provided water for the villagers. One tree was special to Amrita and she vowed to always protect it. When the majarajab ordered the trees to be cut down to build a fortress, Amrita tried to prevent the man from cutting it down by encircling the trunk with her arms. The tree went down in spite of her efforts, but the whole village rallied to prevent the others from being cut, risking their lives. When the majarajah saw their courage, he spared the villagers and the forest. Rose's adaptation has a happier ending than the story upon which it is based, but today one of India's most dedicated environmental groups is known as the "Chipko Movement". Its members support the nonviolent resistance to the cutting of trees. Saflund's bordered watercolor illustrations are lush with rich blues and crimsons.

■ **Thoreau, Henry David. WALDEN. Edited by Steve Lowe. Illus. by Robert Sabuda. Putnam, 1990. 32pp. (LB 0-399-22153-0) Nonfiction.** Interest Level: Ages 9–13
Outstanding linoleum cuts evoke the beauty of nature around Walden Pond where Henry David Thoreau spent two years, two months, and two days in 1845. For young readers not familiar with Thoreau's famous experiment, these illustrated selections from *Walden* will not completely enlighten them about Thoreau's philosophy and environmental ethic. But, it is a visually stunning and accessible way of introducing to young, but not too young, readers to this writer and philosopher, who was an important influence on the American environmental movement. Use the book with Berchick's biography, *A Man Called Thoreau*, which brings out the quirkiness in Thoreau's personality, and with George's *My Side of the Mountain* in which a young

boy lives by himself on a mountainside for a year, inspired by Thoreau's Walden Pond experience. While the picture book format may put some off, the illustrations enhance Thoreau's communion with nature.

Award: NSSB, 1990

■ **Tolan, Sally. JOHN MUIR. Stevens, 1990. 68pp. (LB 0-8368-0099-0) SERIES: People Who Have Helped the World. Nonfiction. Interest Level: Ages 10–14**
Tolan traces Muir's life from his youth in Scotland to Wisconsin, where his family emigrated in 1849 to farm. After attending the University of Wisconsin, he worked and traveled, eventually settling in California where he became a champion of wilderness preservation and was influential in the formation of the national park system in this country. He also helped found and was first president of the Sierra Club. Muir was active on many fronts; he wrote articles and books, he lectured, and lobbied. Throughout his life he spent much time out-of-doors, and returned again and again to Yosemite, his spiritual home. Tolan covers a lot of territory in the book. Readers looking for a quick-read biography may find the high picture-text ratio appealing, but with quotation-filled margins and no table of contents, it looks a bit cluttered. A map of lands designated as national parks, national wilderness preservation areas, and national wildlife refuge areas is appended although no reference to it is made in the text or index. The index is skimpy. Charles P. Graves' biography for younger readers, *John Muir* (Crowell, 1973) is out of print but better captures Muir's spirit. Eden Force's biography, *John Muir* (Silver Burdett, 1990) will appeal to a slightly older group.

■ **Vandivert, Rita. TO THE RESCUE: SEVEN HEROES OF CONSERVATION. Photos by William Vandivert. Warne, 1982. 119pp. (LB 0-7232-6215-2) Nonfiction. Interest Level: Ages 11–14**
In an attractive book with black-and-white photographs, author Vandivert portrays seven men, most of them British, who have worked in different ways to save endangered species over the past 125 years. She portrays Gerald Durrell, author and founder of the Jersey Wildlife Preservation Trust, a breeding center for rare animals; Joe Henson, who through the Rare Breeds Survival Trust, works to save rare breeds of domestic animals from extinction; Len Hill, a conservationist whose interest is birds; Peter Scott, once a hunter, who established the Severn Wildfowl Trust; Father Armand David, a nineteenth century Jesuit priest from France who collected unknown species of animals in China; the first Duke of Bedford, who collected

and bred rare mammals; and Fairfield Osborn, the only American included, who was influential in the development of zoos in this country. Vandivert provides some information on each person's background but concentrates on their conservation activities. Vandivert's writing is dry, but this is a good source of information on some relatively unknown conservationists here and abroad. A list of further reading is appended. The book is indexed.

5

It's Your Turn

Activities, Explorations, Activism

The books in the first four chapters do several things: foster positive attitudes about the environment; acquaint children with principles of ecology; inform them of environmental issues; and introduce them to differing attitudes toward nature. Many of these books discuss serious, sometimes frightening issues.

It seems fitting to conclude *E for Environment* on a hopeful note. Books in Chapter Five are a diverse group of hands-on books written to help children (and adults working with them) become actively involved in learning about and protecting this fragile earth. Users will find children's titles interspersed with a handful of adult books. Parents, teachers, youth leaders, and other nature educators will find these books helpful when planning classes, programs, and other nature and environmental activities with children.

Discovering includes books with solar experiments, seasonal activities, storytelling, recycling ideas, even environmental science fair projects. In *Exploring*, readers will find suggestions for urban explorations, wildlife watching, and nature detecting. *Tending the Earth* books guide and instruct young gardeners whether they are city dwellers or country kids. The titles in *Taking Action* were chosen from the group of recent activism books for children. They offer ideas, opportunities for empowerment, and hope.

Discovering: Nature and Environmental Activities, Experiences, and Experiments

■ Adams, Florence. CATCH A SUNBEAM: A BOOK OF SOLAR STUDY AND EXPERIMENTS. Illus. by Kiyo Komoda. Harcourt, 1978. 77pp. (0-15-215197-4) Nonfiction. Interest Level: Ages 12 up
With continued dependence on fossil fuels raising environmental and political concerns, this selection has a ready audience as the search for energy alternatives stretches on. Adams begins this thoughtfully constructed guide by looking to the past with chapters including activities that illuminate sun theories of the ancients, progressing to eventual, hard-won acceptance of the sun as the center of the solar system. Ensuing sections and activities describe and demonstrate ways the sun can work for us, and camping out with the sun. Projects range widely in terms of complexity, from telling time with the sun, to building a simple desalination system, to constructing a parabolic solar grill, to building a solar furnace. The latter two projects very likely would require adult assistance. Instructions are clear and concise, augmented by precise line drawings. This brightly jacketed collection of sixteen solar projects is a challenging, hardworking guide to hands-on solar study for young energy scientists and adults alike. This book is recommended for larger middle schools and most public library collections. A comprehensive glossary and an index are included.

■ Allison, Linda. THE WILD INSIDE: SIERRA CLUB'S GUIDE TO THE GREAT INDOORS. Illus. by author. Little, 1988 (repr. of 1979 ed.). 144pp. (paper 0-316-03434-7) Nonfiction. Interest Level: Ages 8–14
What does the distribution of dust puppies tell you about your house? Do you know the source of your water? Did you know that sounds can raise your blood pressure? This imaginative tour of the great indoors is an entertaining, thought provoking introduction to our most immediate environment. From molds in the refrigerator, to the beetle under the carpet, to the gypsum in the plaster, Allison's keen eye and creative, ready-for-fun style, informs and involves the reader. Four chapters of explorations begin with a "Shelter" section, briefly describing various types of structures humans have fashioned to survive the elements. "Wild and Not So Wild" includes, for example, discussions of insects, the occasional spider, mice, pets, molds, house plants, seeds, bulbs, roots, and the like. "Indoor Geology" considers the amazing number of rocks an indoor geologist can find, while "House Happenings" treats such topics as heating, lighting, plumbing, waste disposal, micro-climate, and a summarizing reminder of the necessity for making choices in and for the home with heightened aware-

ness of the impact on the environment at large. Experiments and ideas for crafts projects appear on almost every page. Projects range from the more predictable, such as measuring the growth of an indoor plant, to assembling an unusual, but no doubt, handy device for amplifying insect sounds. Simple, sometimes comical, line drawings supplement step-by-step instructions, and complement the breezy text. Here's indoor fun with a go-lightly environmental message that probably will not have to wait on the shelf for a rainy day. An outdoorsy counterpart: Linda Allison's *Sierra Club Summer Book* (Little, Brown, 1977, 1989) is a collection of animal facts, summer activities, craft projects, and nature discussion with an *out*door focus.

■ **Arnosky, Jim. DRAWING FROM NATURE. Illus. by author. Lothrop, 1982. Unp. o.p. Nonfiction. Interest Level: Ages 10 up**
"Drawing from nature is discovering the upside down scene through a water drop. It is noticing how much of a fox is tail. Drawing from nature is learning how a tree grows and a flower blooms. It is sketching in the mountains and breathing air bears breathe," says artist, author, naturalist Jim Arnosky who wears his heart on his sleeve and allows a glimpse of his soul in creating this lovely book. In four sections dealing with water, land, plants, and animals, elegantly spare prose, and beautifully designed pages of supporting drawings provide both artist and non-artist with poetic visual experiences. Glistening beads of moisture on a spider web, a raccoon track in mud, delicate tendrils grasping a stem, and the hissing sound of air escaping as a box turtle closes up tight—these are the images and impressions shared by a contemplative Arnosky. Drawing instructions touch on fundamentals, but focus more on the artist's vision and interpretive techniques. There are no step-by-step instructions here; instead, Arnosky discusses drawing animals, for example, in a broadly applicable way by highlighting basic musculature, which lines should be heavier or lighter, how to put gleam into eyes, the shine on moist noses, and the growth and layering of scale, feather, and fur. A wonderful companion volume, *Drawing Nature in Motion* (Lothrop, 1984), continues and expands Arnosky's insightful lessons on observation and drawing finesse.
Award: ALA Notable Children's Book, 1982

■ **Arnosky, Jim. SKETCHING OUTDOORS IN WINTER. Illus. by author. Lothrop, 1988. 48pp. (0-688-06290-3) Nonfiction. Interest Level: Ages 10 up**
There's a shiver in these pages. As temperatures dip and snow blankets his farm, Jim Arnosky ventures outdoors for another season of drawing from life. His other books include *Sketching Outdoors in Spring* (Lothrop, 1987),

Sketching Outdoors in Summer (Lothrop, 1988), and *Sketching Outdoors in Autumn,* (Lothrop, 1988). Standing on showshoes, sketching with woolen-gloved fingers, cold air on his face and in his lungs, Arnosky finds the season exhilarating. He muses, "Winter makes you think of essential things—warm life and cold death. It is the season to sketch solitary objects. Against winter's stark background, everything stands out as strikingly individual." Here is an artist-naturalist's portrait of a New England winter: snow swept hillsides, bare branches supporting abandoned nests, full-body mouse tracks, a thick frosting of snow over a stream bank, and an off-course snowy owl. Two page spreads with two tiers of text include a pencil sketch, observations and reflections in larger type, tips and techniques for the artist in smaller, bold italicized type. For each drawing, Arnosky first focuses observation, and then cues the artist that, for example, an eraser can be used to "lift out" shaded areas for a highlighting effect, or that a snowy look can be added later with paint spattered from a toothbrush. An ode to winter, this lovely book will inspire nature observers and artists alike to experience the season's beauty with fresh awareness.

Award: ALA Notable Children's Book, 1988

■ **Beller, Joel. EXPERIMENTING WITH PLANTS: PROJECTS FOR HOME, GARDEN, AND CLASSROOM. Simon & Schuster, 1985. 154pp. (paper 0-668-059-915) Nonfiction. Interest Level: Ages 11 up**
Do marigolds repel certain insects? Do electromagnetic fields affect seed germination? What is the effect of acid rain on root growth? While the environment is not the primary focus of this project guide, science teacher and science fair judge Joel Beller's selection of plant experiments provides numerous worthwhile opportunities for assessing the effects of a variety of environmental factors on plant growth and for investigating organic growing methods, soil and hydroponic. After a weak introductory section, Beller presents a helpful outline of planning, library research, and an example of a carefully developed and executed experiment. An additional preliminary chapter is devoted to horticultural basics. Experiments follow, ranging from simple assessment of the effect of flower pot shape on plant growth, to use of an elaborate airtight chamber, which is designed to expose plants to controlled amounts of sulphur dioxide—this to be attempted only with adult assistance. Some experiments are presented step-by-step, others are questions, or ideas for further investigation. Line drawings are useful, but black-and-white photographs are unattractive. A significant chapter detailing display and reporting of project results is misplaced at the very end of the book. A bibliography and index are included.

■ Bjork, Christina. LINNEA'S ALMANAC. Trans. by Joan Sandin. Illus. by Lena Anderson. Farrar, 1989. 60pp. (91-29-59176-7) Nonfiction. Interest Level: Ages 8–12

It's June. Linnea and her friends, Mr. Bloom and Mr. Brush, don floral garlands to celebrate the solstice with a garden party. Mute swans are tending downy cygnets, a bumblebee visits red clover, and the rhubarb is ripe, perfect for a compote. Christina Bjork's lively youngster shares an entire year of nature lore and activities: a January restaurant for birds, a search for the first flower of spring, a beach treasure hunt, autumn star gazing, a year's end blooming amaryllis, and more. This celebration of seasons is woven around a substantial core of interesting information and advice. Linnea's herbarium project involves cautious collection and careful analysis of specimens. She enjoys using her vocabulary of Latin names for familiar plant and animals. As an apartment dweller, most of Linnea's activities take place in an urban setting and make this especially appealing to city girls. This book combines artful pastel illustrations with conversational prose.

■ Bonnet, Robert L, and G. Daniel Keen. ENVIRONMENTAL SCIENCE: 49 SCIENCE FAIR PROJECTS. TAB Books, 1990. 124pp. (0-8306-7369-5) SERIES: Science Fair Projects. Nonfiction. Interest Level: Ages 10–14

With growing interest in environmental topics for science fair projects, this selection will be a welcome addition to school and public libraries—despite some limitations. In an introductory section and first chapter, science teacher Bonnet and computer consultant, Keen, discuss science fair fundamentals. They provide a single page definition and description of environmental science. No additional information sources are listed here or elsewhere. A stop sign symbol used to indicate when adult supervision is required is highlighted along with laboratory safety guidelines. No mention is made of the need to obtain permission before entering or disturbing a natural area, or of the necessity of leaving those areas just as they were found. There are seven chapters, each consisting of seven projects: soil, habitat and life cycles, pest control, recycling, decomposition, indoor environment, and "Mankind and the Environment." The activities, demonstrations, and experiments are interesting and varied, ranging from testing the effectiveness of tannin as an herbicide, to sampling airborne particulate matter in the home, to making fuel bricks from tree litter. Well-organized project pages include an overview, list of easily obtained materials, procedures, and ideas for further investigation. Line drawings are helpful; data charting format is often included, but no guidance is provided for reaching a conclusion. Occasional errors in word usage and awkward sentence structure detract from this book. Both a glossary and an index are included. Students and teachers of environmental studies will find several more related projects in the authors' *Botany: 49 Science Fair Projects* (TAB, 1989).

■ Bowden, Marcia. NATURE FOR THE VERY YOUNG: A HANDBOOK OF INDOOR AND OUTDOOR ACTIVITIES. Illus. by Marilyn Rishel. Wiley, 1989. 225pp. (0-471-50975-2) Nonfiction. Interest Level: Adult
Using a seasonal arrangement, Bowden presents an array of nature activities designed primarily for use by preschool or nature center educators, but readily adptable for use by parents and other friends of the younger child (preschool through second grade). Preparatory and follow-up activities for field experiences, with insightful, practical suggestions for turning nature outings into purposeful, focused activity are the strengths here. While the author promotes adaptation of the content to more urban situations, many ideas seem singularly suited to those with access to field and forest environments. Recipes, stories, songs, poetry, even reproducible line drawings are gathered by theme or topic with basic educational goals and concepts outlined. A bibliography and an index are included.

■ Burnie, David. HOW NATURE WORKS: 100 WAYS PARENTS AND KIDS CAN SHARE THE SECRETS OF NATURE. Reader's Digest, 1991. 192pp. (0-89577-391-0) Nonfiction. Interest Level: Ages 11 up
One hundred natural history/biology projects "devised so that the whole family can join in," are very attractively presented in Dorling Kindersley, Ltd. ("Eyewitness Books" and "My First") style. Step-by-step instructions and photographs illustrate the projects. Beginning with a look at the chemistry of life and at simple organisms; touching on evolution and ecology; discussing fungi, flowering plants, trees, life in fresh and salt water, insects, birds, and reptiles; the book concludes with a section devoted to mammals, a substantial portion of which deals with humans. Burnie's smoothly written narrative helps tie together this ambitious book. Concepts and vocabulary will challenge upper elementary and many middle school readers. Exciting presentations are used to invite and sustain interest. Sometimes unnecessarily complex or elaborate, but always intriguing projects include demonstrations and activities such as transect and quadrant plant surveys, age and height measurement of a tree, trapping underwater night life, seeing inside a shell, building a moth trap or a formicarium, examining owl pellets, and making a model lung. Projects requiring adult assistance and/or special safety precautions are clearly labelled. A naturalist's "Look, learn, and then leave alone." motto is noted in an introduction, but reinforced only sporadically in the text. Initial appeal not withstanding, flair and format

overshadow practicality and substance. This substantial volume will be chosen where budget allows and in response to heavy demand for this type of resource. Both a glossary and an index are included. (The book jacket promises a forthcoming *How Ecology Works.*)

■ Caduto, Michael J, and Joseph Bruchac. KEEPERS OF THE EARTH: NATIVE AMERICAN STORIES AND ENVIRONMENTAL ACTIVITIES FOR CHILDREN. Illus. by John Kahionhes Fadden and Carol Wood. Fulcrum, 1988. 209pp. (1-55591-027-0) Nonfiction. Interest Level: Adult
This fine collection of 25 legends from 20 different Native American cultures provides a structure and a thematic context for environmental education. The authors say, "This is a book about learning, loving, and caring: a collection of carefully chosen North American Indian stories and hands-on activities that promote understanding of, empathy for, and responsibility towards the Earth, including its people." A fundamental belief "that all living and nonliving parts of the Earth are *one* and that people are part of that wholeness" is reflected in ancient wisdom and preserved in oral tradition. The authors, an ecologist and a storyteller, orient parents, teachers, and nature center educators to this inter-disciplinary, holistic educational approach (designed for use with children ages five through twelve) in several preliminary pages of helpful background information, storytelling tips, techniques, and "Steps for Using This Book Effectively." Each retold story is followed by discussion and questions. Accompanying activities, presented in a lesson plan format, focus on environmental themes, or expand—somewhat less successfully—on related scientific concepts. Another section, "Extending the Experience," includes additional project and activity ideas. Note: Access to natural areas is assumed. Full-color cover art and line drawings have an appealing, mystical quality. Map, glossary, pronunciation key, and index are included.

■ Cornell, Joseph. SHARING THE JOY OF NATURE: NATURE ACTIVITIES FOR ALL AGES. Dawn (14618 Tyler Foote Road, Nevada City, CA 95959), 1989. 167pp. (paper 0-916124-52-5) Nonfiction. Interest Level: Adult
From the repertoire of a prominent outdoor educator, this pleasantly designed, clearly written sequel to the classic *Sharing Nature With Children* (Ananda, 1979) includes many additional nature games and activities for children and adults. Cornell introduces his systematic yet flexible "Flow Learning" concept, a structure that facilitates planning and presentation by grouping games and activities in four stages to (1) awaken enthusiasm, (2) focus attention, (3) direct experience, and (4) share inspiration. Cornell greets a group with playful, high energy activities, provides opportunities

for focused observation and direct involvement, and closes with inspiration drawn from the shared experiences of the group or from the words of a great naturalist such as John Muir. "The goal of Flow Learning is to give everyone a genuinely uplifting experience of nature . . . each person feels a subtle, enjoyable new awareness of his oneness with nature and an increased empathy for life." Each activity can be quickly accessed by referring to shaded boxes which provide: stage, concepts, attitudes, and qualities taught by the game, number of players, age range, and materials. Line drawings, effective photographs, and anecdotal experiences supplement clearly presented activity how-to's. The games include "Natural Processes," "Build a Tree," "Sound Map," "Camera," and "Birds of the Air." They involve body, mind, and senses. A summarizing chapter detailing a "Flow Learning" experience precedes a final "Bring Out the Best in Others" chapter. Appended materials include a short story by Jean Giono, "The Man Who Planted Hope and Grew Happiness," and a "Flow Learning Activity Chart," that categorizes games from this selection along with those from *Sharing Nature with Children* and from *Listening to Nature* (Dawn Pub., 1987). A bibliography includes books which inspire, resources for teachers, and references for specific activities. There is an index to quotations. This book is highly recommended for outdoor educators, teachers, and youth group leaders.

■ **Dekkers, Midas. NATURE BOOK: DISCOVERING, EXPLORING, OB-SERVING, EXPERIMENTING WITH PLANTS AND ANIMALS AT HOME AND OUTDOORS. Trans. by Jan Michael. Illus. by Angela de Vrede. Macmillan, 1988. 95pp. (0-02-726690-7) Nonfiction. Interest Level: Ages 8–12**
Midas Dekker's special talent for gathering interesting and fun ideas for intermediate level nature explorers, coupled with generous use of Angela de Verde's wonderful watercolors and charmingly detailed and accented line drawings, yields a very successful collaboration by author and illustrator. Here is an eclectic gathering of nature observation, experimentation, and craft activities, that provides a catalog of possible explorations. Organized in nine thematic chapters, each of the usually multi-faceted or phased activities is presented on two opposite pages with text, illustrations, and layout equalling a stylish, unified whole—aesthetically pleasing and easily referenced. Early chapters are devoted to observing and collecting with tips for keeping a nature logbook, making a convenient device to protect binocular lenses, tape recording nature sounds, assembling a stick and clothespin stand for a closer look at specimens, and adapting a garment by adding pockets, tabs, and gadgets for use as an expedition jacket. Collecting is to be done with respectful discretion; greater emphasis is placed on collecting

facts or observations. Although a substantial portion of the book is devoted to focused observations at home, at the zoo, and afield, activities involving spore prints, growing what has collected on one's shoe soles, making a nature orchestra, and weaving a basket from rushes will satisfy the experimenters and crafts oriented student. Directions include minimal step-by-step coverage, rely on visual cues and clues, and may need to be supplemented. A final "Lend Them a Hand" chapter discusses environmental activism, suggesting ways to feed and house birds. The book concludes with some simple observations and activities designed to help assess environmental pollution. Written in Dutch and translated by a Briton, American readers will note some variance in plant species and differences in vocabulary. The material is indexed.

Award: OSTB, 1988

■ EARTHWATCHING III: AN ENVIRONMENTAL READER WITH TEACHER'S GUIDE. Inst. for Environmental Studies, Univ. of Wis. (15 Science Hall, 550 N. Park St., Madison, WI 53706), 1990. 160pp. (paper 0-936287-01-2) Nonfiction. Interest Level: Adult
This fasinating book brings together short 200-word scripts about the workings of nature, scientific inquiry and discovery, and environmental concerns of the past, present, and future. Based on a popular radio series "Earthwatch" produced at the University of Wisconsin, *Earthwatching III* covers topics that range from ocean pollution to energy conservation, climate change to endangered species, and hazardous waste to outdoor recreation. Tailored especially for teachers, it includes a teacher's guide that explains how to use the book throughout the curriculum for students in elementary through high school. An index is included.

■ George, Jean Craighead. THE WILD, WILD COOKBOOK: A GUIDE FOR YOUNG WILD-FOOD FORAGERS. Illus. by Walter Kessell. Crowell, 1982. 182pp. Nonfiction. Interest Level: Ages 10 up
From fiddlehead (fern) pie to rosehip jam, this award-winning author has collected four seasons of recipes sure to intrigue the foraging set. Opening with a cautionary statement, as well as some general guidelines, George presents description and habitat for each of 39 edible plants, followed by recipes carefully and clearly outlined for less-experienced cooks: each recipe includes a list of ingredients and utensils, with directions in numbered order. Kessell's delicate, shaded line drawings enhance botanical descriptions, complete with scientific names, and harvest months. Interesting details, such as which violets taste sweetest, abound. Appealingly jacketed, pleasing layout, the book includes an index.

■ Herman, Marina Lachecki, et al. TEACHING KIDS TO LOVE THE
EARTH. Illus. by Carolyn Olson. Pfiefer-Hamilton Publishers (1702 E.
Jefferson, Duluth, MN 55812), 1991. 175pp. (paper 0-938586-42-4) Nonfiction. Interest Level: Adult
Thoughtful and wise, this aesthetically pleasing guide springs from the
shared vision of four collaborating naturalists whose philosophies, teaching
styles, and "Sense of Wonder Workshops" are inspired by Rachel Carson's
classic, *A Sense of Wonder*, (Harper, 1956, 1987). Carson's belief that it is
more important to nurture feelings about the natural world than to teach
specific knowledge of it, is reflected in this collection of 186 earth-caring
activities. From a wet-footed hike in search of a fictional Abberwocky, to
collecting maple sap and making syrup, to taking a stand for an environmental cause, these tested activities were designed for use by families,
teachers, naturalists, scout leaders, and other adults involved with children.
Experiences are organized in chapters based on the authors' "Sense of
Wonder Circle," curiosity, discovery, sharing, and passion. Each activity
section is introduced by a stage-setting story, followed by an activity outline
including purpose, age/number/setting, materials, and how-to. "Did You
Know?" provides additional background information and rationale; "Other
Ideas" is a listing of one-, two-, or three-sentence suggestions for related
experiences. The "Resources" sections are noteworthy—including carefully
chosen, timely selections. Very fine charcoal sketches by Carolyn Olson
portray the beauty, joy, and wonder engendered here. A superb selection on
its own, or as a companion to books by Joseph Cornell, this guide warrants
a place on the shelves of most public libraries; teachers will appreciate
finding a copy in the school library media center as well. There is no index.

■ Hillerman, Anne. DONE IN THE SUN: SOLAR PROJECTS FOR CHIL-
DREN. Illus. by Mina Yamashita. Sunstone, 1983. 31pp. (paper 0-86534-
018-8) Nonfiction. Interest Level: Ages 6–10
This slimmest of volumes greets primary and younger intermediate level
solar investigators with a laughing sun on a bright yellow paperback cover.
A brief forward and just seven paragraphs of background information about
solar energy preface the activities. Each project is introduced with a little
scenario involving Sarah, Kevin, and Peggy, whose dialogues provide context for the activity to follow. Peggy, for instance, is assisted in creating an
almost-no-budget birthday gift for her mother, a sun projection, yielding a
silhouette portrait. Each activity also includes an easily referenced list of
readily available materials and well defined step-by-step instructions and
helpful simple line drawings. Questions and answers skillfully designed to
reinforce or expand on demonstrated concepts follow. Projects include
Peggy's shadow tracing, observation of the effects of sun and shade on

water temperature, sun tattoos, comparison of heat reflective and absorbent colors, controlled fading of colored paper, sun tea, salt crystal garden, sundial, solar cooking, and desalination. All can be accomplished with minimal or no adult assistance; busy teachers will recognize that these are accessible blueprints for process-oriented science curriculums. Perhaps eclipsed by previously published solar experiment books in terms of breadth of coverage, this collection of projects is uniquely well suited and designed for its intended audience.

■ Markle, Sandra. EXPLORING SPRING: A SEASON OF SCIENCE ACTIVI-
TIES, PUZZLERS, AND GAMES. Illus. by author. Macmillan, 1990.
122pp. (0-689-31341-1) Nonfiction. Interest Level: Ages 8–12
As breezy and unpredictable as a spring day, Sandra Markle's newest seasonal collection of trivia, riddles, games, investigations, plant and animal facts and lore, and things to make and do, zigzags in unexpected directions, but always leads to fun. As with her previous winter and summer volumes, the pleasures of the season are extolled within loosely structured chapters; here, for instance, the opening "Spring Fever" section associates the tradition of Spring clean up with the science of soap and a soap test, moving next to super bubble fun, moving to solid waste disposal issues, recycling, and then to making recycled paper—all of this activity occurs on pages nine through 15. The prose style is suitably lively, characterized by short sentences, and whirlwind transitions. This is a brainstorming, energetic approach with ideas and activity aplenty for a lively age group and for those who work with them. The science content is enrichment-oriented. Bits of trivia are here and there accents; riddles pop up in unexpected places. Black-and-white line drawings are integrated to good effect and enhance especially the "Buds and Blooms" section. Build a nest the way the birds do, go a-Maying, plant some strawberries; while this book is not a "must" purchase, it will be enjoyed by school and public library audiences. There is an index.

■ Milord, Susan. THE KIDS' NATURE BOOK: 365 INDOOR/OUTDOOR
ACTIVITIES AND EXPERIENCES. Illus. by author. Williamson, 1989.
158pp. (paper 0-913589-42-X) Nonfiction. Interest Level: Ages 8–12
From especially appealing cover art, to the charmingly designed, appended "notes" section, this environmentally conscientious nature book is thoughtfully organized and carefully crafted. An almanac arrangement groups activities seasonally, with individual weeks typically focused on a single theme or subject, for example, a "True Love" week for mid-February. This includes drawing a habitat diagram, reflections on people's impact on

nature, making an edible Valentine for birds, reading a story or poem about loving nature, showing respect for all living things, learning about endangered species, making ecologically sound decisions/changes, and joining an environmental group. Two-page, seven column layouts display a week at a glance; a liberal sprinkling of winsome, small drawings provides a decorative accent, while additional more utilitarian line drawings supplement typically short, two or three paragraph selections/instructions. While the calendar organization affords an ideal structure for using this guide, an index ensures quick access to specific subjects from acid rain to zoos. Additional print resources are cited in context, supplemented by an appended bibliography. Appended materials also include listings of environmental organizations and science and crafts suppliers. An overall tone of respect and caring infuses this excellent book.

■ **Pellowski, Anne. HIDDEN STORIES IN PLANTS: UNUSUAL AND EASY-TO-TELL STORIES FROM AROUND THE WORLD TOGETHER WITH CREATIVE THINGS TO DO WHILE TELLING THEM. Illus. by Lynn Sweat. Macmillan, 1990. 93pp. (0-02-770611-7) Nonfiction. Interest Level: Ages 10 up**
"Like the floss of dandelions and milkweed, these stories should continue to be sent floating out into the wide world . . . By telling them, we keep alive our wonder at the tremendous variety of life on our planet." Whether retold in forest, field, garden, kitchen, or classroom, storytellers, nature center educators, parents, or teachers, their audiences will delight in this international collection of charmingly simple tales about daisies and violets, ferns and palms, popcorn and peas, thorns and trees. Captivating as well as clearly illustrated crafts cleverly transform a leaf or pea pod into a boat, fallen branches into a leafy tent, various garden flowers into a "doll for a day," or pine cones, seed pods, and grasses into a rhythm band. Stories and crafts complement one another and tell of pleasant occupations for gentle times. Judicious picking of plants is advised, or better still, use of fallen seeds, leaves, blossoms, and branches. Cautions about irritating or poisonous plants seem sufficient, but parents and teachers should be forewarned that some people are highly allergic to seemingly innocuous plants. Master storyteller Pellowski closes with source and resource bibliographies, and a list of "Holidays and Other Special Times to Celebrate Plants." There is no index, but an expanded table of contents offers adequate access.
Award: OSTB, 1990

■ **Rainis, Kenneth G. NATURE PROJECTS FOR YOUNG SCIENTISTS. Watts, 1989. 142pp. (LB 0-531-10789-2) SERIES: Projects for Young Scientists. Nonfiction. Interest Level: Ages 12 up**

Providing ideas and direction for the neophyte nature experimenter, this book opens with a brief, cogent introduction to basic scientific method, outlining the planning, procedures, and care involved in executing a valid investigation. Biologist and science fair judge Rainis stresses the concept of, and provides a blueprint for, science as a "process of inquiry." Since many of the projects require access to a microscope, instructions are provided for building a simple "flea glass." (With few exceptions, project materials are readily available.) Chapter one preliminaries also include basic safety information and reminders appear in bold print wherever appropriate. Project chapter subjects include bacteria, fungi, one-celled organisms and other protists, plants, invertebrates, vertebrates, and "Nature at Large—" experiments relating to soil conservation, design of a closed eco-system, biomes, succession, and acid rain. Many activities are presented step-by-step, while others are suggestions or starting points for further investigation. Prose is appropriate, clear, and interesting; new terms and concepts are defined in context. Helpful diagrams and black-and-white photographs are logically placed. Chapters conclude with bibliographies. There is an appendix of science suppliers and an index. Students of environmental science may find additional ideas for investigation in the uneven Projects for Young Scientists series: Martin J. Gutnik's disappointing *Ecology* (Watts, 1984) and Robert Gardner's *Energy* (Watts, 1987) that includes energy conservation and alternative energy projects, but is aimed at an older audience.

■ **Rights, Mollie. BEASTLY NEIGHBORS: ALL ABOUT WILD THINGS IN THE CITY, OR WHY EARWIGS MAKE GOOD MOTHERS. Illus. by Kim Solga. Little, 1981. 125pp. (0-316-74576-6) SERIES: Brown Paper School. Nonfiction. Interest Level: Ages 8–12**
Here is an energetic, freely ranging guide to exciting experiences, activities, and explorations for the young urban naturalist. Rights finds nature everywhere: in the supermarket, under a board in the backyard, on the windowsill, in a sidewalk crack, or in the limbs of an adopted tree. Beastly neighbors are introduced in cleverly titled chapters relating to food resources: worms, ants, and cockroaches; weeds and trees; mice, rats, birds, and wildlife. A just-right balance of boxed, clearly illustrated and described activities and experiments using readily available materials dots the conversational text. Representative projects include: pollinating a flower, teaching a cockroach to navigate its way through a homemade maze, building a window bird feeder, or duplicating one of Charles Darwin's experiments—observing the response of earthworms to a piano concert. On the heels of this whirlwind tour of plant and animal adaptation and survival in the urban setting, Rights forges ahead with additional sections devoted to air, water, waste disposal and recycling, green spaces, community activism, and gardening. Accompanying activities suggest ways to assess and/or respond to environmental

problems. The type and drawings are an attractive brown on buff throughout; pleasant line drawings complement and supplement the text. The arrangement is cheerily idiosyncratic, but this zestful introduction to the complex world of urban ecology is right on target with ideas for active learning opportunities. There is no index. Linda Allison's *The Reasons for Seasons: the Great Cosmic Megagalactic Trip Without Moving from Your Chair* (Little, 1975), is a similarly eclectic selection of activities for both children and adults.

■ **Robinson, Sandra Chisholm. THE WONDER OF WOLVES: A STORY AND ACTIVITIES. Illus. by Gail Kohler Opsahl. Roberts Rinehart, 1989. 52pp. (paper 0-911797-65-3) Nonfiction. Interest Level: Ages 8 up**
Children playing in the attic find a wolf ceremonial mask; this discovery re-awakens their grandfather's memories of his proud Nootka heritage and prompts him to share recollections of his boyhood. Drawing on the beautiful kindred relationship a people perceives with "brother wolf," an otherwise prosaic story gains strength. A child's response to the aging chief's words affirms the preservation of a rich tradition.

Building on concepts and information woven into this story, the activities section conveys a substantial amount of information about wolf biology, habitat, and social behavior. Facts are gradually introduced, integrated with projects, engaging reader to the very last page. While some activities are cut, color, or fill in the blank, many can be experienced without dismantling or marking the book. A page to be held to the light provides a look inside the wolf at skeletal structure; a wolf pack can be folded from newspaper, and a checklist wolf observation guide—designed for zoo visits—synthesizes and applies new learning. Watercolor and line drawing illustrations, from a full-color cover, to black and gray within, are a bit sentimental, but handsome. A justifiable selection for even the most modest-sized collection, this story/activity book will be appreciated by the younger child sharing with an adult, independent intermediates, and teachers. There is a bibliography for both children and adults.

■ **Rockwell, Robert E., Elizabeth A. Sherwood, and Robert A. Williams. HUG A TREE: AND OTHER THINGS TO DO OUTDOORS WITH YOUNG CHILDREN. Illus. by Laurel J. Sweetman. Gryphon House, 1983. 106pp. (paper 0-87659-105-5) Nonfiction. Interest Level: Adult**
"What better gift can we as parents and teachers give this precarious earth than a generation of children who have learned to know and love the natural world?" This trio of educators have collaborated in producing a practical, logically organized, appealing, and accessible guide to environ-

mental education for busy parents and teachers of preschoolers. Preliminary pages are comprised of a brief overview of how the young child learns, organizational logistics, and a fine, if somewhat dated, resources section. Also included here is disavowal of any notion that access to the deep, dark woods and open meadows are prerequisites for meaningful outdoor experiences, although visits to more complex environments may play a role in programming at some point. Activities are arranged in chapters that focus on aesthetic and affective experiences, observation, counting, classifying, and recording—measurement, change, and time—and a final "Hodge Podge," a catchall for crafts, poison ivy awareness, and other miscellaneous information. Each activity is labelled to indicate the age group for which it is geared; experiences are sequentially arranged, but may be used in the order that seems appropriate. "Spyglass Treasure Hunt," "The Texture Collector," "Grow a Sock" (seed dispersal), and "Wash Out" (soil erosion) are a few of more than fifty-five outlined activities. Each project includes a brief introduction, materials list, glossary directions, and suggestions for additional activities. Line drawings are pleasant and helpful. This excellent guide belongs in preschool and day care center professional collections and public libraries. An index is included.

■ Schwartz, Linda. **EARTH BOOK FOR KIDS: ACTIVITIES TO HELP HEAL THE ENVIRONMENT.** Illus. by Beverly Armstrong. Learning Works, 1990. 184pp. (paper 0-88160-195-0) Nonfiction. Interest Level: Ages 8 up
These "activities to help heal the environment" reflect the carefully coordinated efforts of a team that has produced more than fifty educational activity books. Well-organized chapters deal with energy, resources, recycling, air, land, water, plants, and animal habitats. One chapter, "More Ways to Make Every Day Earth Day" includes background information about environmental issues with suggestions for earth-friendly activities, arts and crafts, experiments, and suggestions for further study. Bold, attention-demanding graphics introduce, illustrate, and supplement both text and clearly detailed how-to's. "Earthwords," includes environmental quotes from a bevy of "quotables" such as Victor Hugo and Margaret Mead are interspersed throughout the chapter. Short biographies of some environmentalists are included, along with discussion of relevant issues or events. While this selection was ambitiously designed for use by "kids, parents, classroom teachers, and youth leaders," it is likely that upper elementary and middle school "kids" segment of its audience will find activities such as, making a paper bag vest, writing a thank you note to a honey bee, or designing an environmental coat of arms "too young" or "schoolish." Some

hands-on projects that may interest the older student include, simulating an oil spill (with a small amount of cooking oil), testing clean-up alternatives, planning a garage sale and donating proceeds to an environmental cause, or becoming a home toxic substances alternatives specialist. Despite some limitations, this optimistic, upbeat workbook is a worthwhile addition for larger library collections. A resources section includes addresses for various environmental groups. There is a glossary and an expanded table of contents, but no index.

■ Simons, Robin. RECYCLOPEDIA. Illus. by author. Houghton, 1976. 118pp. (paper 0-395-24380-7) Nonfiction. Interest Level: Ages 8 up
A tried and true resource, a book based on experiences and workshops of the Recycle Center of the Boston Children's Museum, *Recyclopedia* is a sure bet for independent young crafters, and for those who work with children. Simon's stated goal is to provide direction, to foster new attitudes and creativity in searching for "found" materials, and in their creative re-use. Beads, buttons, boxes, and bottle caps (and the like) scrounged from around the house and rescued from cooperating businesses are incorporated in creation of games, a water microscope, a rubber band spring scale, weaving, puppetry, printing, constructions, musical instruments, etc. Directions are clear and concise, illustrated with line drawings. One note of caution: use of matte and X-acto knives may require adult supervision. Crafters are encouraged to improvise, experiment, and adapt; ideas for making model wheeled vehicles, for instance, include mechanical fundamentals, plus imagination-stimulating lists of possible items for use as bodies, axles, and wheels. While this selection is found amongst the craft books in most library collections, its usefulness for science and invention fairs should not be over-looked. There is no index; the table of contents is logically organized: games, science, and crafts, each with a list of the projects included and page number.

■ Sisson, Edith A. NATURE WITH CHILDREN OF ALL AGES: ACTIVITIES & ADVENTURES FOR EXPLORING, LEARNING, & ENJOYING THE WORLD AROUND US. Prentice, 1982. 195pp. (paper 0-13-611542-X) SERIES: Spectrum Books. Nonfiction. Interest Level: Adult
This book is derived from the experiences of an outdoor educator and her colleagues at the Massachusetts Audubon Society, but is designed for use by a broader audience of less-expert parents, teachers, and youth leaders. This classic collection of nature activities includes tips, and pointers that will enable beginners to perform with confidence while providing inspira-

tion and new ideas even to those with more established repertoires. Tested explorations and easy-to-follow project instructions are organized in chapters devoted to trees, other green plants, seeds, invertebrates, amphibians, birds, mammals, seashore, ponds, wetlands, winter, ecology, and living in harmony with the environment. Each chapter provides select, focused background information as well as an excellent, though now-dated, bibliography. Activities include lists of simple, readily available materials along with clearly written procedures. Line drawings supplement text and instructions as needed; black-and-white photographs are helpful and attractive. The author does not suggest age levels for activities, believing that the experience of an individual or group is a better measure of suitability. Access to natural areas is desirable, but many crafts and studies such as making grass whistles, blowing dandelion bubbles, bird gardening, and squirrel watching can be done close to, or at home and school. Sisson's supportive, friendly, accessible style and wise "Everything is hitched to everything," ecological theme pervade and enrich this practical handbook. An index is included. Highly recommended selection for even the smallest school and public library collections. (Note: This wonderful guide is more recently sporting an attractive, glossy new photograph cover (1990), but content is unchanged.)

■ Thomson, Ruth. AUTUMN. Photos by Peter Millard. Watts, 1989. 32pp. (LB 0-531-10732-9) SERIES: Starting Points. Nonfiction. Interest Level: Ages 6–10
Focusing primarily on familiar aspects of plant and animal change and adaptation, this photo essay and the accompanying text depict and describe the colors and textures of the season. Suggested nature activities and crafts are interspersed, for example, collecting, mounting, and identifying fallen leaves; decorating a papier-maché woodland mask with leaves, cones, and feathers; creating an autumn picture from leaves, seeds, and twigs; planting a tree seed indoors, and patiently waiting for a sprout. Directions are sketchy, supplemented in some instances by an in-progress and/or final product photograph. Following a brief festivals section, Thomson summarizes with an autumn quiz and a listing of autumn words. Page design is crisply contemporary; good-to-excellent photography dominates the simple, factual text. *Autumn* is one of a quartet of seasonal "Starting Points" books. With books about seasons in constant demand, this fresh looking pictorial series, which creatively combines nature observation and crafting, will be of interest despite some unevenness. The *Winter* entry (Watts, 1989) is disappointing and includes some rather unattractive projects and unhappy-looking young crafters. *Spring* and *Summer* (Watts, 1990) are of more consistent quality. All four seasonal volumes include tables of contents and indices.

■ Tilsworth, Debbie J. RAISING AN EARTH FRIENDLY CHILD: THE KEYS TO YOUR CHILD'S HAPPY, HEALTHY FUTURE. Illus. by Karen Stomberg. Raven, 1991. 194pp. (paper 0-9627446-7-0) Nonfiction. Interest Level: Adult

"To encourage you and your child to live in harmony with the environment," this author has devised fifty-two parent initiated and guided, interactive projects for use with children ages three to twelve. Following an enthusiastic introduction and a four page overview of environmental fundamentals, activities designed to illustrate, demonstrate, or help alleviate environmental problems are presented in no particular order. Each sparsely or non-illustrated game, story, puzzle, or writing project is outlined in a lesson plan format with deliniated background, goal, age range, materials, suggested process or procedures, and variations. "Sinking Cities," for example, involves five- to eight-year-olds in (Activity 1) building a play dough city on a square of aluminum foil covered wood; the project continues (Activity 2) with the child placing the city in a sink and gradually adding water while discussing what people in coastal areas might do, or where they might go, as water levels rise due to global warming. Activity 3 suggests brainstorming ways to stop global warming, writing a list of these, and taping the list next to the child's bed. Tilsworth offers a wide range of activities from burying cloth and disposable diapers for six months to compare biodegradability, to a paper and pencil word search and a recycling maze, to a tale about a monster rising out of a landfill, and a you-write-the-ending story about a desperate seal, Suzie, with a carelessly discarded plastic ring around her neck, to games called "Shopping Boo Boos," "Ecology Cop," and "Laudromat Star." A final question and answer section, resources list, and index are included. There may be a public library audience for such broad strokes, and this guide may be selected as demand warrants.

■ Wilkes, Angela. MY FIRST GREEN BOOK. Knopf, 1991. 48pp. (LB 0-679-91780-2) Nonfiction. Interest Level: Ages 5–9

The dramatically large format with studied and slick overall design along with vivid, life-size color photographs characteristic of the "My First" books are in evidence in this new volume. This book treats junior environmentalists to a small but well-balanced selection of simple experiments and activities relating to environmental issues. An opening "Being Green" section sets a tone of quiet concern, promotes a hands-on approach to understanding environmental problems, and establishes a positive "Everyone can do something to help." theme. The "Green Experiments" that follow relate to various aspects of air and water pollution, biodegradability, solid waste disposal, recycling, soil, wildlife gardening, tree planting, and the role of green plants in air quality. The rain forest, assembling a campaigner's kit, and keeping a Green Diary are other topics. Visual emphasis extends to the presentation of all aspects of each activity, for example, in the list of materials required, ordinary household items look extraordinary because they are all new and color coordinated. Most of the projects can be completed without adult assistance, however, precautions are noted. Results are illustrated with photographs. The text is limited to a paragraph or two of introduction, captions, and a brief explanation of results. Two or three single sentence "How You Can Help," are also included. Projects such as comparing acid concentrations in water are given an interesting new twist with instructions for making litmus paper. A water cleaning activity graphically demonstrates aspects of water treatment, while a less-than-adequate explanation of soil composition introduces a project that illustrates differences in three distinct soil types. Attractive two-page spreads of garbage beautifully arranged in pre-sorted rows, packaging, and green shopping represent a litany of eco-do's and don'ts. Consumers are encouraged to choose recycled paper products that "look like the things made from new paper, but no trees have been cut down to make them." Despite a couple of minor inaccuracies or mis-statements, this effective and beautiful book will inspire and guide the primary school child in *understanding* environmental problems and in abiding by Wilke's concluding "Green Code." The book is highly recommended for public and school libraries.

■ Wilkes, Angela. MY FIRST NATURE BOOK. Knopf, 1990. 48pp. (LB 0-394-96610-4) Nonfiction. Interest Level: Ages 3–8
Fresh, and strongly visual, the text is dominated by brilliantly colored photographs. This beautiful book is sure to motivate and inspire the young and those who will wish they were. Life-size, distinctive photographs enliven and renew a small selection of familiar nature activities for the preschool and primary audience. Using an oversize format with step-by-step photographs, crisp and efficient layout, and concise instructions, this is an exciting introduction to nature crafting. Working with simple and accessible materials, even pre-readers can follow the pictured directions. Instructions for making a jar worm farm, for example, include a box with line drawings of required equipment, photos of materials needed (including a close-up of sieved soil and sand that appears almost three dimensional), photographs and a line or two of text describing each step in the process, and a final photograph of the finished project. Wilkes reminds readers to return earthworms to where they were found after observation. Topics such as bird feeding, pet watching, flower pressing, and seed sprouting seem new again,

given this enticing visual treatment. Wilkes closes with a "Country Code" of six rules for courteous, eco-conscientious observors and collectors.

■ **Wilkins, Marne. LONG AGO LAKE: A CHILD'S BOOK OF NATURE LORE AND CRAFTS. Illus. by Martha Weston. Chronicle, 1990 (repr. of 1978 ed.). 160pp. (paper 0-87701-632-1) Nonfiction. Interest Level: Ages 10 up**
Homespun reminiscences of a 1930's childhood in small town Wisconsin, close to farms, wood lots, prairies, forests, and lakes, reign here. These details furnish a rich backdrop, shaping Marne Wilkin's collection of nature lore and crafts. In an introductory chapter, the author establishes two points of emphasis, *seeing* and *being ready;* the ability to observe detail and change, however small or subtle, coupled with learning basic know-how. This ensures safe and enriching outdoor experiences. Readers view a variety of habitats through the eyes of a devoted outdoorswoman and acquire new skills with interspersed project instructions and diagrams. Construction of a reflector oven, knot tying, flower drying, dyeing with lichen, weaving a pine needle basket, and tanning a prime hide are representative of the range of crafts included. Chapters devoted to water, meadows and prairies, forests and trees, and sky are peopled by a lively extended family and Chippewa friends, and are further enlivened by tales of annual trips to a secret lake and by such vividly-recalled adventures (or misadventures) as a runaway horseback ride, a forest fire, and a tornado. The prose style is sometimes unpolished. A nostalgic, yet evergreen delight in the natural world infuses the whole book. Weston's delicate, detailed line drawings are the perfect old-fashioned touch. There is a dated bibliography and a crafts index.

■ **Wyler, Rose. SCIENCE FUN WITH MUD AND DIRT. Illus. by Pat Stewart. Messner, 1986. 48pp. (LB 0-671-55569-3) Nonfiction. Interest Level: Ages 6-10**
These easily followed, soil experiments and activities, demonstrate soil composition and types; how plants grow in different soils; and how soils are used in forming clay pots and robin nests, in road building, and in construction of concrete skyscrapers. A concluding "Rich Soil, Poor Soil" section describes nature's own soil enrichment process and also includes activities that demonstrate soil erosion and conservation measures. Home composting is strangely absent from this chapter, but children are encouraged to apply soil erosion prevention measures, which involve building dams to block gullies. The text is simple and lively; terms are defined in context. Line illustrations are appropriately earth-toned, competently supplementing the text. There's a special appeal and equation here involving kids, learning, and

fun. For example, children can discover that the pleasure of mixing dirt with water to make a mud pie teaches science. Collect soil samples, watch for animal footprints in the mud, try to build a bird nest, mix up some adobe, or discover how plants prevent erosion. At home or at school, these activities will motivate and teach.

Exploring

■ Arnosky, Jim. CRINKLEROOT'S BOOK OF ANIMAL TRACKING. Illus. by author. Bradbury, 1989 (rev. ed.). 48pp. (0-02-705851-4) Nonfiction. Interest Level: Ages 6–10
With his pet snake coiled around the crown of his hat, our woodsy guide Crinkleroot (a character first introduced in *I Was Born in a Tree and Raised by Bees*, Bradbury, 1988) sets off for a tramp in the forest. Keen observers will already have noticed a border of Crinkleroot's own tracks–punctuated by little round marks made by his walking stick–crossing preliminary pages. A fellow who can "spot a mole on a mountain" points out tracks and signs left by a variety of woodland animals. Crinkleroot's casual, but informative commentary is supplemented by full page insets for each mammal discussed. Insets present a balanced combination of animal facts and tracks (to scale) and track patterns. (A two-page spread of life size tracks is included near the end of the book.) Arnosky's lively ink drawings, some shaded in gray, others with colored pencil, merge flawlessly with the text; a cutaway peek into a beaver's lodge and environment in a winter pond, complete with frogs hibernating in the mud below, and rabbits bounding over the snow above the ice, is representative of Arnosky's ability to support and summarize the text. This is a revised edition of *Crinkleroot's Book of Animal Tracks and Signs*, 1979, spruced up with a larger format, more white space, introduction of subtle color, judicious editing of the text, page numbers, a table of contents, and an index.

■ Arnosky, Jim. CRINKLEROOT'S GUIDE TO WALKING IN WILD PLACES. Illus. by author. Bradbury, 1990. Unp. (0-02-705842-5) Nonfiction. Interest Level: Ages 4–10
When lively, robust woodsman Crinkleroot wakes up one summer morning with "feet itching" to take him places, join him for a ramble over fields and in the woods, a wade in a stream, and a climb over rocks. Crinkleroot dresses appropriately (Well, almost. His brightly colored shirt soon attracts a hornet); he's alert for ticks and poisonous plants, looks for signs of pollution before wading amid toe nibbling minnows, spots a miniature forest in a rock crevice, and notices animal pathways through the forest.

Our guide's narrative is good-humored and friendly, but economical; occasional full page insets and an informational last page fill in a few more details about ticks, ferns, Crinkleroot's own charmingly modest collection of nature treasures, stinging insects, potential encounters with wild animals, and poisonous plants. Pastel watercolored line drawings brim with life and engaging detail. Double page layouts lend an expansive feeling to this vicarious great outdoors experience. A canary yellow cover, plus continued emphasis of yellow and yellow green tones within, is a sunny tonic. The youngest nature observers will delight in keeping track of the changing whereabouts of Crinkleroot's pet snake and of two chickadees who usually flutter nearby. Parents and teachers preparing children for outdoor experiences will value this picture book size selection as an introduction to respectful, safe, and educational explorations.

■ **Arnosky, Jim. SECRETS OF A WILDLIFE WATCHER. Illus. by author. Lothrop, 1983. 64pp. (LB 0-688-02081-X) Nonfiction. Interest Level: Ages 8–14**
"When you witness an intimate tidbit of a wild animal's private life, glean all you can from the experience. Pay attention to the detail, and wonder about what you see." Gifted wildlife artist, author, naturalist Jim Arnosky shares his strategies for getting closer to and watching wildlife in this generously illustrated guide. Sections on "Finding," "Stalking," and "Watching" include the requisite basics such as animal ranges, signs, and feeding habits; observation helpers such as binoculars and blinds; things to watch such as animal grooming, posturing, and natural enemies. Laced throughout are simply, vividly recounted observations of such sounds and sights as a startled beaver slapping its broad tail on the water; the curiosity of a doe advancing on Arnosky's blind; and the drama of a daytime crow attack on a roosting owl. Cream colored pages are bordered or wreathed by graceful, black on white drawings; a selected few are tinted in restrained hues. Textures, curves, and nuances of this artist's pencil communicate beyond mere words or photography. Arnosky-style guidance provides young naturalists with an accessible, easily acquired information base that will help focus observation and enhance future outdoor excursions. While Arnosky's observations take place in the Vermont woods, he concludes by reminding wildlife watchers to be alert for animals even in the urban setting.
Award: ALA Notable Children's Book, 1983

■ **Carson, Rachel. THE SENSE OF WONDER. Photos by Charles Pratt. Harper, 1987 (rev. ed.). 95pp. (paper 0-06-091450-5) Nonfiction. Interest Level: Adult**

"If a child is to keep alive his inborn sense of wonder . . . he needs the companionship of at least one adult who can share it, rediscovering with him the joy, excitement and mystery of the world we live in." Rachel Carson's timeless message inspires and guides parents (and other friends of the young) to embrace and share the sights, sounds, smells, and feel of the natural world. This lovely book is an appreciation, too, of the rugged Maine coast and woods where Carson and her young nephew Roger experienced the power of crashing waves, enjoyed flashlight hunts for ghost crabs, watched the full moon rise over the silvery bay, and delighted in a long walk through rain-drenched woods. City dwellers are reminded to watch the sky, listen to the wind, feel the rain, and "ponder the mystery of a growing seed, even if it be only one planted in a pot of earth in the kitchen window." Naming, classifying, and explaining are not essential: ". . . it is not half so important to *know* as to *feel.* . . . It is more important to pave the way for the child to want to know than to put him on a diet of facts he is not ready to assimilate." Finally, Carson explains the value of nurturing and preserving a sense of wonder: "Those who dwell, as scientists or laymen, among the beauties and mysteries of the earth are never alone or weary of life." Sensitive color and black-and-white photography by Charles Pratt interprets and illustrates Rachel Carson's own enduring sense of wonder. This book is an essential selection for nature center and public library collections.

■ Docekal, Eileen M. NATURE DETECTIVE: HOW TO SOLVE OUTDOOR MYSTERIES. Illus. by David Eames. Sterling Publishing, 1989. 128pp. (0-8069-6844-3) Nonfiction. Interest Level: Ages 8–12
Real adventure lies just ahead: in the woods, at the shore, or in the back yard; exciting things are happening. Look for clues. The only "equipment" required: eyes, ears, nose, and curiosity. Here is a reminder: "Good nature detectives leave only footprints." You're on the case.

Everyone loves to play the sleuth, and this enjoyable book encourages and guides actual outdoor investigation. There is also immediate involvement for armchair explorers with fifteen problems or cases to be investigated and solved on the spot. Nine chapters with headings such as "Mysterious Visitors," "Hidden Havens," and "Name That Tune" include a brief introduction, suspects, clues, and a case or two. Docekal cleverly introduces a phenomenal amount of information in this fashion, with rapt attention of aspiring detectives virtually assured. While colored line drawings are important and abundant, they are uneven; animal drawings are wooden. Cover art is attractive, but bears no relation to the North American flora and fauna in the book. Chapter one animal tracks are disproportionate; no scale is provided. Despite shortcomings, this is an appealing concept and the aura of mystery will spark requests for this natural world page turner—a good choice for public libraries and school collections.

■ **Herberman, Ethan. THE CITY KID'S FIELD GUIDE. Simon & Schuster, 1989. 48pp. (0-671-67749-7)** SERIES: **A NOVA Book. Nonfiction. Interest Level: Ages 10–14**
Indoors and outdoors, in the backyard, downtown, in a park, or in a so-called vacant lot, plants and animals survive—and sometimes flourish—in the city. This appealing, accessible guide is organized like a classy junior news magazine hybrid—soft cover, a basic two columns per page format with pastel side bars and block insets of line drawings or additional related "articles"—all complemented by a generous selection of superb color photographs. What's more, high interest content is as excellent as the cover, layout, and format are slick. From centipedes patrolling the basement floor, to peregrine falcons nesting atop skyscrapers, to an estimated eighteen million stray or wild dogs in the United States, Herberman provides fascinating glimpses of the wildlife in our midst. This is not comprehensive field guide information in the tradition of Audubon, Peterson, Zim, et al; instead, this is a look at representative plants and creatures with the idea of showing where and how to look in your own locale. No species is considered in isolation; a unifying thread of interrelationships is neatly woven, merging with the full fabric of urban ecology. This outstanding selection from the producers of the NOVA television series introduces and reinforces important environmental concepts. There is an index.
Award: OSTB, 1989

■ **Kohl, Judith, and Herbert Kohl. PACK, BAND, AND COLONY: THE WORLD OF SOCIAL ANIMALS. Illus. by Margaret La Farge. Farrar, 1983. 114pp. (0-374-35694-7) Nonfiction. Interest Level: Ages 12 up**
Drawing from field experiences of observers of animal life, the Kohls masterfully portray three journeys of discovery—one following a wolf pack over its wide territory, another to where lemurs live in trees fifty feet above ground in the jungles of Madagascar, and a third to East African termite cities where the insects spend most of their lives within a complex nest. Exceptionally well-written, handsomely designed with margins wide enough to accomodate small illustrations and definitions of scientific terms, and beautifully enhanced by precise black-and-white pen and ink drawings, these fascinating accounts of animal social life and behavior will engender new levels of understanding and insight for young naturalists, and provide important models and structures for observation experiences. A synthesizing final chapter reflects on the pleasure of understanding animal societies; on the

limitations imposed on observation by human body size, speed, agility, and senses; on one's own social context and humanity; and on the need to preserve a balance so that diverse life forms can continue to be part of a shared world. Sources are cited on a concluding page, followed by an excellent bibliography. Nature observers will also want to read the authors' National Children's Book Award winner *The View from the Oak* (Little, 1988), an exploration of the unique ways creatures experience space, sense time, and communicate.

■ McVey, Vicki. THE SIERRA CLUB WAYFINDING BOOK. Illus. by Martha Weston. Sierra Club, 1989. 88pp. (0-316-56340-4) Nonfiction. Interest Level: Ages 8–14
Lost in the Coast Range, Jesse gratefully realizes that his dog will lead him home. Carolina Islanders navigate with a song map. Kalahari Desert dweller Dikai accurately times a lioness' passage by studying her tracks. Wayfinding with cultural geographer, cartographer Vicki McVey is more than compass, grid, and map skills—although these, too, are covered. In a facile, easygoing fashion, this fine author describes how people use their senses, landmarks, maps, navigation, and knowledge of the natural world to find their way. Thought-provoking chapters such as "How Do We Know Where We Are?" and "Gathering Information" help readers recognize and hone innate abilities and learn new skills to sharpen awareness of location cues in the environment. By involving all of one's senses, by attending to animal, plant, cloud, wind, and even taste clues, a wanderer can find the way. Urban wayfinding involves special skills, and "What If You Do Get Lost?" includes foreign cities. McVey shines as she integrates stories and examples to illustrate her instructions. Pencil drawings are pleasing; McVey's maps are a decided asset. Chapters conclude with related games and activities, ranging from a conventional exercise using a watch as a compass, to "Mr. Bloodhound", which demonstrates the acuity of the human sense of smell. Teachers will consider this book a treasure trove of ideas; prospective intermediate and older orienteers will read it from cover to cover. There is an index.
Award: ALA Notable Children's Book, 1989

■ Selsam, Millicent. HOW TO BE A NATURE DETECTIVE. Illus. by Ezra Jack Keats. Harper, 1966. 46pp. (LB 0-06-025301-0) Nonfiction. Interest Level: Ages 6–10
Here's a collection of whodunits that will intrigue the youngest nature detectives with a series of engaging nature puzzlers. An opening drawing of a tall, trench-coated figure lends an aura of mystery to a simple explanation

of what detectives do and how. Aspiring sleuths begin their investigations right at home with a closer look at cat and dog tracks, comparing and contrasting patterns of locomotion as well as paw prints. Readers visit a variety of habitats to discover clues pointing to the presence and activities of foxes, rabbits, deer, snakes, frogs, sand pipers, sea gulls, and other animals. Selsam's consistent, clear prose progresses across open, uncluttered pages—predominantly double page spreads—sustaining an expansive feeling throughout a reader-sized volume. Keats' richly textured, dynamic two-color drawings appear somewhat dated, but are, nonetheless, perfectly attuned to the text; vivid red-orange coloration is particularly arresting on an unsuspecting raccoon, but color intensity is toned down and very effective elsewhere. Young problem solvers will delight in their newly acquired and promptly applied expertise; this fine selection will focus awareness and explorations, forging a bond with the natural world. Graduates of Selsam's nature detective school will enjoy Jean George's ecological mystery *Who Really Killed Cock Robin* (Harper, 1990). Recommended for school and public library collections.

■ Shaffer, Carolyn, and Erica Fielder. CITY SAFARIS: A SIERRA CLUB EXPLORER'S GUIDE TO URBAN ADVENTURES FOR GROWNUPS AND KIDS. Illus. by author. Sierra Club, 1987. 185pp. (0-87156-713-X) Nonfiction. Interest Level: Ages 12 up
Shaffer and Fielder see the city as an integrated, functioning organic entity; this vision, their seasoning as environmental educators, their exceptional knowledge of learning styles, strategies, and group dynamics, and their creative energies are combined in formulation of this guide. With chapter topics relating to observation and change, wild places, city streets and people, downtown, city systems, and community activism; adults working with a child or children—and even independent young explorers—will enjoy a participatory learning experience. Innovative activities set the stage for, enhance, and follow up on a wide variety of field experiences like exploration of a vacant lot, a financial district in "deepest downtown," or a lush community garden. En route, the authors share insights that will alter readers' perceptions of the bond between nature and the city; for example, notice the dandelion thriving in a sidewalk crack. "Not so obvious are the riverbeds, alpine peaks, and redwood forests transformed into concrete sidewalks, granite siding, and wooden doors and window frames." Eye-opening tours of landfill and sewage treatment facilities are suggested to augment a city systems chapter, "Taking Care of Leftovers." Possible follow-up activities include trash sculpting, compilation of an oral history of household recycling, growing a garden from leftovers, and city-style composting in a covered trash can. A final "Taking Action" chapter reports on

children's community improvement projects and provides a blueprint for action. Black-and-white photographs and Fielder's line drawings are sprinkled over nicely designed pages. Appended materials include a roundup of field trip fundamentals, directions for making clipboards and day packs, and an extensive resources section. This book and Herberman's *The City Kid's Field Guide* (Simon & Schuster, 1989) are a dynamic duo for school and public library collections.

■ Simon, Seymour. EXPLORING FIELDS AND LOTS. Illus. by Arabelle Wheatley. Garrard, 1978. 64pp. (LB 0-8116-6108-3) SERIES: Easy Science Projects. Nonfiction. Interest Level: Ages 6–10
This clearly written primer will guide young nature detectives as they explore plant and animal worlds of a field, park, backyard, or vacant lot. A series of simple experiments and activities involve explorers in elementary yet scientific projects: measuring marked differences in climate within a small area; observing the effect of sunlight on plants; identifying plants and studying plant parts; setting up a terrarium of grassy plants; watching tiny creatures through a magnifying glass; and making and using an insect net. Each project is preceded by a list of readily available materials; background and procedure are effectively combined in ensuing paragraphs. Focus is on respectful observation, rather than unnecessary collection. Two-color line drawings provide supplementary how-to's and assist with identification. Emphasis throughout is on process, stressing the importance of careful observation, of asking questions, and of keeping a journal or log of observations and findings. This excellent selection will guide solo explorers and will be of special interest to primary level teachers. Recommended for most school and public library collections. There is an index.
Award: OSTB, 1978

■ Svedburg, Ulf. NICKY THE NATURE DETECTIVE. Trans. by Ingrid Selberg. Illus. by Lena Anderson. R & S, 1988. Unp. (9-12-958786-7) Nonfiction. Interest Level: Ages 8–12
Wide-eyed, bespectacled Nicky is drawn by talented Lena Anderson who also collaborated with Christina Bjork in illustrating the delightful Linnea books. This time, Anderson lends her eye for detail and her lovely pastel pallette to protray four seasons of observation through the eyes of a budding naturalist, Nicky. Each seasonal section begins with a two page spread including a stage setting poem borrowed from the likes of Thomas Hardy or Ogden Nash; next Svedburg briefly outlines the season's happenings pertaining to trees, birds, plants, insects, and other animals. (Originally published in Sweden, this is a thoroughly North American edition that includes characteristic flora and

fauna.) In autumn, for instance, Nicky learns what happens to seeds and where all of the falling leaves go; how spiders spin their webs, but manage not to get caught in them; how animals prepare to survive the winter; and why birds migrate. There are a limited number of activities sprinkled throughout the text, but the primary focus is on observation of selected subjects. Early on, Svedburg reminds readers: "But Nicky can't show you everything—only a little bit of what she finds interesting." Suggested aids include field guides, binoculars, and a magnifier, but "All you need is a good pair of eyes and ears." Nicky concludes by suggesting a trip to the library for additional nature books and includes her own brief bibliography.

■ Williams, Terry Tempest, and Ted Major. THE SECRET LANGUAGE OF SNOW. Illus. by Jennifer Dewey. Pantheon, 1984. 129pp. (LB 0-394-96574-4) SERIES: A Sierra Club Book. Nonfiction. Interest Level: Ages 10 up
For the relatively new field of snow and winter ecology, scientists are developing a universal snow language by borrowing words from various snow peoples. The Kobuk Eskimos of northeastern Alaska are one such source; their language is rich with descriptive snow words such as *annui* for falling snow, *api* for snow on the ground, *upsik* for wind beaten snow, and *siqoqtoaq* for crusted snow. Williams and Major structure their scientific yet poetic look at snow and the snowy season by focusing on observations of several different kinds of snow as described by the Kobuk. Chapters devoted to each of ten snow types discuss the impact of each variety on the people, animals, and plants of the Far North. *Upsik,* for instance, is both friend and foe; this snow can become so compacted that an axe cannot break it—useful for building igloos, but an impenetrable barrier for most grazing animals. Graceful pen and ink drawings on almost every page sensitively portray a way of life and the beauty of the Arctic world. Readers will subsequently experience snowy conditions with sharpened awareness, and will appreciate how language affects perception. This natural and seemingly effortless blend of snow observation with accompanying ecological and multicultural themes belongs in most school and public library collections, and is a must-read for leaders of snowy environment field experiences. There are both a bibliography and an index.
Award: ALA Notable Children's Book, 1984

Tending the Earth

■ Bjork, Christina, and Lena Anderson. LINNEA'S WINDOWSILL GARDEN. Trans. by Joan Sandin. Illus. by Lena Anderson. R & S, 1988 (1978). 59pp. o.p. Nonfiction. Interest Level: Ages 8–12

Delightful Linnea likes everything that grows. Even though she is named after a little pink woodland flower, she's an "asphalt flower—" a city dweller. With grandfatherly Mr. Bloom as her mentor, Linnea cultivates a variety of seeds, bulbs, cuttings, and plants including a unique sprouting contest in which split peas are buried in plaster of paris, and are observed to see which one breaks out first. Readers will gain basic understandings of what plants require for healthy growth as Linnea shares watering, fertilizing, potting, and organic pest control tips. Linnea's green thumb is complemented by an artist's eye and a generous heart: her plants are imaginatively displayed throughout her apartment, while her Lizzie cuttings and garden cress cheese make lovely gifts. The slim volume concludes with the *Green Gazette*, a potpourri of interesting plant facts and a useful checklist for diagnosing plant problems. Appealing, shaded black-and-white illustrations accented with green blend successfully with the friendly, but highly informative text; the cover design is fresh and inviting. The book was originally published in Sweden. Linnea's friends will also enjoy *Linnea's Almanac* (R & S/Farrar, 1989).

Award: ALA Notable Children's Book, 1988

■ **Brown, Marc. YOUR FIRST GARDEN BOOK. Illus. by author. Little, 1981. 48pp. (0-316-11217-8) Nonfiction. Interest Level: Ages 4–8**
Gardening is great fun! On the windowsill, on a roof-top, a fire escape, or even in a sidewalk crack; in all seasons, indoors or outdoors; in the city or in the country, the plant projects depicted in this gently humorous book will inspire a wave of green activity among the picture book set. Mostly familiar growing projects are simply described with numbered, single sentence step-by-step instructions, and by bold, brightly colored drawings; talking cats and rabbits (beans and potatoes, too) appear on almost every page with cartoon balloons injecting additional tidbits of information or a silly riddle. Indoor growing has a slight edge in terms of numbers of projects here, with activities involving sprouts, cress, a desert garden, bulbs, potatoes in a bucket, and herbs. Container gardeners are advised to improvise and recycle—cans, cartons, and boxes, even an old drawer—can be used. Country garden soil preparation and planting are described on a single page, with another full page devoted to soil improvement via a pit-style compost system. Plant your own perfect pumpkin, grow a salad, or initiate a sunflower "race;" get on your mark, get set, garden! There is a listing of suppliers, a glossary, and an index.

■ **Ehlert, Lois. PLANTING A RAINBOW. Illus. by author. Harcourt, 1988. Unp. (0-15-262609-3) Fiction. Interest Level: Ages 2–6**

Flowers are the stars of this exuberant picture book that celebrates a year-long love affair with a flower garden planted by a mother and child. Gardening begins in the fall when bulbs are planted and continues in winter when packets of seeds are ordered from catalogs. When the bulbs sprout in spring, it's time to sow the seeds, purchase and plant seedlings . . . then watch the garden grow. Ehlert's simple text in large type supports a colorful, stylized cutaway of the garden where bulbs, seeds, and flowers are all carefully marked with garden markers, planted at appropriate depths, and bloom in succession just as they do in nature. *Planting a Rainbow* offers a lesson in the life cycles of plants as well as in color identification. Following brilliant spreads of the garden in full bloom, several pages of varying width picture the flowers grouped by color, with a red tulip, carnation, and rose on one page followed by an orange tulip, zinnia, tiger lily, and poppy on the next and on through the "rainbow." Ehlert has a clean and bold graphic style and she uses primary colors to great effect. Young children will respond to the colors, shapes, and names of common garden flowers and will look for them in their own gardens. Ehlert paints a vegetable garden even more boldly in *Growing Vegetable Soup* (Harcourt, 1987).

Award: OSTB, 1988

■ **Huff, Barbara A. GREENING THE CITY STREETS: THE STORY OF COMMUNITY GARDENS. Photos by Peter Ziebel. Clarion, 1990. 61pp. (0-89919-741-8) Nonfiction. Interest Level: Ages 8–12**
Travel with Barbara Huff and Peter Ziebel to Manhattan, an island awash in concrete and tall buildings crowding taller buildings. Now visit Sixth Street and Avenue B, on and tour a community garden—an oasis of green located where "crumbling tenements were once the headquarters for drug dealers and other criminals." Four-by-eight-foot, intensively gardened, raised bed plots belonging to the nearly one hundred members of Six and B (including students from an elementary school nearby) are sited beyond an open area furnished with benches and tables. A meetinghouse/tool shed provides space for gardening classes and a stage used by a children's theater group. Lovely flowers, healthful vegetables, fruit trees, and herbs flourish here, along with a sense of belonging and empowerment. Having fully described this prime example of community gardening, Huff proceeds to detail the history and evolution of community gardening, as well as some of the challenges and problems community gardeners encounter. A final "Harvesting All Year Long" chapter describes just that, gardening and other activities that happen at Six and B during "non-growing" seasons. Color photographs and some black-and-white are central to the telling of this uplifting, urban success story; prose is conversational, nicely conveying hopeful mes-

sages about cooperation and environmental healing. A bibliography, a listing of gardening organizations, and an index are included.

Award: OSTB, 1990

■ **Kuhn, Dwight. MORE THAN JUST A FLOWER GARDEN. Photos by author. Silver Burdett, 1990. 40pp. (LB 0-671-69642-4) Nonfiction. Interest Level: Ages 6–10**

The world of garden ecology is beautifully introduced through the lens and words of talented Dwight Kuhn. Glossy, close-up photographs of thirsty hummingbirds and butterflies; of rapidly multiplying aphids and newly hatched praying mantises; of sunflowers and goldfinches; of color adaptable crab spiders and anole lizards; and of seed to seedling, bud to blossom, and blossom to seed sequences, depict relationships, dependencies, and life cycles. Annuals, biennials, and perennials are defined and flower parts identified. The pages are dominated by stunning photography; the text is intelligent and informative. A final "Starting Your Own Flower Garden" section provides photo-illustrated, step-by-step instructions for starting seeds indoors and transplanting to garden or window box, and for planting seeds directly in the garden. A combined glossary and index appears on the last two pages. This selection and an equally appealing companion volume, *More Than Just a Vegetable Garden* (Silver Burdett, 1990), an Outstanding Science Trade Book for Children, would be excellent multi-use additions to most public and elementary school library collections.

■ **Ocone, Lynn, and Eve Pranis. THE NATIONAL GARDENING ASSOCIATION GUIDE TO KIDS' GARDENING: A COMPLETE GUIDE FOR TEACHERS, PARENTS AND YOUTH LEADERS. Illus. by Elayne Sears. Wiley, 1990. 148pp. (paper 0-471-52092-6) SERIES: Wiley Science Editions. Nonfiction. Interest Level: Adult**

Successful, youth gardening projects take root and flourish here; this attractive, well-organized guide sets a course for fledgling projects and may even enhance ongoing programs. With renewed interest in development of youth gardening projects and with a history of lending support and expertise to these efforts, the National Gardening Association offers this revision of a 1983 edition. Equipped with environmental communications, agriculture, and life sciences backgrounds, authors Ocone and Pranis effectively communicate the expertise and perspective they have gained working with local projects and in leadership roles with the National Gardening Association Youth Gardening Program. From Pete Seeger's foreword, a hopeful poem about kids, gardening, growth, and miracles, to an excellent final resources section, pertinent topics and concerns are addressed in a down-to-earth fashion, with an underlying "gardening grows good kids" philosophy. A focusing first chapter outlines and discusses six basic challenges for youth gardening projects: leadership, land, funding, vandalism, continuity, and motivation, followed by chapters relating to planning, site development, and design. A "Gardening Activities for Fun and Knowledge" section provides suggestions and/or step-by-step instructions for more than one hundred experiments, crafts, and games. Indoor and container gardening are detailed in Chapter 6, followed by a reprise of sorts, a chapter devoted to descriptions of representative youth garden projects from all over the country. A colorful cover, pleasing graphics, good page design, and effective use of black-and-white photographs are additional reasons why this bible for youth gardening program leaders will be consulted again and again for many growing seasons to come. The book has an index.

■ Oechsli, Helen, and Kelly Oechsli. IN MY GARDEN: A CHILD'S GARDEN-ING BOOK. Illus. by Kelly Oechsli. Macmillan, 1985. 32pp. (0-02-768510-1) Nonfiction. Interest Level: Ages 4–7
This bright, little primer in a pleasant picture book format will guide the youngest of gardeners from site selection to harvest. Instructions focusing on the essentials are logically sequenced, clear, and direct. Soil preparation, planting, weeding, and thinning instructions precede a section describing easy-to-grow vegetables. Indoor gardening alternatives are explored. "Garden friends who keep out pests" is an attractive two-page spread with simple labels identifying ladybugs, a toad, praying mantis, and other insects. Soil enrichment for next year's garden comes from making a compost pile. Cheerfully colored illustrations throughout augment the text, and add an amusing touch. An attentive rabbit appears here and there, sharing extra tidbits of information, and is shown in a final "fruits of our labors" illustration, napping beneath a tall lettuce leaf. This author-illustrator duo has raised a family together, has "always had a garden," and has collaborated to create a lively, friendly guide.
Award: OSTB, 1985

■ Raftery, Kevin, and Kim Gilbert Raftery. KIDS GARDENING: A KIDS' GUIDE TO MESSING AROUND IN THE DIRT. Illus. by Jim M'Guinness. Klutz Pr., 1989. 87pp. (0-932592-25-2) Nonfiction. Interest Level: Ages 8–12
Here's an eye-catching, colorful garden inhabited by, among zany others: a purple elephant, a chorus line of cucumbers, and an armadillo wearing a ten gallon hat. There's fun afoot; readers will discover a solid core of information here that will support beginning gardening experiences—with interest-

ing accompanying activities to boot. Organized in five sections that include gardening fundamentals, vegetables, flowers and herbs, kitchen gardening, and "non-edibles," crops and activities are generally afforded double page spreads. Initial pages deal with gardening basics such as site preparation, starting seeds, soil enrichment, composting, weeding and mulching, and garden pests. Each vegetable or flower crop is presented with step-by-step instructions for indoor or outdoor container gardening and/or outdoor gardening. Companion projects are inserted immediately following related crops, for example, seed roasting instructions follow pumpkin culture, a recipe for ranch dressing follows salad vegetables. Gardeners will also find instructions for making refrigerator pickles, herb tea, and drying flowers. A kitchen gardening section features the familiar avocado pit and sweet potato vine fare, but also includes more unique ideas such as growing and braiding garlic and planting popcorn seeds from the pantry. "Non-Edibles" consists of how-to's for establishing a worm farm, and for adding a traditional finishing touch for gardens, a scarecrow. Open flat, spiral binding and heavy coated paper mean that this guide may be conveniently referenced even outdoors. Page design and cartoon-like drawings throughout the book are appealing—bold with vivid splashes of color; the upbeat text is hand lettered. While this book is marketed with packets of seeds and a plastic trowel, librarians may consign these items to a story time prop collection. This guide will attract neophyte gardeners with its winning combination of growing guidance, related activities, and good humor. There is no index.

■ Tilgner, Linda. LET'S GROW! 72 GARDENING ADVENTURES WITH CHILDREN. Photos by John M. Kuykendall. Storey Communications, 1988. 208pp. (0-88266-471-9) Nonfiction. Interest Level: Adult
"A child plants a tiny seed and watches a sunflower or a bean pole teepee grow into a giant that towers above him. What a sense of power and awe that creates!" This efficient, thorough, and enriching book on gardening with children (from tots to pre-teens—even for those with special needs) is a rewarding read for parents, teachers, and youth leaders. Packed with practical suggestions and guidance, the pride and satisfaction of a successful and memorable growing experience is virtually assured. Organic gardening basics like soil preparation and enrichment are clearly presented along with creative growing ideas like planting corn, bean, and squash seeds ("three sisters") in a single hill as Native Americans did, growing a cucumber in a bottle, or planting a patchwork salad quilt. "Popcorn Fireworks," corn husk doll making, throwing a nibbling party, and building a scarecrow are representative of companion projects. Deft touches of plant lore and mini botany lessons further enhance this friendly guide. Tilgner sets readers sights beyond the garden by including tree planting, maple sugaring, flower

arranging, grape vine wreath making, and foraging for wild foods. Indoor gardening is not overlooked; many examples of seed and plant activities and experiments are included. Teacher, parent, and gardener, this author has a rare knack for finding worthwhile and enjoyable approaches to gardening, and for choosing and integrating projects that relate gardening to developing awareness of the natural world. Nicely designed pages are generously illustrated by appealing black-and-white photographs of busy young gardeners; line drawings supplement clearly presented directions. A glossary, resource list, and an index are included. This book is a strong selection for most public library collections—and a fine addition to the school library media center as well.

■ **Verey, Rosemary. HERB GROWING BOOK. Illus. by Barbara Firth, Elizabeth Wood, and Jane Wolsak. Little, 1980. 41pp. o.p. Nonfiction. Interest Level: Ages 10 up**
This crisply written, very British pictorial guide introduces many different herb varieties, and provides instructions for growing herbs indoors or out. Double-page spreads of labelled, pastel-toned drawings depict herbs growing on windowsills or in window boxes, informal patches, or elegantly configured geometric plots. Accompanying text briefly describes distinguishing characteristics of individual herb varieties, cultivation and propagation notes, and uses. Illustrated, captioned, step-by-step instructions for garden planning, planting outdoors, container planting, and other points follow. Detailed, well-illustrated directions for herb drying, and for making a lavender bag, a nosegay, a pomander, potpourri, and tea are interjected here, before "Helpful Hints," which actually supplement horticultural directions. An attractive, useful plant chart, which includes herb height, propagation, light needs, adaptability to container gardening, harvest times, use and plant part used, precedes an index. Coordination problems beset this otherwise excellent guide: arrangement is choppy, contrasting pallets are employed by three different illustrators, and two symbols are included in a "How To Use This Book" section, which are not used elsewhere. While a more unified new edition would be welcome, young gardeners and adults will find this unique guide helpful.

■ **Waters, Marjorie. THE VICTORY GARDEN KIDS' BOOK. Photos by Gary Mottau and George Ulrich. Houghton, 1988. 148pp. (paper 0-395-46560-5) Nonfiction. Interest Level: Ages 8 up**
The competent, caring, and confident young gardener will have copy of this splendid guide for ready reference. Companion to the popular *Victory Garden* television program, and based on actual first gardening experiences of a racially diverse group of Holliston, Massachusetts children; the book's

initial appeal is a combination of name recognition blended with generous use of color photographs of kids in action. Best of all, coverage throughout is thorough and thoughtful; in clear and careful prose, a wealth of information is adroitly presented. Divided into two main sections, "How to Garden" and "Kids' Crops," beginning gardeners will find step-by-step guidance from planning to harvest, and on to preparations for the next growing season. Initial digging, soil enrichment, composting, plant selection, organic pest control—the full range of gardening concerns and questions—is explored. Soil preparation and testing receive their just due. Gardeners are reminded to have their site tested for lead: "Lead is poison. It will get into your plants, and then into you." Photographs of proud gardeners share best the joy and wonder of growth and harvest. "Kids' Crops" is a browser's delight with bold graphics of ready-to-pick-sized vegetables and color photographs of other crops suitable for beginning gardeners. Gardening suppliers are listed in context. There is an index.

Taking Action

■ **Bellamy, David. HOW GREEN ARE YOU? Illus. by Penny Dann. Crown, 1991. 31pp. (LB 0-517-58447-6) Nonfiction. Interest Level: Ages 5–9**
Join Friendly Whale on a tour of the kitchen, the bathroom, the supermarket, and the garden, with "side trip" assessments of overall home energy use, what goes into the trash can, transportation alternatives, and neighborhood environs; here is an amiable introduction to environmental awareness and activism for older read-to-me's and younger readers. By saving *W*-ater, preserving *H*-abitat, keeping the *A*-ir clean, saving plants and animals from extinction (*L*-ife), and conserving *E*-nergy, readers can help make the planet a healthier place for whales *and* for people. Nicely designed picture book-sized pages are filled with facts, definitions, and activities; busy, pastel toned cartoon-style drawings complement and supplement the text. The supermarket scenario, for example, consists of a two page spread filled with shoppers choosing organically grown food, recycled paper products, and biodegradable washing powder, but passing up disposable diapers and over-packaged products. Environmentally conscientious actions are captioned and identified with color-coded and lettered whale symbols. (The initial need to frequently re-reference the W-H-A-L-E key pages may be distracting.) Environmental terms and concepts are introduced gradually, defined simply, and re-enforced subsequently. Text is generally excellent; the tone is quietly concerned and positive. First published in Great Britain, North American audiences will notice cars being driven on the "wrong" side of the street, and some minor differences in vocabulary. A misleading statistic for

water consumption was supplied to the illustrator and passed over in copy editing. This very appealing, accessible guide will be appreciated by families with young children, and is a solid selection for even the smallest school and public library collections. Although the book is not printed on recycled paper, the publishers didn't waste a page. Library jacketing may obscure the index, which is economically printed on the endpaper.

■ **Dehr, Roma, and Ronald M. Bazar. GOOD PLANETS ARE HARD TO FIND! AN ENVIRONMENTAL GUIDE, DICTIONARY, AND ACTION BOOK FOR KIDS (AND ADULTS). Illus. by Nola Johnston. Earth Beat Pr. (P.O. Box 33852, Station D, Vancouver, B.C. Canada V6J 4L6), 1989. 40pp. (paper 0-919597-09-2) Nonfiction. Interest Level: Ages 10 up**
Even reluctant readers will be drawn to this appealing, colorful, very slim A to Z compendium of environmental concepts, issues, and ideas for action. Each clear, succinct definition is comprised of one or two paragraphs that appear in colored boxes superimposed over full color illustrations (e.g., Amazon rain forest, an African savanna, or a coral reef). Some definitions are also supplemented by charts, diagrams, and smaller inset illustrations of the marine food chain, greenhouse effect, and a geothermal plant. Most definitions are followed by one or two single sentences, achievable ideas for taking action to protect the environment. One exception to this pattern is letter I: *"I* is for how *I* can make a difference to the planet. Remember it's the little things that count." Following are two pages of familiar ecological maxims. Letters Q,X,Y, and Z consist of summarizing questions and quizzes. Without sentimentality or heavy-handed moralizing, cooperation, joy, love, and war are included amongst the CFCs, polystyrene, and ultraviolet rays. This remarkably inclusive, upbeat little paperback is a fine introduction to environmental studies and activism. Appended is a comprehensive international listing of environmental organizations and agencies.

■ **Earthworks Group. 50 SIMPLE THINGS KIDS CAN DO TO SAVE THE EARTH. Edited by John Javna. Illus. by Michele Montez. Andrews & McMeel, 1990. 156pp. (paper 0-8362-2301-2) Nonfiction. Interest Level: Ages 10–14**
Slim and compact, this selection offers quick pickup appeal, a limited overview of environmental problems, and mostly achievable ideas for action by emerging eco-activists. Prefaced by notes on empowerment, the guide goes on to very briefly introduce seven environmental issues ("Acid Rain, Air Pollution, Disappearing Animals, Too Much Garbage, Greenhouse Effect, Ozone Hole, and Water Pollution"), followed by quotes from children that serve as a bridge to the body of the text. Grouped in chapters by subject, with headings such as "Guarding Our Buried Treasures," "Keeping the

Earth Green," and "Spending Energy Wisely," most of the "fifty simple things" suggested are afforded two page layouts comprised of "Take a Guess," "Did You Know," "What You Can Do," and "See for Yourself." Interesting facts and comparisons abound, organized in a bits and bites fashion with minimal elaboration. Breathless over-use of exclamation points is somewhat distracting. Seven easily accomplished eco-experiments conclude the text. Generous use of attractive line drawings and pleasing layout combine to provide visual appeal throughout. Names and addresses of some environmental organizations and their publications are mentioned in context. References to further sources of information are limited; there is no glossary, bibliography, appendix, or index. No details are provided about the primary author nor the Earthworks Group.

■ **Elkington, John, et al. GOING GREEN: A KID'S HANDBOOK TO SAVING THE PLANET. Illus. by Tony Ross. Penguin, 1990. 111pp. (0-670-83611-7) Nonfiction. Interest Level: Ages: 8 up**
First published in Great Britain as *The Young Green Consumer Guide* (Gollancz, 1990), this new title more accurately reflects an ambitious agenda. Beginning with an exhortation that ". . . you have the power to change the world!," familiar environmental concerns such as the greenhouse effect, ozone depletion, air pollution, and acid rain are simply described in adequate prose. Moving would-be activists to a more involving level, the book provides information and structure for conducting a "green audit" of home, school, and community; the more complex community at large is given least coverage. A "Things You Can Do" section is an A to Z compilation of environmental do's and don'ts: "A, Adopt Something; B, Boycott a Product," and so on—a potpourri of suggestions for action. Finally, "Where to Learn More" includes a brief bibliography, a listing of environmental organizations, and an index, very useful, given the organization of the "Things You Can Do" section. Pleasing format and colorful, lively (sometimes irreverent) illustrations by Tony Ross provide both initial appeal and keep-reading fun.

Award: NSSB, 1990

■ **Goodman, Billy. A KID'S GUIDE TO HOW TO SAVE THE PLANET. Illus. by Paul Meisel. Avon, 1990. 137pp. (paper 0-380-76041-X) Nonfiction. Interest Level: Ages 9–13**
"Saving the planet is a team effort. Probably the most important step you can take is to learn more about the environment." Emphasis here is on background, definition, and description of selected environmental problems with less space devoted to eco-do's and don'ts. Goodman sets the stage by

looking first at the origin and history of the planet, putting issues to be discussed (overpopulation, energy and climate, food supply, waste disposal, and endangered species) into context and perspective. Focus is on the understandings necessary to more fully appreciate the seriousness of many environmental problems; discussion of energy and climate, for example, defines and describes acid rain, providing background information about pH, and a useful chart to further illustrate the concept. Examples of successful actions or activities undertaken by young people in defense of the environment are an interesting addition to this guide. Chapters are concluded with a page or two designated as "What You Can Do;" all activities are readily achievable by the intended audience. Black-and-white illustrations by Paul Meisel are inconsistent, alternating with black-and-white photographs of uneven quality. Additional sources of information are not included. Both a glossary and an index are included.

■ **Hynes, H. Patricia. EARTHRIGHT: WHAT YOU CAN DO IN YOUR HOME, WORKPLACE, AND COMMUNITY TO SAVE OUR ENVIRONMENT. Prima Publishing, 1990. 236pp. (1-55958-028-3) Nonfiction. Interest Level: Ages 12 up**
Activist, environmental engineer, Director of the Institute on Women and Technology, and an instructor at the Massachusetts Institute of Technology, H. Patricia Hynes blends a wealth of knowledge, experience, and insight with a credible, lucid prose style to produce this satisfying and thought-provoking guide. Hynes has limited the scope of her book to five topics: pesticides, solid waste, drinking water, ozone layer, and global warming. Facts, charts, drawings, anecdotes, quotations, and resources are effectively interwoven with description and prescription. Educators seeking to integrate resource-based teaching will find the "Resources," (names of projects, agencies, organizations, and publications), which conclude each chapter, of special interest. Capable middle schoolers will appreciate this thorough but accessible coverage, and empowering suggestions for, and examples of, "informed action." A generous proportion of white space and wide margins are eye pleasing, and help to make this more sophisticated, comprehensive guide less daunting for a younger audience eager for rationale and direction. Hynes reminds her readers that the actions she recommends are necessary in order to live on Earth in ways that are *"just, appropriate, most favorable,* and *genuine* (all meanings of the word right)." The book is indexed.

■ **Lewis, Barbara A. KID'S GUIDE TO SOCIAL ACTION: HOW TO SOLVE THE SOCIAL PROBLEMS YOU CHOOSE—AND TURN CREATIVE THINKING INTO POSITIVE ACTION. Illus. by Steve Michaels. Free Spirit, 1991. 144pp. (paper 0-915793-29-6) Nonfiction. Interest Level: Ages 10 up**

"Meet the kids from Jackson Elementary School in Salt Lake City, Utah, whose efforts resulted in the cleanup of a hazardous waste site, passage of two new laws, planting of hundreds of trees, and sidewalk improvements." And, meet their teacher, Barbara A. Lewis who dedicates this upbeat guide "To kids everywhere. May you be *seen* and *heard.''* To empower would-be movers and shakers, Lewis details the experiences of her students and relates stories about other young people who are making a difference in their communities. She shares a codified ten step process for solving social problems; guides to power skills such as letter writing, speech making, fund raising (including grantsmanship), and handling media coverage; procedures for initiating or changing local, state, and national laws; and "Resources–" addresses and phone numbers for government agencies and various social action groups, as well as a listing of national groups that recognize contributions kids have made to their communities. A classified "Books" section lists briefly annotated titles concerning government and citizenship, the environment, and problem solving, followed by a singularly useful "Tools" chapter that includes to-be-copied or adapted forms for telephoning, letters, interviews, petitions, surveys, proclamations, news releases, and the like. A colorful collage cover, crisp overall design, effectively utilized black-and-white photographs, and efficient yet interesting and accessible prose style, all suggest resolve–a seriousness of purpose–with an occasional light touch provided by cartoonlike illustrations. This selection will find a ready public library audience of students, teachers, and a broad spectrum of community-minded individuals; order a copy for the school media center, and prepare for action. An index is included.

■ **Lewis, Scott, and the Natural Resources Defense Council. RAINFOREST BOOK: HOW YOU CAN SAVE THE WORLD'S RAINFORESTS. Edited by Dwight Holing. Illus. by Mercedes McDonald. Living Planet Pr. (558 Rose Avenue, Venice, CA 90291), 1990. 112pp. (paper 0-9626072-1-5) Nonfiction. Interest Level: Ages 12 up**
"Tropical rain forests are a rich and animated celebration of the diversity and wonder of life. Unfortunately, celebration is quickly turning to tragedy." In a concerned, but matter-of-fact manner, energy and environmental analyst Scott Lewis and the Natural Resources Defense Council provide basic information about rain forests, why they are important, how they are being destroyed, and what can be done to preserve them. A colorful cover, dramatic black-and-white illustrations, and effective page design enhance this informative guide. A "Red, White, and Blue Rain Forests" chapter focuses on tropical forests on Hawaii, Puerto Rico, the U. S. Virgin Islands, and American Samoa to emphasize that not all deforestation occurs in Third World countries. "To See the Forest for the Trees" goes on to present advice to consumers, a charge to spread the word, the importance of becom-

ing involved with the work of environmental organizations, and the challenge of persuading governments, corporations, and individuals that their actions must favor preservation of this vital eco-system. Sources of additional information appear in a final "Natural Resources" chapter with listings of organizations involved in rain forest issues, corporations already engaged in or about to embark on questionable actions vis-à-vis rain forest ecology, and book and audiovisual selections for adults and children—with a special resources section for teachers.

■ Miles, Betty. SAVE THE EARTH: AN ACTION HANDBOOK FOR KIDS. Illus. by Nelle Davis. Knopf, 1991 (rev. ed.). 118pp. (LB 0-679-91731-4) Nonfiction. Interest Level: Ages 10–14
Buy this book. If a tight materials budget allows for purchase of just one or two selections from this category, this thoroughly researched, highly readable guide should be a first choice. *Save the Earth* initially appeared in 1974, also to an enthusiastic reception. Drawing again on informed, deeply rooted conviction, Miles clearly and capably develops chapters related to land, atmosphere, water, energy, plants and animals, and people—including overpopulation, distribution of resources and wealth, and reduction of consumption. Each of these chapters consists of three to five pages of background information, followed by a one page list of pertinent "Amazing Facts," some examples of actual organized environmental actions undertaken by young people, projects related to the issue at hand (diagramming population growth, "catching" a shower, and starting a bike rack campaign), and a quick check list of eco do's and don'ts. A final "Getting to Work" section is an activists's tool kit; considered here are research skills, organizations to join, changes to make at home, community organizing, public speaking, letter writing, holding a press conference, choosing a focus, and environmental careers. A rather attractive, brightly colored cover is followed by less appealing black-and-white illustrations. Numerous photographs are effectively integrated. There is a glossary, a bibliography, an annotated listing of environmental groups, and an index.

■ Newton, David E. TAKING A STAND AGAINST ENVIRONMENTAL POLLUTION. Watts, 1990. 157pp. (LB 0-531-10923-2) SERIES: Taking a Stand. Nonfiction. Interest Level: Ages 12 up
Newton's deliberate, reasoned overview of environmental problems and activism prepares and equips readers with historical perspective and background required to take a more informed stand on a variety of environmental issues. Several renowned environmental activists and leaders like Henry David Thoreau, George Perkins Marsh, Gifford Pinchot, Rachel Carson, and Justice William O. Douglas are profiled; Newton draws encouraging paral-

lels to the activities and contributions of Lois Gibbs (Love Canal Homeowners Association), teenager Meadow Makovin (Ocean Sanctuary Movement), "The Monday Group" (Florida high school students who preserved a swamp)—all "typical of that person-next-door who has kept the environmental movement alive in the United States for three hundred years." A "Getting Started As an Activist" chapter discusses the importance of demonstrating personal commitment in one's own life style, becoming better informed, polishing communication skills (including listening), and knowing what to expect from and how to function as a member of an environmental organization. A final chapter presents detailed procedures for teenagers who want to start their own environmental group. There are black-and-white photographs, many of historical interest. An annotated listing of environmental organizations, notes, an annotated bibliography, and an index. This is a good starting point for researchers and activists, a valuable addition for middle school, high school, and public libraries.

Appendix
Environmental Classics
Suggestions for Further Reading

Adults and older students interested in reading more about the environment may wish to consult the following list, which includes many environmental "classics" and a sampling of recent titles that reflect the diversity of literature about nature, environmental issues, and "ecophilosophy."

This list is by no means exhaustive; hundreds of other fine books on various aspects of the environment have been published. In addition, most of the authors cited here have written several—in some cases, many—excellent books with environmental themes; the selections in this bibliography are generally their best-known titles or, in the absence of a standout, are representative of their contributions to the genre.

■ Abbey, Edward. DESERT SOLITAIRE: A SEASON IN THE WILDERNESS. McGraw-Hill, 1968; Ballantine, 1985 (paper 0-345-32649-0).
Abbey combines vivid nature writing with western gruffness and irreverence for humanity in this classic journal about his first summer as a seasonal park ranger in Arches National Monument, Utah.

■ ————. THE MONKEY WRENCH GANG. Avon, 1976 (paper 0-380-00741-X).
In this rare, unabashed "environmental" novel, an unlikely, sometimes comical group of saboteurs launches a self-styled counterattack against billboards, bulldozers, and other artifacts of the assault on nature in the desert southwest. Abbey's sequel (*Hayduke Lives!* Little, 1990) was published posthumously.

■ Anderson, Lorraine, ed. SISTERS OF THE EARTH. Vintage, 1991 (paper 0-679-73382-5).
An excellent anthology of poems, essays, stories, and journal entries about nature by more than 90 women writers, from Emily Dickenson to Denise Levertov, followed by an extensive annotated bibliography.

■ Berry, Wendell. THE UNSETTLING OF AMERICA: CULTURE AND AGRICUL-
TURE. Sierra, 1977; Revised ed. Sierra, 1986 (paper 0-87156-772-5).
The nine essays in this book by Kentucky farmer-writer Berry constitute a critique
of modern agriculture's exploitation of the land and an examination of its ties with
the larger culture. Berry's proposals for change are often controversial but always
passionate and eloquent.

■ Bookchin, Murray. REMAKING SOCIETY: PATHWAYS TO A GREEN FUTURE.
South End, 1990 (0-89608-373-X).
Bookchin, a long-time social critic and political historian who wrote one of the first
comprehensive surveys of modern environmental problems (*Our Synthetic Environment.* Knopf, 1962), contends in this culminating volume that most ecological woes
are tied directly to social problems and will not be solved until society changes in
fundamental ways.

■ Brown, Lester R., et al. STATE OF THE WORLD. Norton, annual (0-393-02934-4;
1991 ed.)
This popular, highly readable series of books, aimed at documenting "progress
toward a sustainable society," examines current international and global environmental issues and offers extensive bibliographies for those who wish to pursue the
information to its origins.

■ Callenbach, Ernest. ECOTOPIA. Banyan Tree, 1975; Bantam, 1983 (paper 0-553-
26183-5).
A fictional visit to a corner of America whose people have taken environmental ills
to heart and changed their way of life accordingly. The sequel (*Ecotopia Emerging.*
Banyan Tree, 1981) is actually a "prequel" about the events leading to the transformation.

■ Carson, Rachel. THE SEA AROUND US. New American Library, 1954. (paper
0-451-62483-1) THE SEA AROUND US: SPECIAL EDITION. Oxford, 1989 (0-19-
506186-1).
One of three books by Carson about the sea, this is a superb and scientifically
accurate description of ocean ecosystems and how they are influenced by humans.
Published a decade before *Silent Spring* (see below), it helped establish Carson's
reputation as a writer of extraordinary talent and skill.

■ ———. SILENT SPRING. Houghton, 1962. SILENT SPRING: TWENTY-FIFTH
ANNIVERSARY EDITION. Houghton, 1987 (0-395-45389-5).
This classic is frequently credited with spawning the modern environmental movement in the United States. Carson exposes the hitherto little-known ecological and
health consequences of the indiscriminate use of DDT and other pesticides before
issuing an impassioned plea for saner treatment of the natural world.

■ Commoner, Barry. THE CLOSING CIRCLE: NATURE, MAN, AND TECHNOLOGY.
Knopf, 1971. o.p.
Commoner emerged as a major spokesman for environmentalism with this book,
which, among other things, helped popularize the notions that "everything is con-

nected to everything else" and blind faith in technology as a solution to all problems is dangerous. Commoner updates his views in *Making Peace with the Planet* (Pantheon, 1990).

■ **Council on Environmental Quality and Department of State (U.S.). GLOBAL 2000 REPORT TO THE PRESIDENT: ENTERING THE TWENTY-FIRST CENTURY, VOLUME 1. U.S. Government Printing Office, 1980; Penguin, 1982 (paper 0-14-022441-6).**
Significant as much for its source as for its content, this report portends of a world "more crowded, more polluted, less stable ecologically, and more vulnerable to disruption" in the year 2000. (For a rebuttal, see: Kahn, Herman, and Julian Simon. *The Resourceful Earth: A Response to Global 2000.* Basil Blackwell, 1984)

■ **Devall, Bill, and George Sessions. DEEP ECOLOGY: LIVING AS IF NATURE MATTERED. Gibbs Smith, 1985 (paper 0-87905-158-2).**
Based on the "deep ecology" premise that human beings occupy no higher status in nature than other living things, this book explores the roots of environmentalism, the human-centered assumptions behind most approaches to nature, the potential for changing those assumptions, and possibilities for direct environmental action by individuals.

■ **Dillard, Annie. PILGRIM AT TINKER CREEK. Harper, 1974; Harper, 1988 (paper 0-06-091545-0).**
In prose as expressive and meticulously crafted as fine poetry, Dillard reflects philosophically on nature and the meaning of human existence from her solitary outpost in the Blue Ridge Mountains of Virginia. This book won the 1975 Pulitzer Prize for nonfiction.

■ **Durrell, Lee. STATE OF THE ARK: AN ATLAS OF CONSERVATION IN ACTION. Doubleday, 1986 (paper 0-385-23668-9).**
A richly illustrated review of the status of wildlife around the world, this book considers the diversity of ecosystems and their wildlife, discusses human impacts on the biosphere, examines threats to the survival of various species, and assesses the growth and impact of conservation activities and organizations.

■ **Ehrlich, Paul. THE POPULATION BOMB. Ballantine, 1968; New revised ed. Ballantine, 1986 (paper 0-345-33834-0).**
Ehrlich's blunt warning about overpopulation of the planet made this one of the top environmental issues of the 1960s and 1970s. Two decades later, in *The Population Explosion* (Simon & Schuster, 1990), he revisits the subject. For contrast, see Ben Wattenberg's *The Birth Dearth* (Pharos, 1987).

■ **Eiseley, Loren. THE STAR THROWER. Times Books, 1978; Harcourt, 1979 (paper 0-15-684909-7).**
Anthropologist, essayist, and poet, Eiseley brilliantly blends scientific knowledge and imaginative vision in this anthology, selected by the author himself and published posthumously, of his many writings on science, nature, and humanity.

■ Foreman, Dave. CONFESSIONS OF AN ECO-WARRIOR. Harmony, 1991 (0-517-58123-X).
Cofounder of the controversial environmental group Earth First!, Foreman calls for a profound shift in people's attitudes toward nature and urges radical political, personal, corporate, and government action "to stop the wholesale destruction of our few remaining wild places."

■ Griffin, Susan. WOMAN AND NATURE: THE ROARING INSIDE HER. Harper, 1978; Harper, 1980 (paper 0-06-090744-4).
Griffin blames the rift between humanity and nature on the dominating and manipulative traits of paternalistic societies and contrasts them with the long-subjugated but powerful holistic, embracing attitudes of women toward nature. It is a heartfelt, stirring, "ecofeminist" appeal for more of the latter.

■ Halpern, Daniel, ed. ON NATURE: NATURE, LANDSCAPE, AND NATURAL HISTORY. North Point, 1987 (0-86547-283-1).
An eclectic anthology of stimulating works by many of the best contemporary nature writers, including essays from Native American and European perspectives. The book includes lists of additional recommended readings—from essays and poems to full-length books—on this subject.

■ Krutch, Joseph Wood. THE VOICE OF THE DESERT: A NATURALIST'S INTER-PRETATION. Sloane, 1954; Morrow, 1980 (paper 0-688-07715-3).
Krutch was so captivated by the desert Southwest on his first visit that he abandoned an academic position at Columbia University and his status as a prominent New York theater critic to move to Arizona. In this book, he explores, with wit and charm, similarities between humans and creatures of the desert.

■ Leopold, Aldo. A SAND COUNTY ALMANAC. Oxford, 1949; Ballantine, 1986 (paper 0-345-34505-3).
Some have called this book the environmentalist's Bible. It begins with a stirring series of nature essays followed, by a thought-provoking discussion of esthetics, the value of natural places, and, finally, the need to extend ethics to nature and to cultivate, in people and society, an "ecological conscience."

■ Lopez, Barry. ARCTIC DREAMS: IMAGINATION AND DESIRE IN A NORTH-ERN LANDSCAPE. Scribner, 1986 (0-684-18578-4).
Lopez immerses himself in the cultures—Eskimo and white, traditional and modern—that cling tenaciously to life on the extreme landscapes and seascapes of the Arctic. He draws contrasts between European descendents, who seem to defy the elements and native people, who live in greater harmony with their environs.

■ Lovelock, James E. GAIA: A NEW LOOK AT LIFE ON EARTH. Oxford, 1979; 1987 (paper 0-19-286030-5).
Scientist Lovelock lays out an intriguing proposition, the Gaia Hypothesis, that the Earth is a single living organism whose constituent parts—oceans, land, the atmo-

sphere, plants and animals, even human beings—function together as elements of a greater, self-regulating whole to assure its survival.

■ **Lovins, Amory. SOFT ENERGY PATHS: TOWARD A DURABLE PEACE. Ballinger, 1977. o.p.**
Though 15 years old and out of print, this book is still provocative and timely. Lovins cleverly debunks conventional wisdom about energy production and consumption and makes an undeniably persuasive pitch for energy conservation and the pursuit of alternative energy sources.

■ **McKibben, Bill. THE END OF NATURE. Random, 1989 (0-394-57601-2).**
A thoughtful treatise in which writer McKibben contends that the potential onset of global warming, the advent of biotechnology, and other recent developments have fundamentally and permanently altered the relationship between humanity and nature.

■ **McPhee, John. ENCOUNTERS WITH THE ARCHDRUID. Farrar, 1971 (0-374-14822-8).**
McPhee is a prolific author of journalistic narratives—at last count, 20—primarily about wild places and the people who dwell and work therein. In this book, he accompanies David Brower, the dean of environmental activists, on battles to prevent development of three still-wild American landscapes.

■ **Marsh, George Perkins. Edited by David Lowenthal. MAN AND NATURE: OR, PHYSICAL GEOGRAPHY AS MODIFIED BY HUMAN ACTION. Harvard, 1864; 1965 (paper 0-674-54452-8).**
This 130-year-old book was the first to challenge the American myth of superabundance and the inexhaustibility of the earth. Though perhaps less well known than other "classics" of the genre, *Man and Nature* remains an important work and has been called "the fountainhead of the conservation movement."

■ **Meadows, Donella, et al. THE LIMITS TO GROWTH: A REPORT FOR THE CLUB OF ROME'S PROJECT ON THE PREDICAMENT OF MANKIND. Universe, 1972; 2nd ed., 1974 (paper 0-87663-222-3).**
This book sparked considerable debate in the early 1970s by predicting dire consequences from, and ultimate limits to, uncontrolled, highly consumptive economic growth. It was among the first to be based on computer modeling studies of the relationships between population growth, agricultural production, natural resource depletion, industrial output, and pollution.

■ **Mills, Stephanie. IN PRAISE OF NATURE. Island Pr., 1990 (paper 1-55963-034-5.**
Brief reviews of many of the best known, most important works in American environmental literature by more than 50 contemporary environmental activists and writers, woven together by introductory essays on the basic subjects and themes.

■ Mowat, Farley. NEVER CRY WOLF. Little, 1963 (0-316-58639-0).
A compassionate and humorous account of biologist Mowat's assignment to watch
and track the activities of a wolf family in northern Canada for the Canadian
government. Mowat's captivating prose successfully bridges the gap between young
and adult readers; it appeals to both.

■ Muir, John. JOHN OF THE MOUNTAINS: THE UNPUBLISHED JOURNALS OF
JOHN MUIR. Houghton, 1938; Univ. of Wisconsin Pr., 1979 (0-299-07880-9).
Muir's legacy as a preservationist today overshadows his notoriety as writer. Never-
theless, he wrote extensively to acquaint the public with American wildernesses and
win support for his cause. This volume exemplifies the inspired notes from which
Muir composed his articles and books and offers insights into the man.

■ Nash, Roderick. WILDERNESS AND THE AMERICAN MIND. Yale, 1967; Revised
3rd ed., 1982 (0-300-02905-5).
Historian Nash traces the evolution of American attitudes about wilderness from the
arrival of the first European settlers, who viewed the harsh, "untamed" American
continent with revulsion and fear, to modern times, when a nation composed largely
of city dwellers increasingly reveres "unspoiled" places. His more recent book, The
Rights of Nature: A History of Environmental Ethics (Univ. of Wisconsin Pr., 1989)
theorizes that human ethics are also evolving to recognize "rights" of other living
and nonliving things.

■ National Wildlife Federation. CONSERVATION DIRECTORY. National Wildlife
Federation, annual.
This comprehensive, annually updated directory of government agencies, citizens'
groups, and educational institutions concerned with natural resource use and management is an indispensable guide to the most prominent organizations and people—
at the state, provincial, national, and international levels—in conservation and environmental protection in the United States and Canada.

■ Olson, Sigurd. THE SINGING WILDERNESS. Knopf, 1945; 1956 (0-394-44560-0).
A collection of elegantly simple first-person essays about the Quetico-Superior
wilderness of northern Minnesota and southern Ontario. This book, illustrated with
simple woodcuts, pleasingly evokes the serene beauty of the north country.

■ Schneider, Stephen H. GLOBAL WARMING: ARE WE ENTERING THE GREEN-
HOUSE CENTURY? Sierra, 1989 (0-87156-693-1).
Climatologist Schneider, a leading authority on the greenhouse effect and global
warming, cogently describes the future risks of rapid climate change and how they
could be minimized by public and private action today.

■ Schumacher, E.F. SMALL IS BEAUTIFUL: ECONOMICS AS IF PEOPLE MAT-
TERED. Harper, 1973; 1989 (paper 0-06-091630-3).
With clarity and remarkable foresight, economist Schumacher criticizes classical
economic theory for its emphasis on materialism and constant growth and proposes

an alternative based on smallness and permanence. His arguments are as relevant to environmental concerns today as they were in 1973. (For a more recent treatment of this subject, see: Daly, Herman, and John Cobb. *For the Common Good: Redirecting the Economy Toward Community, the Environment, and a Sustainable Future.* Beacon, 1989)

■ **Stobaugh, Robert, and Daniel Yergin, eds. ENERGY FUTURE: REPORT OF THE ENERGY PROJECT AT THE HARVARD BUSINESS SCHOOL. Random, 1979; 1983 (paper 0-394-71063-0).**
Analysts at the nation's premiere business school make a solid economic case for pursuing energy conservation and solar energy development rather than increasing the nation's dependence on oil, coal, natural gas, and nuclear power.

■ **Thoreau, Henry David. WALDEN; OR, LIFE IN THE WOODS. Ticknor & Fields, 1854; Anchor/Doubleday, 1973 (paper 0-385-09503-1).**
Nearly a century and a half after its publication, *Walden,* whose philosophical musings about simplicity of lifestyle and strict idealism emanated from Thoreau's two-year retreat to a lakeside cabin in Massachusetts, is still considered one of the cornerstones of American environmental literature.

■ **Udall, Stewart. THE QUIET CRISIS. Holt, 1963. Revised ed. THE QUIET CRISIS AND THE NEXT GENERATION. Gibbs Smith, 1988 (0-87905-333-X).**
A straightforward, informative historical account, by a former U.S. secretary of the interior, of the exploitation of America's land and water and those who struggled to temper it.

■ **Ward, Barbara, and Rene Dubos. ONLY ONE EARTH: THE CARE AND MAINTE-NANCE OF A SMALL PLANET. Norton, 1972 (0-393-06391-7).**
Commissioned by the United Nations Conference on the Human Environment in 1972, this book was among the first to explore the social, economic, and political dimensions of global environmental problems. Unlike many "official" reports, *Only One Earth* is, at times, lyrical and contemplative as well as thorough and authoritative.

■ **Wilson, Edward O., ed. BIODIVERSITY. National Academy Pr., 1988 (paper 0-309-03739-5).**
The product of a National Forum on Biodiversity held in 1986, this book features articles by many of the world's best known ecologists on current subjects ranging from the extinction of species and the human need for biological diversity to the emerging field of ecological restoration.

■ **World Commission on Environment and Development. OUR COMMON FUTURE. Oxford, 1987 (paper 0-19-282080-X).**
This final report of a high-profile international commission examines global environmental and development issues—population, food security, species loss, energy—and recommends further international cooperation to improve the care and management

of natural resources. Its worldwide popularity prompted a follow-up volume by Linda Starke (*Signs of Hope.* Oxford, 1990).

■ **World Resources Institute. WORLD RESOURCES. Oxford, biannual. (paper 0-19-506228-0; 1990–91 ed.).**
More encyclopedic in format and content than the Worldwatch Institute's *State of the World* reports, this biannual series is perhaps the most comprehensive single source of current data on environmental problems and issues of international and global scope available today.

Author Index

Authors are arranged alphabetically by last name. The names are followed by book titles—also arranged alphabetically—and the page number.

Title Index

This index contains all annotated titles, followed by the author's last name and the page number.

Subject Index

All annotated titles are listed within specific subjects. Subjects are arranged alphabetically and subject heads may be divided into nonfiction (e.g., Animal rights) and fiction (e.g., Animal rights – Fiction). All numbers refer to page numbers.